AI, Healthcare and Law

Series Editor
Jean-Charles Pomerol

AI, Healthcare and Law

Edited by

Guilhem Julia
Anne Fauchon
Rushed Kanawati

iSTE

WILEY

First published 2024 in Great Britain and the United States by ISTE Ltd and John Wiley & Sons, Inc.

ISTE Ltd
27-37 St George's Road
London SW19 4EU
UK

www.iste.co.uk

John Wiley & Sons, Inc.
111 River Street
Hoboken, NJ 07030
USA

www.wiley.com

Library of Congress Control Number: 2024933558

British Library Cataloguing-in-Publication Data
A CIP record for this book is available from the British Library
ISBN 978-1-78630-909-9

Contents

Preface

Back in 2017, when I first asked my colleagues at the Faculty of Law, Political and Social Sciences at Sorbonne Paris Nord University to support my candidacy to become the faculty's dean, I was invited to organize a trans-section symposium. Some colleagues complained that the faculty's private lawyers and publicists (not to mention political scientists and sociologists) did not sufficiently discuss the results of their research work. Once elected, I became aware of the richness provided by the multidisciplinary nature of our institution and realized that it would be even more interesting to propose a trans-faculty meeting around a topic that would likely bring together speakers from other research units (UFRs, *Unités de formation et de recherche*) and institutions. The only missing task was to find a common subject: this being artificial intelligence (AI), as it perfectly integrated one of the strategic axes defined in the university's agreement, that is, activities related to digital technology.

With the support from my colleague Guilhem Julia (Research Assistant Dean) and the participation of other teachers/researchers (from various faculties of our institution), a first symposium, "Sciences and the meaning of artificial intelligence", was held at the *Maison des sciences de l'homme* (Sorbonne Paris Nord) on November 19, 2019. The minutes of the symposium were published by Dalloz editions under the "Thèmes et commentaires" collection.

In view of its success, a second edition was agreed on, this time focusing on AI and health, a topic at the heart of the news, which was regularly making the headlines. In the special issue from *Le Monde, Science et médecine*, dated October 26, 2022, the front headline stated: "Artificial intelligence, a new search engine". It was held on November 22, 2022, at the beautiful conference center on Condorcet campus. This research center, dedicated to human sciences, was the perfect setting for a topic closely related to the human being, even if mediated by the question of AI.

Thanks to the assistance from our colleague Rushed Kanawati, you can access the minutes of the symposium and appreciate the contributions from my colleagues at the DSPS research unit (law, political and social sciences), privatists and publicists (two laboratories, IDPS (Institute of Public Law, Political and Social Sciences) and IRDA (Research Institute for Attractive Law)), as well as those from the SEG research unit (economic sciences and management), the SMBH (medical health and human biology), Galilée Institute and Villetaneuse University Technology Institute.

Anne FAUCHON
Faculty of Law,
Political and Social Sciences
Université Sorbonne Paris Nord
Villetaneuse

Introduction

The need for reflection on the rationale and purposes of law in the field of artificial intelligence and health

Definitions and experimentation

Artificial intelligence (AI) can be defined as a "theoretical and practical interdisciplinary field aiming to understand cognition and reflection mechanisms, as well as their imitation by a hardware and software device, for the purpose of assisting or substituting human activities"[1]. For ease of reference, the expression "algorithmic medicine" will designate the use of tools and systems in the medicine field, based on algorithms associated with computer processing (Lambert 2019). The notion of health has been described by the World Health Organization as "a state of complete physical, mental and social well-being, and not merely the absence of disease or infirmity". The present contribution strictly focuses on medical science, considering the notion of "well-being" to be rather ambivalent and inaccurate[2].

Each in their own way, medical acts such as prevention, diagnosis and care, as well as prognosis, invite contributions from "medical AI". A few examples illustrate the diversity of situations involved (for an understanding of the use of AI in the field of health, through experiments and scientific

---

Introduction written by Céline BLOUD-REY.

1 Commission for the enrichment of the French language, Vocabulary on artificial intelligence, JORF, December 7, 2018.

2 Preamble to the Constitution of the World Health Organization. Available online on the WHO website.

collaborations, refer to Chassagne et al. (2021)). First of all, in terms of medical imaging, experiential feedback is "promising", not only due to the increase in data resulting from the devices' technical progress, but also due to the application of a global data management standard (Chassagne et al. 2021, No. 50). Research on the pre-interpretation of mammograms is being explored in relation to AI, its purpose not being to replace the radiologist, but to facilitate diagnosis by identifying the points of attention to be prioritized and assessed by the imaging specialist (Chassagne et al. 2021, No. 62 *sqq.*). Furthermore, AI is being used in certain innovative medical devices for the diagnosis of sleep pathologies (e.g. the detection of sleep apnea at home. See Chassagne et al. (2021, No. 57 *sqq.*)). More generally, the refinement of medical and surgical techniques, as well as the improvement of patient care and the strengthening of remote care, are among the objectives of algorithmic medicine[3].

The use of the "goal law"

All decision support systems and medical devices incorporating AI require the most accurate and reliable algorithms (for a technical and legal analysis of the challenges raised by decision support systems, see Desmoulins-Canselier and Le Métayer (2020)). In terms of data collection, the purpose is to acquire the most diversified data. Data also need to be cleaned, structured, formatted and sometimes enriched. In this context of innovation and research requiring significant investment, GAFAM and BATX[4] appear as the health data "big players" for the first time. The public authorities have not remained indifferent to this factor. They had recourse to the law and, in a privileged way, to the law understood as an instrument at the service of certain ends. This was referred to as the "goal law" (expression coined by Paul Cuche (1919) and quoted by Oppetit (1999)):

> To speak of the goal and final cause law, whether we like it or not, is to announce a metaphysical problem. […] The legislator

3 For example, regarding the intensification of daily digital practices during the Covid-19 epidemic. Activity report from the French National Commission for Computing and Liberties (*Commission nationale de l'informatique et des libertés*, 2020 edition, p. 21); Medical Diagnosis and Artificial Intelligence: Ethical Issues. CCNE-CNPEN Joint Opinion, CCNE Opinion No. 141, CNPEN Opinion No. 4. November 2022, p. 19 *sqq*.

4 GAFAM, acronym for Google, Apple, Facebook, Amazon and Microsoft. BATX, acronym for Baidu, Alibaba, Tencent and Xiaomi.

> who develops a legal rule – a goal law, as we have said – must have taken sides on the value of the goal pursued […] the legislator must have developed a certain conception of social progress; otherwise, how could he/she enforce a legal constraint, encouraging some directions on human activity while prohibiting others? (Cuche 1919)

Reflection on "the goal law", its purposes and rationale

The equilibrium of a "goal law" can be fragile, either because the goals pursued by the legislator are likely to elicit conflict, or because they have been insufficiently considered upstream. Where appropriate, it is necessary to investigate the ethical, anthropological, sociological or practical grounds underlying the law, beyond legal reasoning. Thanks to this approach, it is possible to gain further insight into the values defended by the law, their content, hierarchy and their nature:

> Issuing a goal law obviously implies that one envisions a certain hierarchy in the goals to be reached! Issuing a goal law involves formulating a value judgment (at least implicitly) on the chosen and imposed goals, as well as on disdained and forbidden goals (Cuche 1919).

This approach is particularly important when "algorithmic medicine" is involved. In fact, the use of algorithms and their regulation primarily concerns a human being, that is, the patient. However, it also challenges the very definition of medicine and has implications for another human being: the doctor. Under these circumstances, it is easy to understand the need for an "anthropological coherence imperative". "Act in such a way that your action does not destroy your human nature!" (Lambert 2019).

Differentiated approaches to "algorithmic medicine" in "goal laws"

So far, "algorithmic medicine" has been approached by the legislator through the prism of health data. While the main texts relating to the protection of personal data apply to the medical field (French Law No. 78-17 of January 6, 1978 (LIL); regulation (EU) 2016/679 known as RGPD), the French Law No. 2019-774 of July 24, 2019 aimed to enhance the value of health data and, ultimately, the deployment of an AI medical[5] sector. It is precisely this "goal law" that is relevant to scrutinize the so-called first objective approach to algorithmic medicine. The data's prism leads to an objectified representation of the patient's health. The human being, in its integral dimension (physical, psychological, spiritual), disappears behind objective knowledge (patient's health data). This way of apprehending medical AI through data must be differentiated from another subjective interpretation.

Algorithmic medicine can be inscribed within the doctor–patient interpersonal relationship. This analysis is based on a certain conception of the person: "The human being is not just a lump of clay; it is a living being, in relation with others" (Aynès et al. 2022, footnote No. 1). In line with this doctrine, civil law strives to characterize the trust relationship between doctor and patient, in order to determine their reciprocal rights and obligations. Recently, health professionals have been held responsible for informing the patient when a medical device relying on algorithmic data processing is used (Article L. 4001-3 CSP). It is on the grounds of this innovation – introduced by Article 17 of the French Law No. 2021-1017 of August 2, 2021 – that the second approach to the so-called subjective algorithmic medicine should be studied.

When questioning the purposes and rationale of the law in the field of algorithmic medicine, two approaches need to be differentiated: an objective approach, based on health data, and a subjective one, at the heart of the doctor–patient relationship.

An approach to algorithmic medicine based on health data

The purposes of the goal law

French Law No. 2019-774 of July 24, 2019, on the organization and transformation of the health system (OTSS), was set within a global strategy for AI[6]. Two specific goals were of particular interest in this sense.

5 French Law No. 2019-774 of July 24, 2019 relating to the organization and transformation of the health system (known as "OTSS"), JORF July 26, 2019. See, in particular, Saison (2019) and Galloux and Gaumont-Prat (2020).

6 French Law No. 2019-774 known as "OTSS", Articles 41–45. See, in particular, Saison (2019) and Galloux and Gaumont-Prat (2020).

First and foremost, health data were considered as data to be valorized. Following the submission of the Villani report, the President of the Republic announced the creation of a Health Data Hub as one of the strengths of the French Artificial Intelligence (AI) strategy (Villani 2018). In June 2018, the French Minister of Solidarity and Health launched a prefiguration mission on this platform for the exploitation of health data. A public interest group, called the Health Data Platform (*Plateforme des données de santé*), was created via the French Law of July 24, 2019[7]. During this time, it was argued that the implementation of the platform, as well as the enrichment of the National Health Data System (SNDS, *Système national des données de santé*), were intended to promote new uses of health data, in particular those related to the development of AI methods:

> In order to increase the use of data from the National Health Data System both in clinical research and in terms of new uses, particularly those related to the development of artificial intelligence methods, the National Health Data System will be enriched with all the data collected during the procedures covered by the health insurance. This enrichment will position France among the leading countries in terms of structuring health data, while maintaining a high level of privacy protection[8].

Structuring an Artificial Intelligence and Health sector was one of the ambitions of the report from the Health Data Hub prefiguration mission:

> The analysts' opinions have converged on a double-digit growth of the market for AI-based products and services until at least 2025 and a market size exceeding $10 billion by 2020. AI could thus become the most dynamic segment of the digital economy sector. However, France currently lacks companies with a

7 French Law No. 2019-774 known as "OTSS": "Chapter I: To innovate by enhancing clinical data (Articles 41 to 43)"; *addendum*, Decree of November 29, 2019 approving an amendment to the agreement, establishing the public interest of the National Institute for Health Data and creating the public interest Health Data Platform, JORF November 30, 2019, text 13.

8 Impact study of February 13, 2019, French Bill on the organization and transformation of the health system, p. 91.

strong reputation in AI and large enough to have a knock-on effect on the technological sector[9].

The goals for supporting research and innovation in the field of health had to be reconciled with another important goal, that of preserving a high level of privacy protection[10]. All legal obligations in terms of security, protection of the rights of individuals and access to data were applicable to the processing of health data, whether drawn from the RGPD, the LIL or the French Code of public health; in particular, the security reference system from the National Health Data System (SNDS)[11].

In its opinion on the bill dated January 31, 2019 on the organization and transformation of the health system which gave rise to the platform, the French National Commission for Computing and Liberties (CNIL, *Commission nationale de l'informatique et des libertés*) drew its attention "to the major problem, in practical terms, of limiting the extent and amount of data by these new processing operations, which evolved in a context of data accumulation to feed AI algorithms"[12].

All things considered, it was challenging to reconcile the development of "voracious" technology in relation to the use of sensitive data; and, on the other hand, the application of legal rules protecting personal data. Beyond these purposes, it was necessary to identify the equilibrium between the law and its underpinning principles.

The equilibrium of the law and its rationale

State-of-the-art personalized medicine

To begin with, we should call into question the project's scope as designed by the legislator in 2019, and the evolution of medicine. The Health Data Hub prefiguration report described a shift from "mass curative medicine" to "personalized medicine"[13]. The perfection of the medical

9 Health Data Hub prefiguration mission, 2018, p. 23.

10 Impact study of February 13, 2019, Health Data Hub prefiguration mission, 2018, p. 23.

11 LIL Articles 64 *sqq.*; RGPD Article 9; CSP 1460-1 *sqq.*

12 French Deliberation No. 2019-008 of January 31, 2019 from the French National Commission for Computing and Liberties (CNIL), providing an opinion on a bill relating to the organization and transformation of the health system (request for Opinion No. 19001144).

13 Health Data Hub prefiguration mission, 2018, p. 11.

model suggested was based on an assumption: the collection of massive amounts of data would enable the implementation of "state-of-the-art personalized medicine". By integrating AI approaches, the massive analysis of health data could contribute to clarifying and specifying "the therapeutic strategy to be adopted, patient by patient"[14]. In its opinion on the ethical issues raised by the use of Big Data, the National Consultative Ethics Committee for Life and Health Sciences (CCNE, *Comité consultatif national d'éthique pour les sciences de la vie et de la santé*) also referred to the "concept of precision medicine", emphasizing that "each patient somehow becomes a unique case"[15]. According to the authority, this precision would be deployed not only in relation to the "prediction of a disease, but most importantly, its prevention, or, when required, the therapy to be applied"[16]. Another salient factor was that thanks to the sharing of possible risk factors, "precision medicine enabled profiling techniques"[17]. Along the same lines, the impact study of February 13, 2019 emphasized the benefit of personalized patient care in an evolving and variable ecosystem (city and country medicine, population aging, diversity of the territorial network, etc.)[18].

Still, the shift from "mass curative medicine" to "personalized medicine" raises some critical questions. First of all, the consideration of the patient as a unique subject has historically been an integral part of the medicinal field. The Hippocratic oath recalls the extent to which the doctor is "admitted into the private lives of patients"[19]. The set of duties towards patients (Articles 32–55 from the French Code of Medical Ethics) translates the special attention devoted to the patient under examination. Article R. 4127-32 from the French Public Health Code emphasizes the doctor's commitment "to *personally* ensure the patient conscientious, dedicated care on the basis of acquired scientific data, and if necessary, to summon the help from competent third parties"[20]. The evolution of Western medicine has been

14 Health Data Hub prefiguration mission, 2018, p. 11.

15 Opinion No. 130 from the National Ethics Advisory Committee for Life and Health Sciences, Massive Data and Health: A new approach to ethical issues, p. 19.

16 Opinion No. 130 from the National Ethics Advisory Committee for Life and Health Sciences, Massive Data and Health: A new approach to ethical issues, p. 19.

17 Opinion No. 130 from the National Ethics Advisory Committee for Life and Health Sciences, Massive Data and Health: A new approach to ethical issues, p. 19.

18 Impact study dated February 13, 2019, p. 88 *sqq*.

19 See: www.conseil-national.medecin.fr/medecin/devoirs-droits/serment-dhippocrate.

20 Italicized by the authors.

constantly striving for a deepening of knowledge, in particular, regarding exploratory instruments (the stethoscope, medical imaging). From this point of view, the rise of “algorithmic medicine” should be positively considered. Nevertheless, it is important to take other practical factors into account, even when these might appear as minor, or even prosaic. In the medical field, no one can ignore the cumbersome administrative procedures imposed by positive law, and in particular the implementation of rules relating to the protection of personal data and, less frequently, non-identifying data. This rationalization phenomenon is characterized by a segmentation of stages and by a formalization of the decision-making process: on the one hand, declarations and/or authorizations, and, on the other, evaluations and recourses[21]. The whole process can be harmful and counterproductive:

> Pushed to extreme limits, the personalized medicine project could encourage a discarnate medical approach, with biological data replacing the first-person narrative and suggestions drawn from algorithmic calculations replacing the medical art (Desmoulins-Canselier and Le Métayer 2020, p. 114).

In the end, the implementation of complex decision-making processes (something which computer language powerfully deploys) could end up distorting the doctor–patient relationship. This phenomenon (the “proceduralization” of human relationships) is not specific to the field of health, and leads to increasing stress, anxiety and even isolation for all of the actors involved, starting with the weakest[22]. The deployment of a technique is never morally neutral, but can be beneficial as long as it is employed at the service of human life in its fullness[23].

Evidence-based medicine

The second level of analysis relates to the very definition of medicine. The development of medical tools equipped with AI has not gone without criticism due to the medicine model it embodies. These tools are derived from evidence-based medicine, a practice requiring the medical

---

21 For example, in terms of medical research, www.cnil.fr/fr/modification-dun-traitement-de-donnees-ayant-pour-finalite-une-recherche-une-etude-ou-une-evaluation.

22 CNIL report, Citizen consultation summary on the ethical issues related to algorithms, Montpellier, October 14, 2017.

23 Benedict XVI, Chapter VI “The development of peoples and technology”. In *Encyclique, L'amour dans la vérité*. Lethielleux/Parole et Silence, p. 167 *sqq*.

decision-making process to rely on preestablished standards. The criticism aimed at this conception of medicine is that it "reduces the margins of maneuver granted to the doctor by standardizing procedures and demanding any individual decision deviating from the rule to be justified" (Cléro 2016). In other words, evidence-based medicine "inevitably takes [the] disease more into account than the patient itself; at the time it compels the doctor to do the same" (Cléro 2016). These criticisms can be refuted, however, by the fact that the doctor, in addition to medical knowledge, "develops an empirical and private knowledge of patients", which ultimately leads to building a trust relationship (Cléro 2016). Finally, the mere recourse to "evidence" ends up impoverishing what medicine actually is. The patient cannot be reduced to measurable[24] characteristics. As for the medical act, it presupposes discernment imbued with wisdom on the part of the doctor. Once again, it is not possible to model what belongs to the very essence of the human being. The encounter with the patient constitutes "the time of gratuitous exposure to the patient's singularity, which, in virtue of its imprint, passively shapes the subsequent decision to be made" (Kempf and Kempf 2016). It is the entire being that is targeted in the doctor–patient relationship.

In short, it appears that in medicine, the algorithmic-based approach is insufficient to shed light on (as well as to protect) what has characterized medicine from time immemorial: the relationship between the doctor and the patient.

An algorithmic-based approach grounded on the doctor–patient relationship

The intentions of the goal law

Article 17 from the French Law of August 2, 2021 on bioethics incorporated a provision into the French Public Health Code (Article L. 4001-3) relating to the use of a medical device involving algorithmic data processing by a health professional. Paragraph I imposes an obligation on the professional to provide information for the benefit of the patient concerning the use of algorithmic processing and, where applicable, the

24 This observation should be related to the contemporary tendency to define the human being on the basis of a "more physicalist model [...] which does not hesitate [...] to reduce the spirit and the soul to a simple neuronal datum" (Ravasi 2021).

resulting interpretation. Paragraph II mentions an obligation of information for the benefit of the health professionals concerned. The third paragraph is aimed at developers, who must "ensure that the operation can be explained to users". According to the last paragraph, after consulting with the administrative authorities, the regulatory power is given the prerogative to determine the nature of the medical devices to be used, and their methods:

> I.-The healthcare professional who decides to use a medical device comprising algorithmic data processing for an act of prevention, diagnosis or care, and for which learning has resulted from the treatment of massive data, makes sure that the person concerned has been informed of this and, where applicable, has been warned about the resulting interpretation.
>
> II.-The healthcare professionals concerned are informed about the use of data processing mechanisms. The patient data used in this treatment and the results are accessible to them.
>
> III.-The developers of the algorithmic processing mechanism mentioned in I will make sure that its operation can be explained to users.
>
> IV.-After consulting with the High Authority for Health and the French National Commission for Computing and Liberties, an order from the French Minister responsible for health determined the nature of the medical devices mentioned in I and their methods of use.

This "legal innovation", expected to place "France in a pioneering position", "went largely unnoticed", eliciting mixed feelings (Bévière-Boyer 2021; Crichton 2021; Desmoulins-Canselier 2021). To further address the question of the goal law, it is necessary to identify the desired ends. In a preliminary way, recourse to the law was presented as "a necessity"[25]. Let us gently remind you of the French propensity to legalism. We should also mention the integration of this provision for AI in the law relating to bioethics, a development which went hand in hand with the extension of the

25 Impact study, French Bill on bioethics, July 23, 2019, p. 34 (point 2 entitled "Need to legislate and goals pursued").

scope of the CCNE[26]. In matter of substance, Article 11 from the French Bill No. 2187 on bioethics aimed "to secure the patient's correct information when the algorithmic processing of massive data was involved ("artificial intelligence" applied to an act of care). It also declined the guarantee of human intervention"[27]. In case of a complex learning mode, the influence that the implementation of an algorithm could exert therefore appeared as the main difficulty to overcome:

> The identified risk lies in the fact that the "scientific/mathematical" character of the conclusion produced by an algorithm seems to impose itself indisputably both on the healthcare professional and the patient.
>
> [The] risk can increase when the decision rule used by the algorithm is poorly explained, when the doctor has feeble knowledge on the new technology, or even when the algorithm's construction is impossible to explain by certain AI learning modes ("deep learning"), or when process for developing the algorithm is opaque ("black box")[28].

Based on this observation, the stated goal of the bill was to "preserve a human guarantee for data interpretation"[29]. The analysis of the legal discourse contained in the impact study still raises some doubts. Admittedly, the legal measure (supposed to constitute a "protection") was intended to benefit both the patient and the doctor. The unique exchange between the patient and the doctor also had to be preserved. In an even more uncertain way, the text states "it *seems* essential that artificial intelligence devices should act as a support for a human decision, but not replace it"[30]. This shift is singular, to say the least: it "*is*" essential for these systems to be considered as simple tools at the service of the actors involved. Finally, mention is made of the legal measure, which should act as a "reminder" that a medical decision cannot result solely from automated processing. In fact, nothing could be further from this.

---

26 French Bill on bioethics, No. 2187, tabled on July 24, 2019 and referred to the Special Commission responsible for examining the bill on bioethics, Article 29.

27 French Bill relating to bioethics, No. 2187, Article 11.

28 Impact study, French Bill on bioethics, July 23, 2019, p. 284.

29 Impact study, French Bill on bioethics, July 23, 2019, p. 282.

30 Impact study, French Bill on bioethics, July 23, 2019, p. 285.

Article L. 4001-3 from the French Public Health Code did not meet the expectations placed on it, particularly considering the richness of the reflections that had been previously encouraged. To take just one example, CCNE Opinion No. 129 recommended the "fundamental principle of a human guarantee over digital health" to be included in the legislation[31]. In a similar manner, the French Council of State proposed enshrining the prohibition of a diagnosis exclusively derived from an AI system without the intervention of a doctor, drawing inspiration from Article 10 of the French Law of January 6, 1978, according to which no decision producing legal effects with regards to a person may be taken solely on the grounds of automated data processing[32]. Proposal Nos. 43 and 44 from the report by the information mission on the revision of the law on bioethics recommended introducing a legislative principle of human guarantee on digital health. Its concrete implementation could be specified by good practice recommendations issued by the French National Authority for Health[33]. Finally, the formal recognition of a principle known as "human digital guarantee" did not appear in Article 17 of the law on bioethics. What weakened the equilibrium of the goal law in its rationale was not so much related to the choice made, but to the vagueness of the ends assigned to the legal measure.

The equilibrium of the law and its rationale

The declared goal of the legal measure proposed by the bill relating to bioethics was to preserve the individual exchange between doctor and patient, and to protect the latter. Beyond this intention, it was the medical decision-making process that was at stake. Medical ethics describes this underlying logic as comprising three successive phases. The first phase corresponds to the exchange between doctor and patient. A temporal space is opened for listening to the patient, for discovering the patient's singularity. The second phase is devoted to medical reflection, while the third one involves decision-making.

31 Contribution of the French National Consultative Ethics Committee regarding the revision of the bioethics law, September 2018, Opinion No. 129, p. 102.

32 Revision of the bioethics law: What options for tomorrow? Study adopted at the general meeting on June 28, 2018, Council of State, report and studies section, p. 207.

33 Information report No. 1572 dated January 15, 2019 filed pursuant to Article 145 of the Rules by the information mission on the revision of the law on bioethics and presented by Xavier Breton, President, Jean-Louis Touraine, rapporteur deputies, p. 265.

Based on the analysis of a specific tool developed by doctors to facilitate decision-making regarding adjuvant treatments for breast cancer, it was possible to demonstrate in concrete terms how decision support systems and, more generally, AI-equipped tools can modify (or even shake up) traditional temporality (Kempf and Kempf 2016, p. 46). The "immediacy" of the results obtained from an AI system and their "univocality" are two characteristics likely to upset the classic three-phase decision-making process (Kempf and Kempf 2016, p. 47 *sqq.*). On the one hand, time is retracted. Therefore, performance concerns can make the user forget that the tools are only means placed at their disposal. On the other hand, software results are lacking in nuances and seem to impose themselves as efficient and effective information sets, capable of finding a solution under any circumstance.

This analysis, drawn from "experience feedback", makes it possible to understand the importance of protecting the decision-making process. Despite this, if one of the purposes of the goal law was to ensure protection for both the patient and the doctor, it is unlikely for Article L. 4001-3 of the French Public Health Code to have fulfilled that mission. Actually, the legal measure seems unbalanced. It has been shown to what extent this type of tool can upset medical practice and medical ethics. The lack of equilibrium in the law is further accentuated by the absence of an information obligation for the manufacturer/producer. As previously pointed out, the law potentially places health professionals "in an untenable situation" (Desmoulins-Canselier 2021, p. 32). The new Article L. 4001-3 from the French Public Health Code imposes a double obligation on the health professional. On the one hand, the doctor may not necessarily master new technologies; on the other hand, even if technologically savvy, the health professional may not be able to communicate this kind of information to the patient due to technical reasons (Desmoulins-Canselier 2021, p. 32). On the patient's side, the situation is no better. Consent to the use of a medical device involving algorithmic data processing is not required (Desmoulins-Canselier 2021, p. 31). Furthermore, the patient is indirectly affected by the fact that the doctor has not been placed in a position capable of exercising the art of healing under good professional conditions.

Ultimately, the goal stated by the goal law would have required reflection on the medical decision-making process and, more broadly, on the definition of medicine, the values defended and their hierarchy. Correlatively, the question on the use of algorithmic data processing by a doctor could have been analyzed in a broader context: that of the legal status of exploration tools used in medicine. Under certain circumstances, it is good for the law to stand back to make way for other standards, such as medical ethics or deontology (Gautier and Perchet 2022, p. 233). Moreover, the regulation of medical ethics by the law is relatively recent, if we consider the history of medicine (Sournia 2004). The time has probably come to aspire to more moderation in the production of "goal laws". This movement advocating for a decrease in legal interventions could ultimately be beneficial for medicine, be it algorithmic or not.

References

Aynès, L., Malaurie, P., Peterka, N. (2022). *Droit des personnes. La protection des mineurs et des majeurs*, 12th edition. LGDJ, Paris.

Bévière-Boyer, B. (2021). Numérique en santé : le projet de loi relatif à la bioéthique a accouché d'une souris. In *Données et technologies juridiques*, Nevejans, N. (ed.). Mare & Martin, Paris.

Chassagne, V., Despatin, J., Pax, F., Tedesco, J. (2021). *Intelligence artificielle et innovations digitales en santé. Transformation des prises en charge et des métiers*. Berger-Levrault, Paris.

Cléro, J.-P. (2016). La décision médicale, la fin des décideurs. *Revue française d'éthique appliquée*, 1, 24.

Crichton, C. (2021). L'intelligence artificielle dans la révision de la loi bioéthique. *Dalloz IP/IT et communication*.

Cuche, P. (1919). *En lisant les juristes philosophes*. BnF, Paris.

Desmoulins-Canselier, S. (2021). Traitement algorithmique de données massives et décision médicale. *Dictionnaire permanent, Santé, bioéthique, biotechnologies*. Éditions Législatives.

Desmoulins-Canselier, S. and Le Métayer, D. (2020). *Décider avec les algorithmes. Quelle place pour l'Homme, quelle place pour le droit ?* Dalloz, Paris.

Galloux, J.-C. and Gaumont-Prat, H. (2020). Droits et libertés corporels. *Recueil Dalloz*, 735–745.

Gautier, P.-Y. and Perchet, C. (2022). De l'abdication de la loi. In *Les métamorphoses de la loi, en hommage à Jean Foyer*, Teyssié, B. and Puigelier, C. (eds). Editions Panthéon-Assas, Paris.

Kempf, E. and Kempf, A. (2016). L'informatisation de l'aide à la décision : la décision médicale est-elle indemne ? L'exemple d'un outil prédictif en cancérologie. *Revue française d'éthique appliquée*, 1, 50.

Lambert, D. (2019). Quelques définitions. In *La robotique et l'intelligence artificielle*. Editions Jésiutes/Fidélité, Paris/Namur.

Oppetit, B. (1999). *Philosophie du droit*. Dalloz, Paris.

Ravasi, G. (2021). La foi chrétienne entre culture et témoignage. *Communio*, 4(276), 11.

Saison, J. (2019). Une nouvelle réforme en faveur de l'unité du système de santé. *AJDA*, 2488–2496.

Sournia, J.-C. (2004). Médicale (éthique). Origine, histoire, développements récents. In *Dictionnaire d'éthique et de philosophie morale*, Canto-Sperber, M. (ed.). Quadrige/PUF, Paris.

Villani, C. (2018). Donner un sens à l'intelligence artificielle, pour une stratégie nationale et européenne. Report, 28 March.

PART 1

Artificial Intelligence to Support Diagnosis

1

Healthcare Applications

France is slowly perishing in the face of the explosion of medical deserts. This observation is not new. The newspaper *Le Monde* recently published a leading article to this effect. These deserts are real political emergencies, especially considering that desertification currently affects peri-urban and urban areas. There are multiple clear warnings in the face of the growing risk of potentially violating the Hippocratic oath. The private sector offers opportunities such as "patient care via telemedicine tools, making it possible to reduce the inequalities caused by medical deserts"[1].

Brought about by Simone Veil in 1971, the challenge of the *numerus clausus* in medicine was an urgent one. Back in 2018, Michel Canévet raised the issue of the dangers of medical deserts to the senate. Their impact was particularly severe in Brittany, on the Côtes-d'Armor, concluding that "42% of Bretons lived in areas of tension regarding the access to healthcare" (Canevet 2018a, 2018b). It was by means of a simple decree issued on September 13, 2021 (Journal officiel de la République française 2021) that the *numerus clausus* was abolished, partially halting the exodus of medical students to Romania.

The French National Council of the Order of Physicians applied a code of professional conduct based on Article 32, making reference to Article R. 4127-32 from the Public Health Code, according to which "once having agreed to meet a demand, the doctor undertakes to personally ensure conscientious and dedicated care to the patient, relying on scientifically

Chapter written by Anne CAMMILLERI.

1 For example, the case of the company CISCO.

acquired data, and if necessary, calling on the assistance of competent third parties". The duties towards the patient are clearly defined in Articles 32–55 of said code. This shows the extent to which, after the global crisis of the Covid-19 pandemic, it became necessary to strengthen intergenerational bonds. In all areas, multiple initiatives thrived to make technologies available and improve the quality of life of people and animals.

However, cybercrime continues to be a fast-growing phenomenon. WannaCry has left its mark in our collective memory, as a highly virulent cyberattack against the British healthcare system in 2017 and 2020, which resulted in the lucrative theft of medical data of over 2,300 people. In 2021, it was France's turn to suffer a brutal data theft, affecting over 1.4 million patients from the AP–HP (*Assistance Publique–Hôpitaux de Paris*), including "the identity, social security number and contact details of the patients tested, as well as the identity and contact details of the health professionals treating them, the characteristics and results of the tests carried out" (Le Parisien 2021).

While the use of applications such as Stop Covid can fulfill this role in the event of a serious threat to public health (Journal officiel de la République française 2020), they can only do so in a limited way due to the fact that using the application is not compulsory. On the other hand, the use of Stop Covid quickly showed its limitations, particularly in regards to the fundamental requirement of privacy protection. The modernity of our era is paving the way for an increasingly greater reliance on digital technology, making room to a variety of healthcare applications.

1.1. The uses of a healthcare application

The Larousse dictionary defines an application as "a limited processing domain for which software is written" or as "software or set of programs intended to assist a computer user for processing a specific task".

The use of digital applications in the field of healthcare constitutes an immense physical and moral contribution, enabling patients to regain autonomy and improve their health through effective self-monitoring. The number of healthcare applications of all kinds has exploded. For example, among the top 50 best healthcare applications, the American search engine Google returns results for "AllergoBox, the anti-allergy health app", which helps people with food allergies or intolerances and contact allergies, It also helps people to identify everyday products compatible with their dietary requirements. The application Health For You is only available on the AppStore. The healthcare application Gluci Check helps to monitor diabetes. Also, at the top of the list, there is the Santé.fr application, the official public service application!

It is clear that, above all, healthcare applications enable a collection of sensitive data. This implies the consent of the person who downloads the application on a mobile device or another computer medium and accepts its installation, fully aware that consent will lead to a processing of their personal data. The most classical and popular application in France is *Mon espace Santé*. This safely stores health documents, including "analysis results, prescriptions, medical certificates, which can be exchanged with healthcare professionals through secure messaging and protect health-related data"[2]. With the patient's consent, healthcare professionals have access to sensitive information. Data cannot be collected without the informed consent of the person involved and must have been completely anonymized. The contents of the results stored in the application may be of interest both to healthcare professionals who will analyze the recorded results and to the patient.

The digitization of the public and private spheres has enabled the development of applications in all fields, and depends on the uses envisaged. In this sense, the healthcare field is particularly sensitive. At the European Union level, the subsection XIV TFEU on public health is ambivalent. Article 168, TFEU states that a high level of human health protection is ensured by the definition and implementation of all EU policies and actions. However, the role of the EU remains legally complementary, insofar as this action only "completes" national policies on the improvement of public health, the prevention of human diseases and illnesses, and the causes of danger to physical and mental health.

The European Union is also held competent for monitoring and combatting serious cross-border threats to health. Therefore, this sphere of action is only limited to cooperation competences, in particular, to improve the complementarity of health services in cross-border regions (Article 168, paragraph 2 TFEU). Complementarity is also related to the adoption of standards on the quality and safety for medicinal products and devices for

2 A health insurance website.

medical use (Article 168, paragraph 4.c TFEU). EU action shall respect the responsibilities of the Member States for the definition of their health policy and for the organization and delivery of health services, medical care or the donation of organs. Medicine is experiencing spectacular progress in all fields. The dematerialization of our activities is a digital revolution and has opened up new fields of action to help those suffering, particularly in the medicine field, thanks to AI. Individuals are gaining autonomy through the remote access to healthcare and innovative technologies. This is how the popularization of healthcare applications for individuals contributes to strengthening their autonomy and feeds their hopes of regaining freedom and independence. If used properly, these applications promote the well-being of individuals and the correct functioning of public and private hospital structures (section 1.2). On the other hand, as regards the sensitivity of processed health data, guaranteeing their integrity requires building powerful cybersecurity strategies to ensure the resilience of applications (section 1.3).

1.2. Applications at the service of hospitals (HR dimension)

We immediately note the exponential development of healthcare applications with the assistance of a web search engine. While the anxiety-provoking context of the pandemic could be somehow related to this, in circumstances where a health crisis is not involved, applications continue to develop widely in all fields.

1.2.1. *Internal staff and patient management applications in public and private hospitals*

The hospital workload is particularly heavy. When it is possible to provide remote healthcare, the use of applications can lighten up the workload in public and private hospitals (section 1.2.1.1). The effective sharing of health data necessarily requires the ability to develop actions to ensure healthcare continuity, mutability and equality (section 1.2.1.2).

1.2.1.1. *Applications to assist human resources in hospitals*

MyGHT is a human resource application for hospital workers. It is a complete modular e-health offer to meet the needs of healthcare institutions, nursing staff and patients. It is also used for patients at French residential care facilities for senior citizens (Ehpad, *Établissements d'hébergement pour personnes âgées dépendantes*). MyGHT Agent was the winner of the 6th edition of the Human Resources Innovation Prize awarded by the French Hospital Federation (FHF), MNH GROUP and the Association for the Development of Human Resources in Health and Social Institutions (Adrhess, *Association pour le développement des ressources humaines dans les établissements sanitaires et sociaux*) on the occasion of the HR Health Meetings back in 2018. This was a successful testimony of the impact of digitization for improving the administrative functioning of the public hospital.

The different solution modules for this application aim to strengthen the link between patients, residents, hospital agents and health institutions through the use of innovative applications, to be used across all media (computers, tablets and smartphones).

The application "comprehensively acknowledges the needs of healthcare institutions by facilitating medical care, patient remote monitoring, care coordination, the analysis or exchange of information between patients and medical or medico-social professionals". MyGHT centralizes all of the information an agent needs (payslips, hour counters, etc.), and provides access to documents and messages from the administration. The agent can easily submit administrative forms online (applications for leave, travel requests) through the application. Information management is facilitated because the administrative staff can manage the information made available to them via the application and centralize every procedure. Following their own initiative, agents can access their account, retrieve professional records and manage the administrative follow-up. As well as from accessing information, MyGHT enables staff to validate their "well-being" at work, from their first login, every day. The data collected and recorded provides the HR department with access to sensitive information. The HR Department can consult statistics on the well-being of agents, and monitor the quality of life at work in hospitals. However, the piece of information relating to the effectiveness of the agent's well-being, collected anonymously, has not been clearly determined. This is likely to truncate the expected information and constitute a serious breach of the GDPR (General Data Protection Regulation). In the search for balance in the French national health policy, the state relies on the classic rules of public law, namely Rolland's laws (section 1.2.1.2).

1.2.1.2. *The effective sharing of health data, scrutinized by Rolland's laws: continuity, mutability, equality*

For any public law specialist, Rolland's laws constitute a reference that is still the cornerstone of the public service: the principles of continuity, mutability and equality can contribute to framing the sharing of health data. How can applications contribute to scientific progress in aid of vulnerable people?

1.2.1.2.1. The continuity of care

This is taken into account thanks to the use of the digital shared medical record (DMP, *dossier médical partagé*). The Minister of Health supports the adoption of the shared medical record, which should enable all patients to access their medical data via the mon-dmp.fr website. With the patient's consent, the consulted doctor can gain access to it, making it easier to reach medical data. By its very nature (intended as the receptacle of all results from health examinations), it contains sensitive data, which justifies cybersecurity concerns and the protection of medical information. In principle, the access to the medical record should be based on the patient's consent, although the latter is not required in the exceptional case of a medical emergency. In fact, the continuity of care offered by the shared medical record favors a secured exchange of patient health data, regardless of the healthcare facility hosting it. Although not exactly an application, the updating of health information on the shared medical record either by the patient or by health professionals works similarly to one: sensitive data are collected, with the patient's consent, in order to ensure the mutability of care based on updated health data.

1.2.1.2.2. The mutability of care

At present, mutability is achieved through connected platforms destined to the health professionals. For illustration, Enovacom, a subsidiary of Orange Business Service, enables teams to share data in order to ensure the continuity and coordination of care. Above all, "for the Orange subsidiary, the intention was to create a common communication channel across clinics, cities and hospitals so as to make the patient's path consistent". The platform should make it possible to enhance the patient's cure/support, ensuring appropriate care practices. Today, many connected health platforms work in this direction. Among the points to be improved upon, let us mention here the availability of medical staff, curbing the growth of the chronically ill and the high cost of treatment. It is also necessary to counter the overcrowding of medical facilities and to compensate for the lack of access to healthcare in rural areas. It is in this sense that we must understand the arrival of connected health platforms, such as Comarch Healthcare. The goal is to offer the patient teleconsultation solutions.

1.2.1.2.3. The equality of care

Telemedicine makes it possible to fight against medical deserts and to bring not only physical, but also moral, comfort to the isolated patients. Equal access to care was enshrined by the preamble of the French Constitution of October 27, 1946. The Republic proclaimed that the Nation should guarantee the necessary conditions for the development of the individual and the family; and, on the basis of paragraph 11 of said preamble, guarantee health protection, material security, and rest and leisure to everyone (in particular, to children, mothers and elderly workers). Any human being unable to work – in virtue of their age, physical or mental state, or economic situation – has the right to obtain suitable means of existence from the community.

1.2.1.2.4. The ethical challenge regarding the use of applications

Although seemingly innovative, the ethical use of technology is an age-old question. In 1990, Jean-Marie Auby wrote:

> the category of contracts relating to human rights, ignored by traditional civil law, currently appears as an important and difficult element rgarding contractual techniques. Given the fact that it concerns a medical act, it is up to the doctor to implement these techniques in the name of the principle of therapeutic freedom, provided that they do not affect public order (Auby 1999).
>
> What is certain is that ethics does not satisfactorily compensate for the absence of legal rules (Auby 1999).

The European Union addressed the needs of vulnerable adults on the conclusions drawn by the Council in 2020 ("Access to justice – seizing the opportunities offered by digitization"), noting "that they should be given special attention to improve their digital skills and their access to information, in order to protect their rights" (Journal officiel de l'Union européenne 2021a). It is in this context that obtaining the person's consent for the processing of sensitive information on a healthcare application is a requirement that has to comply with the GDPR, a legal binding that no practitioner can be exempt from. As sedentary lifestyles evolve, applications can be a useful resource to combat isolation and vulnerabilities (section 1.2.2).

1.2.2. *Helpful applications to counter isolation and other vulnerabilities*

The Hippocratic Oath reminds doctors that their "primary concern shall be to restore, preserve or promote health in all its elements, physical and mental, individual and social" and that the doctor "will inform patients of the decisions envisaged, their groundings and their consequences". Modern software applications are an extension of that oath. Without overriding the diagnosis and recommendations preliminarily determined by the doctor, the development of applications allows many people to recover their motor skills for achieving greater freedom and dignity (section 1.2.2.1), and to overcome isolation (section 1.2.2.2).

1.2.2.1. *Recovering motor skills for greater freedom and dignity*

1.2.2.1.1. Through the use of virtual hypnosis

There are several applications to support human and animal welfare. People do not react in the same way to illnesses, physical accidents or moral trauma.

While a few years ago paralysis could permanently immobilize a person, today several applications allow humans, as well as animals – sensitive beings – to regain hope and recover their independence through the mastery of their body. Applications can be extraordinary tools to stimulate atrophied body portions. It is as if the body was sculpted to encourage the brain to regain balance. The world of start-ups is fully invested in research areas for the development of virtual[3] reality therapies, based on applications that facilitate hypnosis.

3 The start-up HypnoVR develops virtual reality therapies.

1.2.2.1.2. Increasing the autonomy of the vulnerable person by mastering technology

The help provided by heart tracking applications

Recovered autonomy can also be achieved "with the help of connected sensors which measure and record muscular strength outputs. The purpose is to provide practitioners with quantified results assessing patient progression in less than a minute"[4]. Many applications help the dependent person to regain moral and physical independence, through health self-monitoring. For example, in the case of heart diseases, some applications enable the recording of an ECG signal, considered to be reliable and secure in the long term. The application Cardiovest, developed by Comarch[5], offers a solution for carrying out preventive examinations. Patients suffering from heart diseases can be diagnosed and monitored through the use of technology that enables a safe, reliable and long-term recording of the ECG signal.

The monitoring[6] bracelet

The monitoring bracelet can be a solution for people in need of constant care, eager to improve their quality of life, and wishing to feel safe. These are remote care services for seniors: each patient is provided with a bracelet[7] and benefits from 24-hour remote support. The implementation of remote care for seniors by local authorities and health institutions helps to improve the situation of the elderly, especially those living on their own, far from relatives. This service seems to cater for dependent patients requiring constant support. The interoperability of digital certificates also helps in the fight against the isolation of vulnerable persons, thanks to free movement rules (section 1.2.2.2).

1.2.2.2. *The critical aspect of protecting information, introduced to the application*

Even though the application *Tous anti Covid*, created in 2020, had a national spectrum of use, its acceptability was difficult to generalize. While many other applications play an essential social role, they are largely

4 Application presented by Comarch.

5 See: www.comarch.fr/solutions-it/plateforme-de-santeconnectee/telemedecine/comarch-cardiovest/.

6 Comarch Life Band Company.

7 Comarch Life Band Company.

outstripped by medical applications, which enable patients to partially recover their physical and mental autonomy.

1.2.2.2.1. Health protection, a national, technical and political goal

Amidst the Covid-19 pandemic, the EU Commission fully played its role as guardian of the treaties in terms of preventive health policy, releasing the sum of 100 million euros under the emergency aid instrument, in order to acquire antigen tests with rapid results. It initiated a joint procurement procedure for over half a billion tests (Berrod 2021; Journal officiel de l'Union européenne 2021b), adding up to the discussions on the multi-annual financial framework adapted to the crisis for the 2021–2027 period.

1.2.2.2.2. The monitoring of essential services by the National Agency for Information Systems Security

In France, the National Information Systems Security Agency (ANSSI, *Agence nationale de la sécurité des systèmes d'information*, set within the General Secretariat for Security and National Defense) plays a crucial role in the functioning of several essential services, including health. A long European process has made it possible to strengthen cybersecurity, particularly in terms of health. Following the exponential increase in cybercrime among the Member States of the European Union, the French government was a driving force for amending and deepening the NIS 1 and NIS 2 directives (Journal officiel de l'Union européenne 2022a). On June 22, 2022, in order to better protect our cyberspace, the Member States, mindful of their sovereign prerogatives, agreed to distinguish the lists of essential services from important sectors in terms of cybersecurity.

Healthcare provided by public and private institutions was qualified as an essential service. Other services and sectors were also deemed to be essential: the postal services; waste management; chemical products; the food sector; electronics; machinery; motor vehicles; digital infrastructure providers; drinking water; education and the entire catering chain; order management; supply and logistics. Although this list, adopted by the consensus of states, is probably not exhaustive, it has the merit of fostering a better protection of health in many ways, by focusing on the interoperability of services. The ANSSI ensured the security of digital vaccination certificates (section 1.2.2.2.3).

1.2.2.2.3. The interoperability of digital vaccination certificates

The ANSSI made it possible to maintain free movement rules, while respecting public order in terms of health and public safety. We should bear in mind that digital certificates stem from a medical act binding the doctor. Hence, health protection cannot be affected by the interoperability of services.

On the other hand, it is up to the European Union to promote "a high level of human health" (Article 168, paragraph 1 TFEU). In 2021, the balance sought between the protection of public health and the respect for the free movement of people enabled the European Union to lift restrictions on free movement, including with regards to Third States such as the Republic of North Macedonia (Journal officiel de l'Union européenne 2021c). Digital vaccination certificates against Covid-19 were interoperable, which led to an improvement in free movement during the pandemic, thanks to the application of the mutual trust principle (Journal officiel de l'Union européenne 2021d). From 2021, the same rule was extended to Ukraine (Journal officiel de l'Union européenne 2021e) and Turkey (Journal officiel de l'Union européenne 2021f). Interoperability can be targeted by various attacks, whose spread could be significant in cyberspace. Therefore, a cybersecurity policy must be clearly stated in an area as sensitive as health. It is thereby appropriate to combine a modern approach in the use of healthcare applications with cybersecurity measures (section 1.3).

1.3. Cybersecurity to reinforce the resilience of applications

Based on the French constitutional traditions and the Declaration of the Rights of Man and of the Citizen, the explosion in the number of applications now available to minors implies an increasing awareness of the need to set up an effective protection of youth against content that could potentially harm their health. In order to achieve this, the use of the regulatory instrument is a strong political signal, considering the urgent need to provide a legal framework for cyberspace, in view of protecting vulnerable people and, especially the health of minor children (section 1.3.1). More generally, the cybersecurity policy must make it possible to better assess the risks associated with the use of modern technologies (section 1.3.2).

1.3.1. *The obligation to protect the health of minor children against content that may harm their health*

A democratic society must promote the physical, mental and moral development of children (section 1.3.1.1) and be able to manage crises or pandemics (section 1.3.1.2).

1.3.1.1. *The substantial interest in the physical, mental and moral development of children*

In formal terms, the entry into force of Regulation 2022/2065 from October 19, 2022 on digital services (Journal officiel de l'Union européenne 2022b) enabled the representatives of the Member States to take into account the convergence of this regulation with the GDPR, placing the person at the center of digital space. The acceptability of technologies integrating AI is in line with the search for scientific progress so dear to Bachelard, and is reflected by the consideration of the substantial interests of the child.

This demand for the primacy of the protection of the children's well-being is a legal and moral requirement. The representatives of Member States ensure that the design and operation of the service are easy for minors to understand, but most importantly, seek to protect them from content that could harm their health, as well as their physical, mental and moral development. The Council particularly emphasizes the obligation to protect children because "such risks may arise, for example, in relation to the design of online interfaces which intentionally or unintentionally exploit the weaknesses and inexperience of minors or which may cause addictive behavior" (Journal officiel de l'Union européenne 2022b, paragraph 80).

It is also necessary to provide a legal framework for the uses of algorithmic systems: operators must take into account the risks of infringement of children's rights by algorithmic systems, which are extensively used on online platforms. European lawmakers attach considerable importance to "the design of online interfaces which intentionally or unintentionally exploit the weaknesses and inexperience of minors or which may cause addictive behavior" (Journal officiel de l'Union européenne 2022b, paragraph 80). Child health risk assessments aim to protect minors. Providers of very large online platforms and of the biggest online search engines have an obligation to ensure that no negative consequences infringe the rights of children, including through an application.

The effective monitoring of the full integrity of minors' health, physical, mental and moral development (paragraph 81) is an essential moral and legal obligation, constantly recalled by the European Commission. It involves taking into account the risk of "serious negative consequences to a person's physical and mental well-being". Particular targets are gender-based violence and the "danger to the minor's health by stimulating behavioral addictions" (Journal officiel de l'Union européenne 2022b, paragraph 80).

1.3.1.2. *Crisis or pandemic management*

Contrary to the providers of very large platforms, there is an obligation to take specific measures in the event of a pandemic and to ensure the adaptation of online content intended for children. In this context, mastering time constitutes the nerve of digital and pandemic warfare.

There is an obligation to adopt specific measures at odds with providers of very large online platforms in the event of a crisis. This covers

> armed conflicts or acts of terrorism, including emerging conflicts or acts of terrorism, natural disasters such as earthquakes and hurricanes, as well as from pandemics and other serious cross-border threats to public health (Journal officiel de l'Union européenne 2022b, paragraph 90).

As guardian of the Treaties, the Commission should be able to require providers of very large online platforms and of very large search engines to initiate a crisis response as a matter of urgency (paragraph 91).

Obligations relating to the adaptation of online content for children are detailed in Regulation No. 2022-2065 on digital services, and specifically impose an adaptation of content and awareness-raising measures. The panoply of these obligations is far from negligible. In particular, it concerns:

– the adaptation of content moderation processes;

– the adaptation of the general conditions of algorithmic and advertising systems;

– the intensification of cooperation with trusted flaggers;

– awareness-raising measures;

– the promotion of trusted information;

– adapting the design of online interfaces.

This search for a balance between the proper functioning of the digital internal market and the effective protection of children's rights is at the heart of the European legislative system. The European Union firmly combats advertising targeted at people in vulnerable situations, in particular, minors (Journal officiel de l'Union européenne 2022b, paragraph 95).

Finally, the mastery of time constitutes the nerve of the digital and pandemic war: in this barely hidden economic war, taking time into account is essential when evaluating different reactions to crises. Those responsible for processing must be able to react within a very short time and in a proportionate manner to the breach of the obligations to protect health. The simplified ergonomics of an application can be a major asset in this sense.

This strategy of controlling time to prohibit practices that could jeopardize health is reminiscent of the method of adopting European acts of secondary law, which are the basis of the intergovernmental common security and defense policy. A community of values clearly emerges between defense actors and internal market "watchdogs", who ensure the proper functioning of the four fundamental freedoms of movement (goods, persons, services and capital) and the ethical behavior of platform managers. However, it is equally essential to be able to assess the risks of harm to health by digital services (section 1.3.2).

1.3.2. *Assessing health risks through digital services*

It is desirable for health actors to find a sustainable balance between the use of digital services and the national health, on the one hand (section 1.3.2.1), while seeking to reconcile the wide distribution of digital services with the security goal, on the other hand (section 1.3.2.2).

1.3.2.1. *The balance sought between health protection and the sustainable inclusion of digital services in the daily lives of European citizens*

1.3.2.1.1. The risks of harm to public health by digital services

On October 19, 2022, European lawmakers adopted Regulation (2022/2065) on digital services, which contemplates a crisis response mechanism (Article 36, Regulation 2022/2065). In the medical sector, health applications help both doctors and patients. These same applications are very popular terrains for cyber attackers, since corporate cybersecurity is sometimes very rudimentary – if not nonexistent – not to mention applications for which finding a hint of cybersecurity is still a challenge. Regarding the scale and intensity of attacks, mentalities are changing, but still often far too slowly! In many regions and cities – among which Rennes is particularly relevant – cybersecurity centers of excellence help ensure that a business ecosystem is firmly rooted in resilient territories to grant the cybersecurity of essential services, including health.

These risks must be "proportionate to systemic risks" and respect the EU Charter of Fundamental Rights. On the basis of Article 34 from Regulation (EU) 2022/2065 on digital services (DSA, Digital Services Act), European lawmakers implemented the use of analysis in compliance with the principle of human dignity, freedom, media pluralism and children's rights (Article 24, Charter of Fundamental Rights), a high level of consumer protection (Article 38, Charter of Fundamental Rights), and the prevention of negative (or foreseeable) health effects related to gender-based violence (Article 34d, Regulation 2022/2065).

A risk assessment is also based on the design of recommendation systems and any other "relevant" algorithmic systems (Journal officiel de l'Union européenne 2022b, Article 34, paragraph 1). In this context, the providers of very large online platforms and large search engines examine whether (and to what extent) certain factors influence systemic risks, and how these are acknowledged. On the basis of Article 34 from Regulation 2022/2065 (DSA), European lawmakers clearly seek to protect "public health and minors, preventing serious negative consequences to the person's physical and mental well-being" (Journal officiel de l'Union européenne 2022b, Article 34, paragraph 2).

In order to legally qualify (or not) a health crisis at the European Union level, European lawmakers rely on internal public law and Article 35 paragraph 2 from Regulation 2022/2065 (DSA), to assess the scope of such a crisis. This is the case when such extraordinary circumstances result in a serious threat to public security or public health (Article 35, paragraph 2 from Regulation 2022/2065-DSA). This reveals a certain community of spirit with the rules of operation of the internal market and the freedoms of movement inherent in it.

While the general rules on the operation of the internal market are similar to those of the operation of a unified digital market, in the name of free competition, there is a certain vigilance against the operation of contestable and fair digital markets for essential services.

1.3.2.1.2. The influence of health on contestable and fair digital markets for essential services

European lawmakers adopted another regulation 2022-1925 on contestable and fair markets on September 14, 2022. In this context, the access controller and the requesting supplier must ensure that interoperability does not compromise the protection of personal data (GDPR). This reflects the desire of European lawmakers to implement specific protective measures for children online, a goal deemed as "important for the EU" (Journal officiel de l'Union européenne 2022, paragraph 38).

The functioning of these markets is scrutinized by the Commission, because they essentially come under the rules of free competition: the freedom to provide services and goods within the internal market.

Moreover, the deepening of the digital internal market is particularly intense in the context of the crisis response mechanism with regards to digital services (Journal officiel de l'Union européenne 2022b, Article 36, paragraph 2). For that matter, in terms of health, the legal protection mechanism implemented is reminiscent of the European Capability Action Plan (ECAP)[8].

As regards crisis management mechanisms aimed at protecting digital services, European lawmakers strictly frame the notion of extraordinary

8 European capability action plan.

circumstances as "a serious threat to public security or public health in the Union or in significant parts of the Union". Nowadays, the European Union still contemplates public health simply as an end, and not as an integration policy. This public health goal is understood as a horizon, an aim of the European Union in its economic, social and environmental dimension, but not as a European health policy (in the same way as the other policies of the unified market). Such an approach simply confirms the Europeans' 'right to health', rather than calling into question the hospital system itself, a system which is still lacking in essential means for the dignified care of patients.

The glaring absence of a real European health policy persists in favor of an unambitious goal: the mere coordination of social protection mechanisms. The so-called European health policy does not exist. At best, there is a Berveridgean or Bismarckian mechanism for coordinating social protection systems (Cammilleri 1992).

Similarly, based on EU Regulation 2022/1925 (Journal officiel de l'Union européenne 2022c, pp. 1–66), lawmakers allow the European Commission to not have to impose an obligation on an essential platform service, for reasons of public order. Under exceptional circumstances – solely justified by reasons of public health or public safety, defined by European Union law and interpreted by the Court of Justice (Journal officiel de l'Union européenne 2022c, Article 10(3)) – the Commission should be able to decide that a given obligation does not apply to a specific essential platform service. It is in this framework that an exemption, for reasons of public health and public safety, can be decided upon.

This exemption is subject to an annual review by the Commission (Journal officiel de l'Union européenne 2022c, Article 10, paragraph 3). It can only be granted for reasons of public health or safety. Only an emergency measure by the Commission can temporarily suspend the application of a specific obligation at any time (Journal officiel de l'Union européenne 2022c, Article 10(4)).

1.3.2.2. *Three national and European entities to support health*

Cyberspace monitoring by two national and European agencies is a substantial guarantee of security.

1.3.2.2.1. Two agencies: a national (ANSSI) and a European entity (ENISA)

In its report published in 2022 on the Panorama of the computer threat in 2021, the French National Agency for the Security of Information Systems (ANSSI) announced that "the number of proven intrusions into reported information systems increased by 37% between 2020 and 2021 (786 in 2020 compared to 1,082 in 2021, that is, nearly three proven intrusions per day" (ANSSI 2022). Major events in France, such as the French presidency of the European Union, the presidential and legislative elections of 2022 and the Paris Olympics in 2024, are all contextual opportunities attackers could seek to exploit.

1.3.2.2.2. At the European level, the ENISA annual report (2021)

This highlights that the Covid-19 pandemic favored cyber-espionage activities and created opportunities for cybercriminals[9]. Covid-19 was an important lure in email attack campaigns. Healthcare-related data breaches multiplied. Regulation (EU) 2019/881 of the European Parliament and of the Council of April 17, 2019 relating to ENISA (Journal officiel de l'Union européenne 2019) provides a basis for legal standards that should allow for the implementation of a certification policy, whose outlines can help strengthen cooperation between all the actors, to increase confidence by seeking a high level of security and transparency vis-à-vis the consumer.

1.3.2.2.3. An independent administrative authority, the CNIL, to support health

On May 11, 2022, the CNIL published its 2021 annual activity report, which confirmed:

> the exponential trend in rule violations […]. In 2021, the CNIL received 14,143 complaints, 12,522 of which were closed down. It carried out 384 controls and the shortcomings noted during some of the investigations led to pronouncing 135 formal notices and 18 penalties, for an unprecedented cumulative amount of fines exceeding 214 million euros[10].

---

9 ENISA Annual Report, p. 12.

10 Sanctions and corrective measures: the CNIL presents the 2022 report of its repressive action on January 31, 2023. See: www.cnil.fr.

With the adoption of the NIS Directive 2 (Journal officiel de l'Union européenne 2022a, p. 80), specific rules are to protect so-called "important" sectors such as postal services, waste management, chemicals, food, medical device manufacturing, electronics, machinery, motor vehicles and digital suppliers.

1.4. Conclusion

Historically, within the UE, health corresponded to a simple and insufficient method for coordinating social protection mechanisms. These could reflect two social models: either the Beveridgian model (identifiable by its universality) or the Bismarckian type, based on an insurance model (Cammilleri 1992). Unfortunately, without really being able to speak of the existence of a European health policy, the Union limits its role to the promotion of public and private healthcare institutions and pharmaceuticals. However, in the event of cyberattacks, the protection of health must result in the use of specific protection tools, because this concern is at the heart of the human being!

1.5. References

ANSSI (2022). Panorama de la menace informatique. Report.

Auby, J.-M. (1999). L'autorité judiciaire gardienne du corps humain ? In *L'unité du droit. Mélanges en l'honneur de Rolland Drago*. Éditions Economica, Paris, 353–367.

Berrod, F. (2021). Le passe sanitaire français et l'enjeu des droits fondamentaux. Université de Strasbourg, Strasbourg.

Cammilleri, A. (1992). *La protection sociale en Europe*. G.L.N. Joly Editions, Paris.

Canevet, M. (2018a). Question orale n° 0441. *JORF Sénat*, 4646.

Canevet, M. (2018b). Réponse du secrétariat d'État auprès de la ministre des solidarités et de la santé. *JO Sénat*, 14043.

Journal officiel de l'Union européenne (2019). Règlement (UE) 2019/881 du Parlement européen et du Conseil du 17 avril 2019 relatif à l'ENISA (Agence de l'Union européenne pour la cybersécurité) et à la certification de cybersécurité des technologies de l'information et des communications, et abrogeant le règlement (UE) n° 526/2013 (règlement sur la cybersécurité JOUE). *JOUE*, L(151), 15–69.

Journal officiel de l'Union européenne (2021a). Conclusions du Conseil sur la protection des adultes vulnérables dans l'ensemble de l'UE. *JOUE*, C(330).

Journal officiel de l'Union européenne (2021b). Déclaration de la Commission. *JOUE*, L211(23).

Journal officiel de l'Union européenne (2021c). Décision d'exécution (UE) 2021/1381 de la Commission du 19 août 2021 établissant l'équivalence, aux fins de faciliter l'exercice du droit à la libre circulation au sein de l'Union, des certificats Covid-19 délivrés par la République de Macédoine du Nord avec les certificats délivrés conformément au règlement (UE) 2021/953 du Parlement européen et du Conseil. *JOUE*, L(297).

Journal officiel de l'Union européenne (2021d). Règlement (UE) 2021/953 du Parlement européen et du Conseil du 14 juin 2021 relatif à un cadre pour la délivrance, la vérification et l'acceptation de certificats Covid-19 interopérables de vaccination, de test et de rétablissement (certificat Covid numérique de l'UE) afin de faciliter la libre circulation pendant la pandémie de Covid-19. *JOUE*, L(211).

Journal officiel de l'Union européenne (2021e). Décision d'exécution (UE) 2021/1380 de la Commission du 19 août 2021 établissant l'équivalence, aux fins de faciliter l'exercice du droit à la libre circulation au sein de l'Union, des certificats Covid-19 délivrés par l'Ukraine avec les certificats délivrés conformément au règlement (UE) 2021/953 du Parlement européen et du Conseil. *JOUE*, L(297).

Journal officiel de l'Union européenne (2021f). Décision d'exécution (UE) 2021/1382 de la Commission du 19 août 2021 établissant l'équivalence, aux fins de faciliter l'exercice du droit à la libre circulation au sein de l'Union, des certificats Covid-19 délivrés par la République de Turquie avec les certificats délivrés conformément au règlement (UE) 2021/953 du Parlement européen et du Conseil. *JOUE*, L(297).

Journal officiel de l'Union européenne (2022a). Directive (UE) 2022/2555 du Parlement européen et du Conseil du 14 décembre 2022 concernant les mesures destinées à assurer un niveau élevé commun de cybersécurité dans l'ensemble de l'Union européenne. *JOUE*, L(333).

Journal officiel de l'Union européenne (2022b). Règlement (UE) 2022/2065 du Parlement européen et du Conseil du 19 octobre 2022 relatif à un marché unique des services numériques et modifiant la directive 2000/31/CE (règlement sur les services numériques). *JOUE*, L(277).

Journal officiel de l'Union européenne (2022c). Règlement (UE) 2022/1925 du Parlement et du Conseil du 14 septembre 2022 relatif aux marchés contestables et équitables dans le secteur numérique et modifiant les directives 2019/1937 et 2020/1828 (règlement sur les marchés numériques). *JOUE*, L(265).

Journal officiel de la République française (2020). Décret n° 2020-650 du 29 mai 2020 relatif au traitement de données dénommé "StopCovid". *JORF*, 0131(17).

Journal officiel de la République française (2021). Arrêté du 13 septembre 2021 définissant les objectifs nationaux pluriannuels de professionnels de santé à former pour la période 2021-2025. *JORF*, 0217(27).

Le Parisien (2021). Diffusion de données piratées à la suite d'une cyberattaque : quels sont les risques et les précautions à prendre ? *Le Parisien*, September.

2

Behavioral Insurance: The Latest Trick of Capitalism?

2.1. Introduction

Many decisions are made with the support of artificial intelligence (AI): for household activities or help with cooking, robots can take care of tedious and repetitive tasks; in the field of romantic relationships, AI can help in the search for a partner. Health is one of the areas in which AI has a broad audience. On the basis of medical records, algorithms are able to produce a rapid diagnosis, and are sometimes even considered to be more reliable than doctors. In the field of medical diagnosis, the mass of collected data is not singularly used for detecting an anomaly (e.g. a pathology, a fracture), which is then combined with a treatment that has proven its efficiency. The interest of using AI in this way is that it works as a "learning through failure" mechanism, but without incurring the risk of failure, since the doctor is not going to experiment with a treatment on the patient. Rather, it is the accumulated experience of others that makes it possible to detect a pathology, and to associate it with a certain treatment. In the field of cancer, for example, an X-ray image can be associated with a type of cancer and its treatment.

AI feeds on the development and sophistication of digital tools. In that sense, it is necessary to have a huge database for the expert system to learn from a large number of available cases having a confirmed diagnosis. The major argument for deploying AI in the field of medical diagnostics is its

Chapter written by Philippe BATIFOULIER and Nicolas DA SILVA.

ability to increase human intelligence, because the expert system can see more things than a human doctor can.

A lesser-known aspect of AI development in healthcare concerns health policies. In that area, AI is used for identifying standards, in order to make decisions deemed to be more efficient. Expert systems can manage the availability of beds in hospitals or decide whether or not to finance a treatment within the framework of the medico-economic assessment, a tool aiming to associate the result criterion (or gain in health) of a health[1] strategy with that strategy's cost. The data collected are used by public evaluation agencies (the *Haute Autorité de Santé*, HAS in France, the National Institute for Health and Clinical Excellence, NICE, in Great Britain, etc.) for calculating the maximum amount to be allocated for a medical treatment or procedure.

A more recent application of AI in the field of healthcare, which will be discussed in this chapter, is that of health insurance. Recently, new tools have flourished, enabling patients to adopt healthy behaviors, deemed more appropriate in relation to public health. In that sense, private insurers (for profit or not) offer products in broad areas: nutrition, quitting smoking, physical activity and stress management, etc.

These products are supported by the development of digital technology and connected objects. They are based on algorithms which are used by health insurers in order to optimize the decisions and behaviors of policyholders. Applications compete in inventiveness to count steps and ensure that they have burned enough calories, or that they are keeping in shape. They can be used for keeping a healthy diet, getting a better sleep, etc. New marketing strategies point to health in the sense of well-being, rather than targeting a specific disease.

While they seek to provide an expert system to decide on the extent of what an insurer should finance (relying on an automatic process), they aim to amplify human intelligence through "self-quantification" technologies. Encouraging healthy behavior (to be adopted by policyholders) is also good for insurers, because this can be translated as fewer expenses to be covered.

1 For example, QALYs (Quality-Adjusted Life Year) technologies. QALY is equal to 1 for a healthy year, and 0 if the person passes away. Thanks to a treatment with variable impact on quality of life, QALY can be set between 0 and 1.

This new health insurance market relies on the proliferation of digital devices prompting policyholders to adopt “good health behaviors” on a daily basis. Not only are they introduced as a new market segment, but they are also tasked with missions at the service of public health. Bearing in mind this assistance to human intelligence in order to maintain or improve a health condition, insurers set themselves in the field of general interest. Therefore, the development of the health insurance market is fostered in the patient’s “highest interest”. The insurer’s register changes. The insurer is no longer expected to pay for the consequences of the disease, but rather becomes the patient’s companion or coach to support the best daily practices.

This chapter seeks to grasp the challenges of this new market. It shows that the use of AI in the field of health insurance to increase human intelligence is seeking to develop a self-quantification market. While these new health insurance techniques are presented as individual and collective health promotion missions, they contribute to the insurers’ business model, enabling them to present themselves as champions of general interest, monopolizing its definition while maintaining inequalities. In this sense, the use of AI in the field of health insurance techniques is a means available to actors in the search for profitability and the wish to expand their power, while presenting themselves as defenders of general interest.

The first part will provide an overview of healthy lifestyle behavior insurance, the behaviors and actors embodying it, as well as the historical and legal context resulting from the reforms on health coverage policies. The second part will discuss the political and philosophical stakes of these new insurance products. Insurance companies arrogate to themselves a definition of the general interest in the name of paternalism and feed on social inequalities in health, which are a lever for the development of these new products.

In conclusion, we will explore the transformations in the definition of health risk portrayed by these new logics. We will observe a shift from a conception of a health risk as a social risk (as in public health insurance systems), to a notion of risk in personal terms, whereby transforming social ills into individual problems.

2.2. A new health insurance market

2.2.1. *Healthy lifestyle behavior insurance: an overview*

The Vitality program, developed by Generali in 2016 in France, is a leading figure in healthy lifestyle behavior insurance. In this system, initially implemented in South Africa and then reproduced in other countries, members adhering to collective health or provident contracts can benefit from a specific program in which all of the actions aimed at health preservation or improvement are rewarded in the form of gifts. Each member sets a personalized goal plan for a healthier and more active lifestyle: the number of steps taken per day, the purchases of fruit and vegetables, preventive medical visits, etc. If the member reaches these goals, points will be awarded, which can then be converted into commercial advantages at well-known and recognized companies, such as Fnac or Decathlon, Weight Watchers, Sephora, or even travel brands such as Club Med or Transat Voyage. The program calculates the number of points earned by the member and sets a hierarchy according to the number of points: bronze, silver, gold or platinum.

This initiative coming from a general insurer (which does not only sell health insurance) is not an isolated case. In 2014, AXA (also an all-terrain insurer) developed a rewards system with partner brands in return for a commitment to reach prevention goals. These were sanctioned by the verdict of an electronic bracelet worn for four weeks.

The Swiss insurer Helsana also put this bonus policy into practice (accumulation of prevention points) by means of a pedometer embedded into a smartphone. The originality of that program was that the points acquired could not only be converted into vouchers, but could also be cashed out or transformed into donations to associations such as the Swiss Red Cross or the Theodora Foundation (for hospitalized children).

We should bear in mind that these arrangements are not health insurance contracts, but addenda or supplements to an insurance contract. They are supplements to collective contracts; in other words, health insurance contracts taken out by the employer for the employees, but not directly taken out by employees on an individual basis.

This is why the rewards are expressed by advantages which are somehow disconnected from the health insurance contract. For example, in France, there is no reduction in the insurance premium if the person meets the agreed health goals. Such a mechanism existed in Germany, known as *franchise cautionnée* (proposed by France Mutuelle in 1996), whereby policyholders, having consumed the least in health expenses, were reimbursed a part of their contributions. However, no deposit was refunded if the healthcare consumption of the insured was significant.

In 2018, the American insurer John Hancock set up a bonus/penalty system that imposed a penalty of 15 dollars in the event of a bad pedometer verdict and a bonus system with a reduction in the cost of the insurance premium of up to 15% of the premium's total amount.

These examples show that behavior-centered insurance has profusely developed since the 2000s, despite strong protests in certain countries such as France, due to the possession (or deprivation) of health data (Ginon 2017; Chelle 2018). As a matter of fact, all of these products assume that the user agrees to share health data for commercial purposes. This type of program reinforces the threat of the use of personal data to strengthen segmentation and as an excuse for charging more for "bad risks" (Jeanningros 2021).

Connected objects play a key role in healthy lifestyle behavior insurance. From "e-health" (information and communication technologies applied to health) to "m-health" (health on mobile devices), innovative health insurance products rely on "digital footprints" left by human behaviors, including the ones that go unnoticed and are part of everyday life (Cappel 2021). It is not enough for the insured person to agree to provide their health data. They must be able to do so (which means being digitally equipped).

This approach to health risks focusing on individual behavior has many advantages for insurers: it differentiates them from competitors by selling innovative connected products aimed at young people and the able-bodied. Adopting a healthier lifestyle, like any preventive action, reduces curative health expenditure and ultimately the cost of health insurance for insurers.

Healthy lifestyle behavior insurance is also presented as "fairer" in the sense that it makes those leading a healthy lifestyle pay less. This modality is similar to the "pay how you drive" car insurance model: drivers provoking no accidents can accumulate bonus points and a reduction in the amount of their premium (and vice versa).

Healthy lifestyle behavior insurance is in fact part of a generic type of insurance mainly carried by for-profit generalist insurers, who sell the whole panoply of insurance. The great ambition of insurers to develop insurance techniques wherever there is sinistrality (without worrying about the insurance content) leads to trivializing health insurance and making it an insurance product like any other. Health insurance is assimilated to automobile, civil liability or home insurance and must obey the same techniques of commercial mutualization. In this perspective, mutualization is to respond to a healthcare cost-effectiveness logic, globalized across all customers or groups of customers. The goal is to erase the "solidarity mutualization" aspect of health insurance, implemented by public systems (such as the Social Security in France), whose mission is to generate social ties and produce collective security. With Social Security, everyone contributes according to their means and receives in function of their needs; whereas, with private for-profit insurance, everyone contributes according to their risk level and receives depending on what they have previously paid. Insurance mutualizes identical or similar classes of risk; whereas, Social Security mutualizes all risks to balance solidarity between the rich and the poor, between big risks and small risks.

2.2.2. *The importance of the institutional context*

The insurer Generali displays outstanding performances for its Vitality program, with approximately 2,000 member companies for a total of 40,000 employees. More developed in the United States, Great Britain or South Eastern Asia than in continental Europe (except in Germany), the program is not present in Latin America. First and foremost, nothing obliges individual employees to join the program, even if the company is an adhering member[2]. The reluctance to provide health data is nonetheless significant.

Only the private health insurance sector is covered by behavior insurance. This is why it is found in the United States and Germany (where health insurance is essentially private for high incomes). In France, the so-called

2 Data drawn from *Argus de l'Assurance*, 2017 [Online]. Available at: www.argusdelassurance.com/acteurs/compagnies-bancassureurs/generali-vitality-les-premiers-enseignements-du-programme.124048.

complementary private health insurance covers 96.4% of the population. It is sold by three types of organizations: nonprofit mutual societies, pension funds, which are jointly managed by nonprofit organizations, and for-profit insurance companies. The latter are the main providers of behavior insurance. Let us emphasize that the boundaries between these three operators are blurred, as the literature has shown (Domin 2021; Da Silva and Domin 2022). The health insurance market is a highly concentrated market where – in order to face competition – mutual societies have had to merge with one another and join forces with non-mutual organizations in order to form large financial groups. This has resulted in significant market standardization, dominated by a limited number of insurance companies who adopt the same management techniques and seek cost-effective coverage. The pooling of new offers accessible to all insurance groups makes it possible to industrialize them and to nuance offers so that they can cater for a wide range of customers. In short, health insurance operators are converging towards a homogeneous risk management mode.

Three elements combine to leverage healthy lifestyle behavior insurance in France: the important and secure place of the private health insurance sector, the development of collective company contracts and the standardization of basic health contracts, which call for innovations in order to stand out and face competition.

2.2.2.1. *Health insurance in France: a protected market*

The organization of health coverage in France is highly original. Alongside the public scheme (Social Security), there is a highly developed private insurance system whose market place is secured. While the market place is often analyzed with regards to its weight (high in relation to the market place of public insurance in the United States, low compared to the United Kingdom, etc.), in France, its nature is striking. Private health insurance is not residual or reserved for comfort or convenience. It was given the privilege to reimburse one part of the public reimbursement price for all care. It is even dominant on certain medical acts related to optics, dental medicine, hearing or hospital facilities. For each medical act, the patient is required to have two insurance modes, one public and the other private. Lawmakers thus secured the private health insurance market by making full coverage of all health costs, subject to the purchase of a private insurance policy.

While French-style complementarity is an institutional originality, it also translates into commercial liveliness. The part of private health insurance accounts for 14% of current health expenditure in France, that is, twice as much as in the Netherlands, three times as much as in Spain and four times as much as in Germany (DREES 2019). This market place (both size and location) is a necessary condition for the deployment of new insurance products. The health insurance market in France represents 38 billion euros in total premiums. This has continued to increase every year, except for during the Covid-19 period (DREES 2021). The market's sound financial health, whose turnover is increasing, creates the conditions for the deployment of behavior-centered insurance products. While this condition is necessary, it is not sufficient.

2.2.2.2. *The development of company health insurance, breeding ground for new innovative products*

A second French characteristic boosts healthy lifestyle behavior insurance. The emphasis placed by the public authorities on so-called collective insurance contracts (namely contracts taken out through the intermediary of the company) gives leverage to new insurance products. As has been shown, new behavior-centered product insurance are often amendments or accessories to collective contracts. Although these have existed for a long time in France, they used to be limited to large companies. Since the national interprofessional agreement of 2013, all companies in the private sector are required to provide private health insurance and to contribute to the cost of the insurance premium paid by the employee. This law (implemented in 2016) does not generalize private health insurance, but is aimed at those who already have complementary insurance. It transforms individual contracts taken out individually into collective ones, acquired through the company.

This change is significant. It makes company insurance the backbone of complementary health insurance. In this market, for-profit insurance companies selling healthy lifestyle behavior insurance are present; whereas, mutual societies traditionally focus on the individual contract market. The new landscape of complementary health insurance in France is reflected in the proliferation of additional guarantees or tariff options added to the basic complementary insurance contract. The complementary contract covers current healthcare costs (co-payment, hospital, etc.). The additional contract offers supplementary quality for a higher price, to cover products related to well-being, particularly healthy lifestyle behavior insurance. Often presented in the form of a "package" (well-being, sports on prescription, fitness coaching, etc.), these enable the buyer (the company) to choose from among various offers in the catalog following the diagnosis established by the seller (the insurer).

The two types of complementary and supplementary contracts (which is somehow complementary to the complementary) are taken out through the company, most often with the same insurer. Fulfilling this health insurance provider role, the company can deploy its human resource policy to motivate and retain its employees (Bruna 2022).

2.2.2.3. *Selling well-being to stand out from competitors*

For innovative products in the area of healthy lifestyle behavior insurance to develop, the presence of profitability perspectives is also required. However, due to hyper-regulation, which obliges private insurers to respect certain social clauses, the health insurance market in France is highly standardized. This includes the prohibition of risk selection, the organization of an increasingly detailed configuration of the services and the levels of guarantee offered in contracts, compliance with specifications prohibiting the exclusion of the most vulnerable people, the obligation to cover a minimum healthcare basket, etc. With the development of such a legal arsenal, private health insurers are now guarantors of the solidarity mission usually associated with the Social Security. An important part of the legislative framework aims to educate the market in solidarity and to raise it to a level of support which is not spontaneously that of its business model (Batifoulier et al. 2021). The "responsible contract" framework, whereby insurers undertake to adopt the same rules of solidarity as the Social Security against social and tax exemptions, synthesizes this standardization movement in health insurance contracts. In theory, the development of innovative products is hindered by this uniformization.

While lawmakers are the masterminds behind responsible contracts, they have also made room for the existence of non-responsible contracts, which are often collective contracts taken out by companies. Non-responsible contracts cover a different type of care from the Social Security (Ginon 2014). This means that they assume a discontinuity with the latter. They are autonomous in that they escape the restrictive specification framework of responsible contracts. They are therefore not covered by complementary insurance, which covers the same thing as Social Security but additional insurance, which intends to cover a whole potential space for innovative insurance products. Healthy lifestyle behavior insurance, and more generally, all innovative insurance products focusing on well-being and health coaching, belong to this category.

By escaping the standardization movement, they offer insurers a way to differentiate themselves and to develop new products to stand out from their competitors and/or enhance their brand image. The portfolio of new insurance products with a digital twist enables private health insurance companies to position themselves as the new pivot of public health by displaying a mission in the name of general interest, emphasizing self-prevention and the development of a "healthy body". Health insurance does not merely sell reimbursements. It now promises – and actively promotes – a healthy lifestyle (Batifoulier and Del Sol 2024a).

2.3. Heading towards a great backward leap in health risk socialization?

2.3.1. *Artificial intelligence at the service of paternalism in insurance policies*

New health insurance techniques seek to encourage policyholders to adopt behaviors which are considered better for individual and collective health. E-health applications are not only presented as commercial products on a market but as means of taking part in a general interest goal: improving the health of the population.

The starting point of the argument considers that new technologies are necessary because they help individuals to make good health decisions, which they would not make on their own. Digital tools associated with behavior insurance products are put at the service of a form of paternalism in insurance policies, whereby insurers know what is "good" for policyholders and their health (Batifoulier and Ginon 2018).

This conception is based on the development of behavioral economics, which breaks away from the standard conception in economics, according to which individuals are perfectly rational beings. Unlike the heroic individual in standard economic theory (who makes good decisions by thoroughly weighing the consequences of the choices to be made), real individuals can make bad decisions. They are far less calculating than standard economics asserts, and their rationality is limited. The question then comes down to admitting that individuals are not cold and cynical beings attached to the figure of the *homo economicus*, but simply human. The behavioral economics current (Thaler and Sunstein 2008) was developed on the basis of this observation and provides the theoretical basis for behavior-based insurance.

Patients, in particular, are awfully human. They make choices that can be bad for their health. They eat foods which are fatty, too salty and too sweet. They do not do enough physical activity, etc. Their fast or impulsive thinking often outweighs their slow or reasoned thinking, in the words of psychologist Daniel Kahneman (2012).

Behavioral economics is not limited to this observation. It considers that unhealthy behaviors are errors or biases people consistently make. They are therefore predictable, and we can try to fight against these biases. All behaviors labeled as deviant are associated with bias. For example, behaviors such as "nutritional delinquency", tobacco consumption or risky car driving are associated with "a weak will", whose social determinants have been clearly identified. Obesity is related to a strong social and cultural determinism, in particular, to the definition of healthy eating. Tobacco addiction primarily concerns working-class circles. Car accidents obey statistical regularities that have social roots (Batifoulier et al. 2018).

For behavioral economics, these phenomena bear less witness to social inequalities than the expression of a "hyperbolic discounting" bias, typical of irrational individuals. Even though individuals know that their practices are unhealthy, they value the present more than the future (present bias). After establishing this diagnosis, therapy seems self-evident: it is necessary to "de-bias" irrational individuals. The objective of insurers is to put people back on the right track by modifying the architecture of choices through a nudging or boosting process. This involves letting individuals decide while inviting them to make the right choice by modifying the way in which the choice[3] is presented. For example, insurance contracts can be prefilled.

3 Harmless examples are often quoted to illustrate this point, such as putting the fruit in the foreground at a self-service kiosk and hiding the chocolate cake in the back, to encourage without forcing. Making organ donation more frequent by changing the way the choice is presented is also a recurring and effective argument. Nudging practices also posed freedom problems when used for justifying exit permits during the Covid-19 period (Arruabarrena 2016) or to fuel anti-abortion campaigns (making people listen to heartbeats in Hungary) (Al-Amoudi and Latsis 2019).

Another possibility is to automatically enroll policyholders in a system so that they make the "right" choice. The ultimate goal is to change choices without the people concerned having to worry about it. Nudging seeks to obtain the recipient's consent by "opting-in" – unless they have said yes, the answer is NO – or "opting-out" – unless they have refused, the answer is YES.

The "right choice" is assumed to be that of the insurer who somehow monopolizes the definition of the general interest. The insurer is supposed to know what is "good" for the patient. This kind of paternalism is described as libertarian or "soft", in that it intends to leave the individuals' freedom of choice intact. It exploits the resources provided by connected objects to encourage policyholders to become their own health entrepreneurs. Proper health standards are defined by performance criteria, which are defined by algorithms and revealed by connected objects. Individuals are thereby reduced to mere data and applications (Rouvroy and Berns 2010). In other words, a panoply of measures is deployed at the service of an injunction to perform and to manage our own health (Sharon 2017).

According to this approach, "right" choices are those which are also right for insurers. The reeducation of policyholders in terms of well-being and self-care must also be good for business, and the architecture of choices has to favor the business model.

2.3.2. *Building on social inequalities*

Behavior-centered insurance feeds on the development of behavioral economics. Health is invoked to encourage individuals to adopt a behavior considered as normal, without any further public discussion or deliberation (Al-Amoudi and Latsis 2019). AI is engaged to reach binding normative decisions, but without discussing and/or criticizing these decisions and their impact on social inequalities in health. The focus is exclusively placed upon individual responsibility, assuming that individuals will seize insurance schemes and digital tools to boost their health capital. This approach is based on the belief that it will suffice to modify the architecture of choices for behavior to change, regardless of social differences. As if simply by reducing the size of glasses, we could fight against alcoholism (Bergeron et al. 2018; Servet 2018).

However, social inequalities are not forgotten, because they are an implicit market argument. Certainly, the target of digitized insurance contracts is made up of a few population segments who can afford the additional quality promised by supplementary health insurance contracts. The policyholders concerned are mainly recruited on the basis of their employment situation within the framework of collective company contracts.

Wellness coaching products, as well as behavior-centered insurance, are aimed at executives rather than workers, in particular, at senior executives. Despite being smaller, this market is made up of a pool of potential customers who consume more. While the goal of healthy lifestyle behavior insurance is to deepen the demand of certain consumers, it does not aim to maximize the number of customers. Health is associated with a symbol of success (Schneider-Kamp and Askegaard 2022). This is why insurance products are niche or "tailor-made" products, as opposed to mass-produced "ready-to-wear" products.

Finally, health insurance contracts fall into two categories:

– responsible contracts, which are complementary insurance contracts covering health costs, reimbursing a basic healthcare basket, ranging from the basic contract to fuller contracts for those who can afford more expensive insurance;

– non-responsible contracts, which are additional insurance contracts, taken out within the framework of the company for innovative products in the field of well-being and health coaching.

In this last category, digital tools are not just technological innovations. They also act as markers of belonging to the same community of values (having a "healthy body", a "beautiful body", seeing sport as a form of self-transcendence, of well-being at work or personal accomplishment). These values highlight joyful affects: while the risk of disease is austere and associated with weakness or incapacity, the promotion of well-being is more radiant and opens onto an enchanted world. Insurance products as healthy lifestyle behavior insurance are presented as "trendy" or "latest fashion" products, shared by an "avant-garde" before the masses seize it and the product becomes "outdated" (Boltanski and Esquerre 2017). They also serve to position the insurance company in the field of innovation and contribute to brand awareness. The desired "wow" effect enables the insurer to present itself as a major player in the market. "Well-being *addenda*" to health insurance contracts act as a lure to sell the brand's other product ranges (Jeanningros 2021).

Social differences are driving the growth regime of this new market. It is clear that the story of the cult of the healthy body and self-concern only address certain categories of the population, who have ease of access to connected objects. The conception of health risks understood in this way instrumentalizes social differences. It organizes policyholders by those who do not wish to comply with the standard or share their data (at the risk of appearing as if they had something to hide), and those who accept or put up with the privatization of public health.

2.4. Conclusion

The development of behavior-centered insurance, thanks to recent advances in AI, raises a number of questions. Is this not a symptom of a great backwards leap in health risk socialization?

After the French revolution of 1789, profit-making insurance on individuals and mutual benefit societies were prohibited (the latter sometimes benefited from the authorities' tolerance). It was not until 1867 (insurance laws) and 1852 (decree on mutual insurance companies) that the collective management of health risks became authorized, without it being public. Even if public policies refused to take steps to improve increasingly difficult industrialization working conditions, the discoveries related to hygiene imposed the idea that health states depend more on the social conditions of existence than on individual responsibility: unsanitary towns, access to drinking water, the quality of housing, food, etc. In 1898, the Workmen's Compensation Act partially defeated the "liberal objection" (Hatzfled 1971), which had led the state to refuse to impose any form of constraint on the employer. In the event of an accident at work, the employer was presumed responsible and owed compensation to the worker. Despite it being decisive, the paradigm shift was partial: in exchange for the presumption of liability, compensation was capped and the management of industrial accident funds was endowed to employers and private for-profit insurers. The two world wars gave the decisive impetus to setting up socialized healthcare systems. The logic of individual provident insurance failed to finance effective healthcare production accessible to the entire population. Rather than the insurance principle, the social insurances of

1928–1930 and the general Social Security system of 1945–1946 were based on the principle of mutualism: everyone contributes according to their means and receives depending on their needs. Here lies the secret of the development of the French health system and of the considerable improvement in the population's health condition during the 20th century (Da Silva 2022).

Healthy lifestyle behavior insurance is part of the trend towards the socialization of health risks observed since the 1980s. From this period onwards, public policy has preferred to organize the development of the complementary health insurance market to the detriment of Social Security. This is not a neutral choice, since existing studies show that complementary health insurance is more costly from a financial point of view and more socially unequal than Social Security. The management costs of complementary health insurance are three to eight times higher than those of Social Security. Due to the existence of a social gradient in health (the richer you are, the less health problems you experience), complementary health insurance increases social inequalities in health, since they offer contracts that provide good coverage to fairly healthy populations, which leaves populations in poor health with mediocre coverage.

Not only does public policy promote inefficient and unequal organization, it also remains silent in the face of the social determinants of health. Recognition and the fight against occupational diseases and accidents at work are not progressing (rather the opposite, with the reform of health, safety and working condition committees). Social ills are not the object of any effective struggle. For example, malnutrition persists because of the weak will to question the agri-food industry, advertisements and the formation of food prices. The health system is not adapted to the promotion of prevention and public health. To take just one example, fee-for-service liberal medicine, a long-standing opponent of healthcare socialization, is unable to implement prevention and to coordinate measures with other healthcare and social professionals. It is not for lack of an alternative organizational project, such as social health (Duvoux and Vezinat 2022).

It is difficult to tell whether healthy lifestyle behavior insurance has good prospects for the future. Will it be limited to a mere gadget? A weakly effective instrument, constrained by legislation on risk segmentation, confined to the role of a marketing tool. Is it destined to become widespread in a context of surveillance capitalism? An instrument to control individual behavior, ready to financially punish and reinforce health inequalities. The only certainty is historical. In the past, the fight against disease was not won by modifying individual behavior but by socializing healthcare financing and through ambitious public policies to fight social ills. Let us remember that all of these victories have involved highly conflicting confrontations between social groups striving to change the spirit and interests of public policy. They engaged in a battle in favor of Social Security!

2.5. References

Al-Amoudi, I. and Latsis, J. (2019). Anormative black boxes. Artificial intelligence and health policy. In *Post-human Institutions and Organizations. Confronting the Matrix*, Al-Amoudi, I. and Lazega, E. (eds). Routledge, London, 119–142.

Arruabarrena, B. (2016). Le Soi augmenté : les pratiques numériques de quantification de soi comme dispositif de médiation pour l'action. PhD Thesis, Conservatoire national des arts et métiers, Paris.

Batifoulier, P. and Del Sol, M. (eds) (2024a). *More Competition Between Health Insurers with Less Protection for Patients? The Health Insurance Market in France*. IODE, Rennes.

Batifoulier, P. and Del Sol, M. (eds) (2024b). *Plus d'assurance santé pour moins de protection ? Le patient face au marché*. IODE, Rennes.

Batifoulier, P. and Ginon, A.-S. (2018). Les métamorphoses de la protection sociale complémentaire : vers un paternalisme assurantiel ? In *Livre blanc : l'assurance face aux défis des nouvelles formes de travail*. La fabrique de l'assurance, 37–39.

Batifoulier, P., Da Silva, N., Domin, J.-P. (2018). *Économie de la santé*. Armand Colin, Paris.

Batifoulier, P., Duchesne, V., Ginon, A.-S. (2021). La construction d'un "marché éduqué" de l'assurance santé : une réorientation de la solidarité ? *La Revue de l'Ires*, 103/104(1/2), 21–44.

Bergeron, H., Castel, P., Dubuisson-Quellier, S., Lazarus, J., Nouguez, É., Pilmis, O. (2018). *Le biais comportementaliste*. Presses de Sciences Po, Paris.

Boltanski, L. and Esquerre, A. (2017). *Enrichissement : une critique de la marchandise*. Gallimard, Paris.

Bruna, M. (2022). La mise en place d'une complémentaire santé par l'entreprise : entre logique d'incitation et inégalités de couverture. *Economie et institutions*, 30–31.

Cappel, V. (2021). The plurality of daily health. The emergence of new form of health coordination. *Historical Social Research/Historische Sozialforschung*, 46(1), 230–260.

Chelle, E. (2018). La complémentaire santé comportementale : un nouveau logiciel assurantiel ? *Revue de droit sanitaire et social*, 674–686.

Da Silva, N. (2022). *La bataille de la Sécu. Une histoire du système de santé*. La Fabrique, Paris.

Da Silva, N. and Domin, J.-P. (2022). La mutualité : histoire d'une lente dépolitisation. In *Plus d'assurance santé pour moins de protection ? Le patient face au marché*, Batifoulier, P. and Del Sol, M. (eds). IODE, Rennes.

Domin, J.-P. (2021). Monopole mutualiste versus concurrence dans le secteur de la prévoyance complémentaire. Retours sur un débat méconnu (1983-1985). *Revue française de socio-économie*, 26(1), 67–86.

DREES (2019). La complémentaire santé : acteurs, bénéficiaires, garanties [Online]. Available at: https://drees.solidarites-sante.gouv.fr/publications-documents-de-reference/panoramas-de-la-drees/la-complementaire-sante-acteurs.

DREES (2021). Rapport sur la situation financière des organismes complémentaires assurant une couverture santé [Online]. Available at: https://drees.solidarites-sante.gouv.fr/publications-documents-de-reference/rapports/rapport-2021-sur-la-situation-financiere-des.

Duvoux, N. and Vezinat, N. (eds) (2022). *La santé sociale*. Presses universitaires de France, Paris.

Ginon, A.-S. (2014). La déconnexion juridique des paniers de soins. *Revue de droit sanitaire et social*, 831–841.

Ginon, A.-S. (2017). L'assurance comportementale : de quoi parle-t-on ? *Revue de droit des contrats*, 2, 321–325.

Hatzfled, H. (1971). *Du paupérisme à la Sécurité Sociale. Essai sur les origines de la Sécurité Sociale en France. 1850-1940*. Armand Colin, Paris.

Jeanningros, H. (2021). Capter, quantifier, gouverner. L'assurance comportementale au service de la prévention ? *Revue française de socio-économie*, 26(1), 47–66.

Kahneman, D. (2012). *Système 1, Système 2. Les deux vitesses de la pensée*. Flamarion, Paris.

Rouvroy, A. and Berns, T. (2010). Le nouveau pouvoir statistique : ou quand le contrôle s'exerce sur un réel normé, docile et sans événement car constitué de corps "numériques". *Multitudes*, 40, 88–103.

Schneider-Kamp, A. and Askegaard, S. (2022). Conceptualiser la consommation en santé grâce à la notion de capital santé. In *Santé, consommation et marchés*, Gorge, H. (ed.). ESM, 61–83.

Servet, J.-M. (2018). *L'économie comportementale en question*. Editions Charles Leopold Mayer, Paris.

Sharon, T. (2017). Self-tracking for health and the quantified self: Re-articulating autonomy, solidarity, and authenticity in an age of personalized healthcare. *Philosophy & Technology*, 30, 93–121.

Thaler, R. and Sunstein, C. (2008). *Nudge: Improving Decisions about Health, Wealth, and Happiness*. Yale University Press, New Haven.

3

Artificial Intelligence and Health: Description of the Ecosystem Required for an Effective Use of AI

3.1. General data ecosystem for data mining and algorithm development

3.1.1. *An ecosystem for a digital "revolution"*

The term ecosystem may seem outdated, hollow or ill-defined. However, in virtue of its polymorphic character, its fuzzy or porous boundaries (what makes a system, what is outside or part of the system?), it seems suitably adapted to the topic of data use in general, health data in particular and health-related artificial intelligence (AI). By means of a single gesture, it makes it possible to free ourselves from one of the salient characteristics of a cleavage between two worlds: the compartmentalization of actors, systems and data; in short, an artificial and strict division corresponds to nothing in a "digital age" sphere. For example, if we follow Baricco and his thesis expressed in *The Game* (Baricco 2019), the digital revolution is unique in that it tends to abolish intermediaries, the figures inherited as essential within a system (the elites, scholars, civil servants, etc.), and redistributes roles, while modifying them. In this sense, data captured in a specific context – web browsing, via a "free" service made available to anyone wishing to use it – will be used, monetized and exchanged for the purpose of targeted

Chapter written by Thomas LEFÈVRE.

advertising (for example, or in another context, by other actors, destined to other users).

Addressing the digital by referring to a nomenclature or rigid classification deprives us from embracing cross-disciplinarity from the very beginning, and risks overlooking the topic's ubiquity, either when discussing its components or its uses: digital technology is cross-disciplinary, and the tensions we may come across in its practical application precisely stem from the encounter between this inherently traversing movement, and the existence of more or less resistant compartments (such as technical, professional, regulatory, cultural, etc.). Here, the term ecosystem will be used in the sense of (beyond historical compartments) evoking components or actors, on the one hand, and the interrelations between them, on the other hand. In no way is the task simple because digital technology has never managed to impose itself so overwhelmingly as through the ultra-fragmented adoption of uses that are simultaneously very simple, targeted and sufficiently malleable (engine research, social networks, etc.). It is offered centrally by a single, strong actor (Google, Meta, etc.): by targeting the individual (regardless of any professional or civic prerogative) and by offering them daily services, often without any constraints or necessities. This involves the free adoption of a tool which, while being relatively limited in functionality, is sufficiently permissive and pleasant, not to say addictive, to use. Individuals are not reunited, organized, unionized around a cause, a need or an activity to be defended. Things get more complicated when it comes to penetrating markets, which are more structured, hierarchical professional organizations: the first examples that come to mind are passenger transport (Uber) or housing (subletting, in reality, historically and mainly: AirBnB). These are emblematic examples in that they accurately testify to the first hitches with a more structured reality. In recent years, lawsuits, demonstrations, bans or sanctions have multiplied for these two companies (Errard 2021; Le Point 2023).

In this respect, the field of health is still one of the most resistant bastions to the digital revolution, at least in its first forms. Many reasons can be mentioned: health is not a "good" in the economic sense as other goods are; financing systems are complex, combining the private and the public in a way not strikingly obvious in practice; the presence/absence of regulatory requirements, presumably and by analogy and aversion to legal risk (and the companies' image), as there are still many voids and vagueness in this matter, perhaps among the highest in all areas; corporatism, the organization of scholars and practitioners, the selection of particularly robust elites; performance and quality requirements are superior to many other areas, especially by reference with one of the historic areas for the new dominant digital players, advertising and marketing segmentation, etc. At present, we are probably in a first phase of confrontation between digital technology and health, in their historical and dated version; however, the DNA of the digital has the quality of circumvention. Where health (in the way it is currently organized) risks breaking up for not knowing how to bend, the digital will not be afraid to come back, tirelessly, in one form or another, through a door or a window. Hence, we talk about an ecosystem: to be able to talk about health, as it is today, in terms of actors, components and functions, and to be able to consider everything that is simultaneously outside this system at its borders, or partly inside this system.

3.1.2. *Some preliminary socio-historical and technical elements*

Having been (and still being) an actor with different roles in the field of digital health in France (institutions, research, use, design, promotion, etc.), what follows will be mainly inspired by the French situation, but we must keep in mind that in terms of the digital and especially AI in the field of health, beyond the regulatory aspects, little can be said or observed. Everything related to the scientific and technical aspects will be inspired in international literature, and therefore, will not be specific to the French case. Socio-historical aspects, which are great boosters of comprehension – or to represent things, which comes to the same thing – will explore the current situation in terms of health-related AI, and primarily address the French context.

3.1.3. *A digital approach from the inside of health...*

We cannot speak of AI without referring to data, although it can be possible the other way around. Data has long been synonymous with information systems. In addition, administrative piloting "through data" – the open path to health management, namely hospitals and the financing of Social Security in the line of sight – was quickly perceived as the Holy Grail, by analogy with the introduction of measurement sensors in factory lines, supporting both task automation and the quantified monitoring of human actors. The French Information System Medicalization Program (PMSI,

Programme de médicalisation du système d'information) was introduced in hospitals, a local system federated into a system on a national scale. This was achieved particularly thanks to the creation and operation of the French Technical Agency for Information on Hospital Care (ATIH n.d.), quantifying the patient's stay through various characteristics (dates of entry and exit, reason for hospitalization, etc.). This system echoed the implementation of another directly oriented to the budgets of French institutions: the creation of a classification of "homogeneous groups of patients", to which unitary costs were associated, serving as the basis for the tariffing of institutions, rather than applying package costs (T2A) (Vie publique 2022). Digital healthcare has seen the introduction of two aspects: on the one hand, the introduction of IT (for example, for data digitization and their interrogation, for drawing data from additional examinations), and on the other hand, the implementation of medico-administrative data systems, initially implemented for managing activities. At the national level, the French National Health Data System (SNDS, *Système national des données de santé* n.d.) emerged, seeking to upgrade the health insurance healthcare consumption database, gradually supplemented with other data sources.

Other historically non-digital data sources existed in parallel, combining research (for example, cohorts) and monitoring functions (such as records). Growing digitization gave hope for standardization through a common denominator: data, exchangeable in a "digital format". Between this dream and reality, however, many obstacles arose and partially persist: there is no universal, obvious or unequivocal "digital format"; there is only one language for representation where captured or existing data are far from being completely digitized or recorded, available or accessible, and even less, shareable. In addition, we quickly realize that "immediately available" data are often insufficient: there is always a missing piece required for calculation or for a search.

Hospitals, whose information systems and digitization have significantly multiplied in recent decades, now perceive themselves as gigantic producers of health data, a product derived from their care activity, that is, from their main mission. In this context, the concept of Healthcare Data Warehouses (HDW) emerged, its purpose being to overcome the fragmentation and compartmentalization of data sources within the same institution, so that all healthcare-related data (with the patient as granularity) could be found at the same physical or virtual place. Thus began the design of data warehouses, as listed, for example, by the French High Authority for Health (HAS) in a recent document (HAS 2022). It is necessary to understand that these warehouses are separate, leak-proof from the rest of the hospital information systems: on the one hand, there is the system supporting daily practice, healthcare, and on the other hand, there is the warehouse, primarily conceived and validated as a research support tool.

Schematically, in the mid-2010s, France witnessed the following situation: the coexistence of the PMSI, the Health Insurance database, hospital data warehouses which were being set up, records and cohorts, as well as a myriad of other small databases, impossible to identify and with limited reusability. This is what was ultimately at stake: the reuse of generated data, in a context where they are used for a different purpose from their initial production, except perhaps for cohorts. This signaled the entry point of a specific characteristic of the digital: we can take advantage of an existing resource in order to achieve something different to what it was initially intended for, based on an obvious advantage: we can virtually multiply the same datum without distorting it ad infinitum. However, the dataset thus constituted was part of the Tower of Babel: nothing was easily communicated and there was no interoperability between data representation systems.

The state wished to organize this dataset, to enhance it, so as not to miss the "digital boat". This involved "Big Data" rather than AI at first, but quickly became a question of AI. Several missions followed one another, either under the aegis of the ministry in charge of health, or the services of the Prime Minister (e.g. the France Genomics plan: another example of the perpetuation of compartmentalization, the France Genomics mission and the Big Data health mission, the latter under the aegis of health, having been prohibited from communicating with one another, despite the fact that they were simultaneous): the Big Data mission in health (2015–2016); the France Génomique plan (2015); the Villani mission on AI (2017–2018), including a component on health; the mission to prefigure the Health Data Hub (2018); etc. At the same time, let us mention here the scientific and financial relevance of cohorts and records, particularly for public health: the IGAS-IGéSR mission on cohorts (2019–2020), the French High Council for Public Health (HCSP, *Haut conseil de la santé publique*) working group, and the referral to the French General Directorate of Health (DGS, *Direction générale de la santé*), relating to a national strategy for records in the digital age (2020–2021). In general, the constitution, organization or reconciliation of these databases intended to facilitate clinical or public health research and, more broadly, to fulfill purposes compatible with a public interest mission. However, it is interesting to note that in practice, alongside this shared general goal, the main uses envisaged and actually processed were of quite a different nature: the fight against fraud (the French National Health Insurance Fund, and more broadly, URSSAF), the possibility of offering an intermediary service between pharmaceutical laboratories and patients to be recruited for clinical trials (Public Assistance Data Warehouse – Hôpitaux de Paris, AP-HP), or even, in the long term, organizing access data to private companies, for example, for training their AI algorithms.

At the center of these initiatives, the Health Data Hub (the national health data platform) acted as a "hub" for reconciling or enhancing several data sources, while easing the access to these data for several actors. Several calls for expressions of interest, calls for projects, data challenges, etc., were organized and quickly followed one another, spanning two to three years. At the same time, 3IA institutes – centers of excellence for AI in France – were created (Ministry of Higher Education and Research 2019). These institutes were dedicated to AI in general and all of its possible fields of application, not just health.

3.1.4. *...and an external approach to health*

The main private actors involved in the digital business (among which none came from the field of health) had been interested in the field for several years. However, do not be deceived, as they were only as interested in it as they were for almost every other field, for which they suspected a market could be developed to foster their privileged position, their material resources and their skills in digital and image technologies. Several initiatives took shape, followed one another, and intertwined. Several companies opted for the classic digital bias: offering a service, an application intended for the individual, betting on the fact that the latter would be able to produce relevant data on their own, usable by the company or a third party. For example, Apple developed its own Health app (Apple n.d.). In a nonexclusive way, other companies bet on connected objects – for example, bracelets or connected watches – for the individual to respond. To date, these initiatives have largely failed, people's active or passive adoption being either short-lived or not massive enough to be meaningful or reliable. Others engaged in the creation of health-related subsidiaries, as did the Google parent company (Alphabet) with Calico (n.d.) (more related to biotechnologies than to health), and attempted to access data which had already been produced within a health system, such as the agreement that quickly caused a scandal between Google and the NHS in the United Kingdom (BBC 2021). Others chose to stick close to their core business, and offered software to health professionals: this was the bet of IBM's Watson, particularly in the context of oncology. AI was to be trained by the healthcare professionals themselves and not by IBM, which thus disengaged itself from most of the liability incurred in the event of a dispute. That case also ended in the withdrawal and sale of Watson by IBM to a company, due to the proposal's failure (Vitard 2022).

There is also a last resort, similar to the one existing in the field of clinical research and medicine, and assimilable to medical products in terms of regulations: the development of algorithms by university or hospital teams, with or without technical assistance from the private sector, as part of a research project. For the past two years, the regulatory authorities have opened the valves for this type of software/medical product, starting with the Food and Drug Administration (FDA) in the United States. However, the number of algorithms authorized on the market to this day is still very low, although it is expected to swiftly increase (FDA 2022).

3.1.5. *The evolution of regulatory aspects*

One of the most particularly powerful brakes on the development of the digital in the field of health, and more specifically of AI, lies in regulatory aspects (not so much in terms of AI, which are often compared to medical products, but in terms of data). This was a major issue, because what had prevailed for long in terms of regulations for the protection of personal data was the data's hosting or processing geographical location, which determined the applicable law: this means that the majority, if not all, more or less, of health-related applications (both serious and fanciful) had or still have their servers in the United States, or in any country similar to a "tax haven" in terms of data regulation.

As far as France is concerned, the French National Commission for Computing and Freedom (CNIL, *Commission nationale informatique et liberté*) was involved in a rather deleterious braking due to excessive conservatism on the part of all actors, with health researchers in the front row. The definition of health data was also problematic, because it did not recognize the advent of AI or any data processing, which could inform us of the higher or lower probability of developing a health condition inspired in "non-health related" information (living environment, average income, etc.). Not only was it necessary to change the definition of health data to acknowledge the particularities of processing (ranging from a "non-health" to a "health" dataset, related to the purpose or nature of the information produced), but also to create a sufficient scope for the development of research and certain supervised economic activities. This is partly what the (European) General Data Protection Regulation (GDPR), which has been in force since 2018, brought about, and the CNIL adhered to (CNIL 2018). At present, there is still the problem concerning the regulations between large countries or economic areas being too different, in particular, between the United States and Europe, even if agreements are trying to be found.

More specifically, the CNIL has given birth to several repositories – reference methodologies, such as MR004 – which have changed the situation in a more favorable direction towards the development of digital health, and even more recently, a repository relating to healthcare data warehouses (CNIL 2021). It is important to note the relative speed at which these datasets move, especially from a legal point of view: in this case, their evolution spanned a 10-year period: practically, the blink of an eye.

To summarize, in France, there is still a very recent and controversial "hub", mainly comprising fast-developing hospital healthcare data warehouses and structuring initiatives around AI and the regulation of data access and processing, which enables a certain number of things, at least theoretically. However, it is clear that this mainly concerns data, that is, the prerequisite for any form of AI. To put it another way, from this state of affairs, how can AI be developed, validated and most importantly, used?

3.2. From data to the algorithm at present: the role of research

So far, a brief socio-historical picture of the organization of health data in France has been drawn out, starting from the birth of the PMSI within hospitals, in parallel with the constitution and consolidation of data sources straddling population and epidemiologic surveillance and research (records, cohorts). In other words, the first elements relating to the conditions of existence and of data mobilization for the development of algorithms have been described. Still, the reader will note that this first type of data mobilization is necessary but insufficient: we have to be able to mobilize other data downstream, matching a different frameworks and frequencies. The following sections will outline the type and role of research in the design and use of health-related AI.

3.2.1. *What kind of research is there for health-related AI nowadays?*

The moment an algorithm has been developed, a question arises: what will be its place of execution, its environment? Even if they are not the only ones, a first reading of these places can be sorted into two types: algorithms, which will be executed in a public or private healthcare facility (in particular, under the supervision of a healthcare professional or at their request), and algorithms that will be used outside these places, virtually almost anywhere, including healthcare facilities. The difference lies in whether it is the patient or the citizen who requests the use of the algorithm, for example, via a connected object (smartphone, etc.). This last place is closely linked to digital DNA, at least partially abolishing one or more intermediaries (for example, the physician: think of the use of applications based on photographs shot by a personal smartphone in order to identify dermatological pathologies). While, in both cases, it is initially indispensable to access quality health data in order to train algorithms, it is quite easy to understand that the main actors behind them are not necessarily the same; and that, at a second stage, the technical constraints weighing on the technical integration of algorithms will be different: in the first case, the algorithm will have to be "plugged" to a hospital information system or computerized patient record; whereas, in the second case, the procedure will involve downloading an application on the *App Store* (so that the algorithm can be executed locally on the smartphone, or remotely, on remote servers from a service provider or data host).

This is also the specificity of digital technology and AI applied to health: most research focuses on what is usually (and in other circumstances) called Research and Development (R&D) or engineering. Until recently, it was no exaggeration to say that the vast majority of published research on the development of health-related AI was done by non-medical journals: in IEEE-type journals (Institute of Electrical and Electronic Engineers), with an excellent reputation in engineering, as well as in preprint standard journals or open archives (not having undergone peer review). The researchers and computer scientists behind these publications are not necessarily less serious or rigorous than their counterparts in medicine; it is simply a question of a different scientific culture.

Unlike medicines, which are immediately protected by a patent so that they can be exploited for commercial purposes exclusively for a given time, the attitude of private or public laboratories in relation to algorithm development is less clear-cut. It seems evident that part of the AI developed in certain fields, including health (e.g. IBM's Watson), remains protected and closed, and that underlying principles and codes are neither published nor made available in libraries. However, we can be reasonably certain that the majority of algorithms developed until now have been at least partially published or made available in the form of a code: even Google and Meta have "offered" their codes to the community. This is an essential point, and a research role that needs to be clearly identified in the development of health-related AI: a priori and unless indicated otherwise, the interest of AI, its performance and usefulness, will not depend so much on its publicly shared principle, as on its concrete application to relevant data, and proven know-how in design and training. This is just the first critical step, and probably applies to around 99% of research published on the subject. However, again by analogy with medicines, the second critical step requires performances to evolve in "real life", to gain external validity (can AI "leave" the laboratory and establish itself in a real environment, while maintaining similar performances – generally not).

3.2.2. *Beyond research, the integration of algorithms in the practitioner's environment*

In a way, the circle is closed: for example, if we were to purchase AI for the diagnosis of cancer from medical imaging, this needs to be "plugged" into the working environment. Once again, there is a switch from the field of research to the field of engineering. A priori, this involves two possibilities at a healthcare facility: AI can either be plugged to what is called the production system – the information system used for care – or AI is integrated into existing software, for example, because the AI seller also manufactures the software, which simply comes down to enriching software functionalities. However, to-date, AI design is a singularly different profession from software design and publishing destined to healthcare professionals. This means that bridges have to be built between AI suppliers and software suppliers, or there should be a diversification/absorption of AI skills among software suppliers.

A third way, which proves the ability of digital technology of freeing itself from classic categories and compartments, is the following: the use of a "classic" connected object (smartphone) and an application on this object by the healthcare professional. AI is then not technically integrated into the practitioner's traditional "professional" environment (production system, computerized patient record, etc.) but into a new tool, at the boundary between civilian life and professional activity. Of course, the access to this resource may be limited, depending on the status of the healthcare professional and may not be accessible to everyone. Additionally, its appropriate use may be subject to the experience and specialized/qualified judgment of the healthcare professional. However, we should not be easily duped: if an application available to the greatest number (albeit certified or not) manages to seduce professionals, they will use it.

Here, there are two major possibilities: on the one hand, integration into the "classic" environment – in the sense of an environment designed by an industry that is more computer-based than in the current digital era – or on the other hand, regulated use and access for an elite of scholars and practitioners (integration through ubiquitous objects, likely to bypass intermediaries). It is difficult to predict whether one will prevail over the other. Probably, initially at least, coexistence will be the rule. We can also draw a new parallel with medicines and the MA (Marketing Authorization): AI may very well have been the subject of an MA equivalent, mainly via integration and certification paths in technically and socially controlled environments (the traditional path), and the practitioner will appreciate the guarantees provided by the "prescription"; that is, the use of an AI in such a context, because they will be protected from the hazards associated with its use. However, AI can just as well exist, be available as an application, regardless of any MA, any certification, and its use by a practitioner will still be not guaranteed: this would be the equivalent of a prescription outside the MA, which is, for medicines, rather commonplace. Why would it not be for AI? Arguing the fear of the "black box" in terms of AI would be acting in bad faith: a priori, the practitioner who prescribes off-label does not have any concluding evidence on the action principles and physiology of the molecule on the patient's body. It is just as much, if not more, of a black box.

3.2.3. *An intermediate case for integrating AI into the practitioner's environment: learning systems*

There is a substantially different specimen from the one discussed so far: the case of so-called Learning Healthcare Systems (LHS) (McDonald et al. 2022). Here, AI can be either integrated into the practitioners' general environment – actually, of everyone attending a health institution with such a system – or used to output data from the information system, but theoretically, re-injecting results into the system. This is an evolution of the generalization of sensors and the automation of assembly lines in industry, and a partial delegation, at least, of certain decisions regarding the organization of the healthcare system: collected data are either used routinely for care, or eventually supplemented with ad hoc data, useful for controlling the system.

LHS certainly have a generalized logistical scope: managing and optimizing material resources as much as possible, and adapting to needs in near-real time. However, their ambition is broader: to adapt all of the components of the healthcare system to ever-evolving constraints and circumstances, based on what is "learned" from collected data. Of course, one of the risks of this type of learning system is similar to other AI and data-based systems: learning in a biased way, and even reinforcing biases, while ignoring what may be the main directions in which the system should evolve. This is a deliberately caricatural vision to illustrate this type of risk. If we wish to optimize (in this case, minimize) hospital stays, data can be informative as to the most serious and critical patients: those likely to pass away within a short period of time will be the preferred, to the detriment of all others.

LHS are yet another example of the integration of AI into the environment of practitioners and users, even if it involves a "systemic" integration, precisely oriented towards the management of the healthcare environment.

3.2.4. *Articulation between research and practice*

To-date, most of the production in health-related AI falls under research, a type of research that can be mainly described as exploratory or prototyping, without considering an entire section. While it may be difficult to quantify, we suspect an important part of it (or most of it?) to be essentially made of "publications just for publication's sake". Due to the relatively easy access to algorithm libraries, to their more or less marginal modification, to free or small-sized datasets accessible to the teams producing them, and because all that is ultimately needed is a more or less powerful computer, depending on the task to be performed, it is rather simple to produce a "research" whose utility will be null or negligible, but which will be effortlessly published in a journal or similar. In particular, this type of production serves to increase the visibility of researcher bibliometrics, a widespread criterion for professional advancement.

Therefore, this type of publication will be left aside in this study, even if in the end, they are not so easily identifiable. The question is quite assimilable to clinical trials for medicines, in the sense that studies are carried out under experimental conditions (in this case: on training data) and aimed at evaluating the algorithm's effectiveness (for example, performances such as accuracy). Unfortunately, the analogy between medicines and algorithms almost ends there, and algorithm evaluation has to match specific needs: validation on other data, adaptation to the environment where it will be used and appropriation (similar to compliance in the case of medicines: will it be used and, if necessary, will this be done in the "right way"?). As in the case of clinical trials or observational studies, recommendations have emerged to try to describe what constitutes "a proper study" in terms of algorithm validation, as well as the suitable reporting of these studies: what elements should be systematically reported in a study or report so that a third-party or external evaluator can get a concrete and precise idea of its effectiveness, as well as its potential usefulness? While clinical trials and observational studies have to follow CONSORT or STROBE guidelines, systematic reviews rely on PRISMA recommendations, etc., and studies on algorithms are evaluated via TRIPOD, CHARMS, etc. (Moons et al. 2014; Collins et al. 2015), most of which overlap.

More specific to AI, considered as a technology in its own right (a technical object or a medical product), it is possible to associate the notion of TRL (Technology Readiness Level) with each algorithm (Tournois et al. 2023). In short, this helps us to assess an algorithm's state of progress, from its concept to its real and routine use, integrated into a given practice.

The concepts of reporting and TRL applied to AI are complementary, and useful for assessing current production in health-related AI. To illustrate this point, section 3.3 will discuss two examples in the context of forensic medicine and at the boundary between psychiatry and forensic medicine, which we had the opportunity to explore with expert collaborators: the use of AI in the diagnosis of post-traumatic stress disorder, and AI for complementary examinations in forensic medicine, intended for forensic scientists.

3.3. Examining the quality of reporting of health-related AI research and the readiness of these AI forms through two medical examples

The focus of our attention was quickly drawn to the quality of reporting studies on health-related AI. On the one hand, there was a genuine scientific interest in practices and integrity in the broad sense, and on the other hand, within our services and laboratories, we were at the forefront of the development of algorithms in several contexts. Sections 3.3.1 and 3.3.2 will report the results obtained from colleagues over the past three years, focusing on two specific examples: the use of AI (versus "classical" methods: the use of determinants and predictive scales) in the context of screening and the "prediction" of post-traumatic stress disorder in populations exposed to any type of trauma, and more specifically in patients having experienced sexual violence (studies conducted in particular with V. Trousset, from the Legal and Social Medicine Department, Jean Verdier APHP Hospital), and the use of AI in terms of additional examinations in forensic medicine, both living and dead, intended for the medical examiner (study conducted with L. Tournois, Biosilicium). Concerning post-traumatic stress, the focus was mainly on reporting; for complementary examinations, interest was placed on TRL (at the mature stage), without neglecting reporting aspects.

3.3.1. *Screening or "predicting" post-traumatic stress disorder with AI*

Post-traumatic stress disorder (PTSD) is a disorder that can be particularly debilitating in terms of psychological, physical and social functioning, over a longer or shorter time period, but can also become chronic. It can follow any potentially traumatic event, although exposure to such an event is not systematically followed by PTSD. Among others, traumatic events include road accidents, mass disasters, armed conflicts, sexual violence, etc. Although not all of these events are reputed to have the same traumatic potential, the scientific literature is not very abundant or precise at the time of quantifying such potential by type of trauma. Nevertheless, it is recognized that sexual violence, in particular rape, is among, if not the most, traumatic triggers of PTSD (according to studies, up to around 20% of victims of sexual violence, for a lifetime) (Trousset and Lefèvre 2022).

While this disorder can be quite frequent in the general population, and especially disabling in the everyday life of the victims, it often goes under-diagnosed, diagnosed with a significant delay or at the end of a diagnostic wandering. Given the exposure to a traumatic event, it is still difficult to "predict". In addition, effective treatments and resources for the victim care (psychologists, psychiatrists trained in psychotrauma) are proportionately rare. It is quite challenging to deploy effective screening methods for an early targeting/orientation of patients likely to develop PTSD.

The classic methods available to the clinician for detecting a future disorder are the existence of determinants (with sufficient explanatory and predictive power), and the development of standardized scales. Their elaboration is statistical, and their application to a particular patient therefore remains statistical. However, the majority of studies focus on the occurrence of PTSD as a result of different mixed traumas in variable and unbalanced proportions. To-date, there are ultimately no clear determinants of PTSD: several results are contradictory, and the few results that seem consistent concern determinants with very low explanatory power. This means they are not sufficiently reliable in current practice. A more targeted look at sexual violence among adults shows that the number of studies drastically decreased to barely 30, including the search for determinants, scales and AI (Trousset and Lefèvre 2022).

Given the inefficiency of conventional approaches, it seemed legitimate to try the path of AI: was it helpful for detecting this disorder, in particular, in a medical consultation situation? Several observations followed. First, a dozen studies identified with AI were able to "predict" PTSD. Among those, only one fulfilled a minimum criterion for quality reporting. Beyond the fact that the majority (if not all of the proposed AI forms) did not reveal an outstanding performance for PTSD screening, according to the way in which these studies were reported and described, they were likely not to be sufficiently well conducted (or robust enough) to support conclusions regarding the AI developed. In some cases, there were crippling flaws and a general lack of information in what was communicated, damaging trust and understandings of the results proposed, as well as the reproducibility of such studies. This was extremely problematic, because it conveyed only a first level in the design of health-related AI: the development and demonstration in experimental conditions greatly differed from real life. Furthermore, performances were not robust enough to hope for a significant contribution from AI to practice. All things considered, to-date (the beginning of 2023), if we solely focus on sexual violence, only one article was identified as pertaining the development of an AI for PTSD screening, and this being quite permissive on what falls within AI or not (the model used here being a multinomial regression).

Regardless of the quality of reporting, the study of these articles highlights what was known beforehand: the need for good quality data adapted to the problem to be treated. The majority of studies focused on the reuse of data, either from general cohorts or from medical records from health institutions. None had undertaken to collect data, or at least partially consolidate the data already available, in a prospective and dedicated manner. The paradigm valuing preexisting data still prevails.

3.3.2. *AI to assist the medical examiner in investigation*

France has significantly contributed to the development of tools and structures devoted to multicentric research in forensic medicine, data collection and formatting. Therefore, the following natural stage was to explore the state of the art in the use of AI in this discipline. Initially, we intended to stick to AI that would be directly designed for practitioners, with a view to developing aid tools, in particular, for decision-making, so that they could be integrated into their current practice.

With L. Tournois, we conducted a systematic review of the scientific literature on the development of algorithms for forensic scientists, to help them in their usual missions. This review followed a first published study (Tournois 2022). Several goals pervaded this review: to identify and map the uses covered by AI, and to assess their readiness via an estimate of their TRL. At the end of the research process for articles published and indexed in the Medline, Scopus and ScienceDirect databases, 35 studies were identified and chosen. The proposed algorithms covered most of the major fields in forensic medicine in varying proportions: mainly, the application of AI techniques to estimating the age of the living, the identification of bodies found dead or the search for causes of death.

The conclusions of this painstaking work were clear: even if the exploration of the potential of AI had gained momentum in almost every branch of a discipline, when data existed for applying these algorithms, reporting studies were still mediocre and their performances quite disappointing compared to expectations; on the other hand, their readiness did not go beyond the stage of developing algorithms from existing data. In other words, algorithms were not validated on external or prospective data, they were not integrated into the physicians' working environment and were not used as part of a routine. Of course, this situation may, and no doubt will in part, evolve over time. A bias also consists of the fact that publications mainly addressed the first stages of the development of an algorithm. However, if regulations impose the equivalent of therapeutic trials for an MA, the corresponding assessment studies on the clinical added value of algorithms will have to be published. Obviously, this point has not been reached yet.

3.4. Integration and appropriation of algorithms

As shown through two specific examples (without claiming to be perfectly representative of all of the state of the art in health-related AI), under the current conditions, the majority of algorithms subject to scientific publications can be characterized in the following two ways: insufficient reporting overall, and a low level of technological readiness. In other words: in most cases, it is difficult (when not impossible) to comment on the quality and probable usefulness of an algorithm on the basis of what has been made public. This is because published algorithms are mainly at the first level of validation, sometimes of external validation. We are therefore generally far from their integration into the environment of a physician or any other health professional. On the one hand, a handful of algorithms escape all or part of this observation, and on the other hand, things may evolve more or less quickly.

This being so, it should not prevent us from discussing their integration within a system and an organization. We should call into question at least two dimensions of this integration: technical integration, and the microsocial integration of an algorithm. As mentioned earlier, by analogy with medicines, once laboratory effectiveness has been certified, it is necessary to evaluate its effects in real-life conditions: the algorithm must be "immersed" in the physician's technical system, and this tool must be integrated, appropriated by the physician and the environment, the practice. This is not obvious: as for medicines and for patient follow-ups, it could represent a major factor in the failure of an algorithm, no matter how precise or performing it may be in theory.

3.4.1. *Technical integration of algorithms, microsocial integration: about appropriation*

Initially, an algorithm will be "trained" over a dataset, either produced for the occasion as for a clinical trial or drawn from an information system or from a larger or general database. We will not delve into the good practice details required to train the algorithm on this dataset, and instead directly emphasize the following observation: the algorithm is not "trained" in "real-life" conditions. What does this mean? It means that once trained and shaped, the algorithm will have to operate in an environment quite different from its first dataset.

The following are two examples. In one case, the "frozen" algorithm takes several variables (for example, patient characteristics), to perform its calculation and return its result. At the same time, it must be able to access these data, and execute the calculation somewhere, then display the result in one way or another: it will no longer work on the computer of the researcher having designed it. The algorithm code must be adapted and inserted within a larger code dataset, for example, a hospital information system, or patient record software. A second case involves resorting to a diagnostic algorithm, based on patient data. The interest of the algorithm is that it can produce results, diagnoses concerning other patients, for example, the patient who has made an appointment for today. This means that the algorithm's code must be able to run in a place with access for physicians, where the data regarding the new patient within the algorithm can be successfully communicated. The algorithm's core code (the one developed and published) must often be adapted, more or less marginally, to be integrated and operate in "real life". This is a question of technical integration.

Once this code has been inserted and integrated into a customary dataset at the physician's working environment, it still has to be used. Performances evaluated at the laboratory are not everything, even if they constitute a prerequisite for using the algorithm a priori. Literature on IT and on digital systems often draws on the notion of acceptability: is a new tool introduced within a professional organization acceptable to its members? This view poses a number of problems. One of these is that it is directly inherited from a technical tradition: the engineer designs something seemingly useful, the manager decides to introduce a new tool and practitioners see it more or less as an imposition (in two ways, imposed on the grounds of a technological tool designed by non-practitioners, and imposed by a managerial decision, for example, due to performance or management issues). Acceptability refers to something quite binary in itself: an artifact is available, its appearance will be accepted or not, without that saying much about its "proper use" (the proper use having been defined by third parties who are not the final intended users).

While the concept of appropriation does not completely solve the problems raised by acceptability, it has the merit of leaving a margin of freedom and action to the presumed users of the algorithm and in relation to its purpose and predetermined "proper use". The question comes down to evaluating not only whether an algorithm will be accepted or not (not so important after all) but of knowing how it will be accepted, and used. Furthermore, appropriation should not be understood as a notion only taking place at the end of the chain (for cases where the algorithm has been developed and fixed upstream), independently from any consideration on final users. Appropriation also involves the process of developing the algorithm, considered not only as a technical object, but as a separate component of an organization which will enrich (modify by its very existence) the set of new interactions it will generate within the organization. Appropriation also designates the nuts and bolts of what technology can possibly bring, from its conception to its actual use, regardless of whether it is ultimately successful. Finally, appropriation also encompasses the notion of diversion: in digital technology, it is common for a technical component to end up being integrated into an environment through changes in its purpose. In practice, the tool is used, but not necessarily according to the use initially envisaged by designers.

Be that as it may, it is necessary to keep in mind the two dimensions (technical and social) of algorithm integration. The evaluation of algorithm efficiency or usefulness must acknowledge these two dimensions. The example presented in section 3.5.2 will refer to the design of an algorithm intended for physicians, together with its technical and microsocial evaluation (appropriation by two actors of the organization where the algorithm will be integrated).

3.4.2. *An example of algorithm integration and socio-technical evaluation: the Big Data Drop IT project*

Forensic medicine lies at the border between health and criminal law. Here, the focus will be on forensic medicine for the living, in particular, on violent situations. A frequent mission of the forensic physician involves assessing the functional impact of violence on a victim. From a criminal point of view, the requesting authority will require a quantification of the total Unfitness For Work (UFW), as expressed by a number of days. UFW is mentioned in the Penal Code, and contributes to qualifying an offense and orienting the competent court to judge the alleged perpetrator of such an offence. Nevertheless, as UFW is not defined anywhere, this has left ample room for a variety of interpretations and practices (for long, and still at present, to a lesser extent perhaps), both from the part of physicians and magistrates. In apparently similar or comparable situations, the number of UFW days can vary greatly, causing unequal treatment. In 2011, through a work group created ad hoc, the High Authority for Health (HAS) proposed a definition of UFW on the basis of case law, expressing the quantification (in number of days) of remarkable unfitness for everyday life activities, whether of psychological or physical origin (HAS 2011). Determining this number of days is essentially a matter of medical opinion, in the sense that there is no opposable reference, no specific study that can serve as a landmark to support a decision. Depending on situations, there is significant variability in the number of days prescribed.

A first idea implied that the use of an algorithm could not make it possible to "predict" the number of days, because no data are available for training such an algorithm. However, we could account for this variability if the algorithm was trained on real data, drawn from several institutions and many physicians. The purpose was to offer assistance, a point of reference for physicians reflecting the practices of peers (and their own) for each "new" situation to be assessed. As already mentioned, several steps had to be taken: accessing data, developing the algorithm in good conditions inspired in such data, having an environment to integrate the resulting algorithm, evaluating the degree and type of appropriation of such algorithms by at least two main actors in the forensic organization: the medical examiner and the magistrate, recipient of the physician's conclusions. These were the goals of the Big Data Drop IT project, funded by the Law and Justice research mission, between 2017 and 2020 (Lefèvre 2021).

Given the scope of this discipline (forensic medicine), the main stages had to be built de novo. On the technical side, the project was an opportunity to develop the equivalent of a health data warehouse, based on the sharing of medical documents among 12 forensic centers, first on a pilot basis, and then, due to its fertility, in a permanent mode. This warehouse was named ORFeAD (*Outils et réseau pour la fédération, l'analyse et l'utilisation de données*), which stands for "Tools and network for the federation, analysis and use of data" in forensic medicine. At the same time, an operational version of a business software was completed, mainly designed and intended for forensic medicine professionals, called Medilegist. On the one hand, its design had the particularity of continuously integrating the contribution from several practitioners in different specialist areas. On the other hand, it eased the integration of AI algorithms. Rendered smooth for the direct use of data recorded during the consultation, and facilitating the restitution of results within the same interface, it required no specific intervention on the part of the practitioner, yielding information in a transparent way. A family of UFW decision support algorithms was then designed, based on data from almost 10,000 victims, examined at seven different centers, using two different approaches, which will not be detailed here. By mixing various methods, an experimental scheme was designed for evaluating the digital representations of two types of actors (physicians and magistrates), as well as their appropriation of the algorithm, integrated both in the practitioner's environment and in practice. Mixed methods designate a quantitative questionnaire, the presentation of use cases following a randomized scheme and semi-structured interviews with a sub-sample. Several possibilities were considered in terms of the practitioner's decision: decision without the intervention of AI ("classic" case), decision with AI and presentation of the UFW estimate without associated uncertainty measurement ("unique number of cases"), and decision with AI and presentation of the estimate of UFW with an associated measurement of uncertainty ("number of days with a range of possible values" case). Then, the practitioner and the magistrate were asked as to what had changed in terms of decision support. At the same time, a qualitative component (through semi-structured interviews) questioned and explored the representations and knowledge of digital forensic physicians and magistrates, as well as their understanding and perceived use/usefulness of this type of algorithm in their current practice.

The main results of these explorations were noteworthy and provided information on the microsocial integration of this kind of decision support algorithm. Two decisions were addressed here, at two stages and of different natures: that of the medical examiner, when they proposed a number of UFW days and the magistrate's decision, who would pronounce a sentence, partly based on this number of UFW days. The fact that the tool was palpable and available did not seem to change much of the fears usually identified in relation to digital technology and AI: AI will replace humans, will eliminate certain professions, opinion practitioners will be challenged by machines, etc. This apprehension was expressed in the form of fears about a future that seems inevitable, albeit distant. Phrased differently, the actors were pessimistic for their successors. From a technical point of view, an important result was that the algorithms obtained showed mediocre performances (in any case, unfit to be of sufficient clinical utility). Regardless of performance, the attitude of magistrates towards the intervention of an AI in the decision-making process was ambivalent, although indicative of a form of strong appropriation. On the one hand, they refused the formulation of any result in the form of probability or quantification of uncertainty (this was synonymous with doubt, and the magistrate did not wish for additional doubt to be introduced, the lawyer's working matter). On the other hand, magistrates immediately reacted by taking advantage of this uncertainty (e.g. a range of UFW days), as it gave them additional freedom to support the conclusion they desired to promote. It was not the algorithm's performance or specifically/initially imagined purpose that made it potentially useful or usable, but a peripheral, formal aspect that offered the magistrates a way to appropriate it on a daily basis.

Finally, a last notable point concerned the selection of variables (characteristics) to be included in the algorithm. The "black box" character of AI is often brought forward by physicians as a factor limiting its adoption, due to mistrust, lack of understanding or explanations on how the algorithm produces its result. This aspect was submitted for consideration among physicians and magistrates: the question of whether explainability was a critical aspect. It turned out that it was not explainability that these actors called into question, but knowing whether a certain characteristic – which, according to them, should be taken into account, or that they thought they took it into consideration during their clinical reasoning – was acknowledged by the algorithm. Therefore, the appropriation of AI was more a question of verifying whether the basic elements of "classic" reasoning had been taken into account (even if this meant refuting them in the chosen model), than about the need to "understand" the functioning of AI.

3.4.3. *The contribution of mixed methods and the interdisciplinary approach for the end-to-end development of an algorithm – the I-ADViSe project*

The Big Data Drop IT project was an opportunity for our team to engage both strong interdisciplinary skills and mixed methods: briefly stated, the use of quantitative and qualitative methods, not juxtaposed but used in a joint and complementary way, in order to cover a research question at several scales and following several modalities. This idea was taken a step further with a new AI project, called I-ADViSe, for screening sexual violence. This project had multiple goals, among which three were particularly relevant: i) to develop a screening algorithm for PTSD in forensic consultation situations, for physicians; ii) to use AI for identifying the profiles and psycho-socio-judicial trajectories of victims of sexual violence, in order to help with their orientation within the various care and judicial systems; iii) to study the appropriation of these algorithms by the various actors concerned (Fedele 2023).

Based on the findings of our previous studies, particularly on AI and PTSD, we opted for a mixed data collection: taking advantage of the data usually collected during medical consultations, and completing and consolidating them with an adapted and prospective data collection. Drawing on data and usual consultation contexts to configure algorithms, we increased their integrability and their possible appropriation. Thanks to the previous Medilegist (at equipped institutions), not only did we succeed in capturing data for this research project, but we also tackled the iterative and technical integration of the algorithms developed, in such a way that they could be evaluated in everyday practice.

From the point of view of AI development and appropriation, the mixed methods approach was also justified by the fact that already recorded data were not sufficient for this project (they had generally been produced in another context and for a different purpose from the ones pursued by the development of this form of AI). In addition to the fact that data could be incomplete/unsuitable in relation to the needs of the algorithm, information systems are crossed by many biases, which means that the algorithm obtained cannot apply to everyone in the same way. On the other hand, it presents multiple blind spots due to quantification/categorization procedures. Two examples illustrate this.

Biases are taken up, amplified and self-reinforced through the use of AI derived from biased data: for example, the gender or ethnicity bias. For example, there is an excellent algorithm for identifying dermatological pathologies, which is highly effective on fair skin. However, data can be biased in terms of the populations concerned (this algorithm does not know how to treat dark skin). The same problem arises for men, who are better represented in the databases than women.

Regarding blind spots in databases, let us reflect on the notion of course, trajectories and recourse to care. If patients are not interrogated from a qualitative point of view, everything that emerges from representations, opinions, etc., regarding the healthcare system will remain unknown, because this is not taken into account or measured by databases. Orientation assistance algorithms will only be useful, if ever, for patients who have already been identified and oriented, overlooking those with a specific need in terms of assistance/orientation.

Accessing this type of knowledge by joint and complementary methods makes it possible to minimize the risks of uselessness, harm (reinforcement of biases and inequities in treatment), while it maximizes appropriation (despite this not being a guarantee of success).

3.5. The integration of AI in a broader ecosystem than the practitioner's immediate environment: questions and perspectives

So far, we have discussed the stages and conditions for the development and appropriation of health-related AI, in what could be called the microsocial ecosystem of an activity relating to health or medicine. At the beginning, we also emphasized the salient characteristic of the digital: to ignore, if not to refuse, classic categorizations and boundaries. If we wish to analyze the irruption of health-related AI, we can only observe it within the restricted and classic perimeter around the health professional: digital technology crosses and goes beyond this perimeter, but the use of AI is circumscribed to a specific task.

3.5.1. *The illusions of immediacy and the dematerialized*

The renewed interest in the use of health-related AI is largely based on the idea that data exist and are available in large quantities, that their access is almost immediate and their operating cost marginal. This idea of immediacy is an illusion we must get rid of. Data are produced, that is certain, but in the current state of technological development, they are neither necessarily suitable for uses in AI, nor technically or legally accessible.

The illusion of immediacy also stems from the idea that only a few existing technical bricks, a few connections suffice to connect data sources, open the floodgates, exploit them, with constant means other than technical ones, producing significant savings in other areas. AI is thought to cost nothing, generating both benefits and savings, while increasing the quality and reliability of the missions rendered. However, as shown by the case of data warehouses (and others), it has become evident that before hoping for an increase in technical or economic performances, material and human investments are necessary. For potentially human tasks wholly or partially delegated to AI, new necessary professions have emerged, possibly more qualified and with scarcer resources than those replaced. Reconfiguration is concomitant with the infiltration of the digital, rather than a simplification or a reduction. It is also this new ecosystem that must be considered.

As regards the illusion of immediacy, the "dematerialized", it is extremely misleading in its statement. Behind any data or algorithm, there is a material and unavoidable structure, of a certain fragility. Servers require very basic and massive attention: they heat up, they have to be constantly cooled down, they have to be protected and they consume a lot of electricity. These energy consumptions are all the more problematic in that they are totally hidden behind the great simplicity of using digital technology (think of our untimely browsing of applications and the Internet, often without any real purpose, and without any particular profitability for anyone in general).

The development of an AI algorithm based on deep learning and the use of thousands, millions and even billions of data is very energy intensive (Trystram et al. 2021). It will quickly become complicated to continue to develop AI with the extremely low yield in terms of sufficient/useful performances without taking into account these materially expensive data.

3.5.2. *An opposite problem: what place for health professionals in an ecosystem conducive to the use of AI?*

AI will find its place in medicine: it is already beginning to show interesting performances for well-defined tasks, in particular, those based on the use of images and video. This will be the case for the expansion of task automation/robotization (as it happened during the industrial revolution), relying on arguments such as reliability, non-fatigability, availability, accuracy, speed and transferability to the patient.

However, AI is not human, and bursts into a medicine that is becoming increasingly technical and over-specialized. It then becomes legitimate to inquire after the future physician's role: what will happen with health professionals as they exist today? What skills, what roles, in what places and at what times will they intervene?

If today we wish to ponder the favorable ecosystem for the relevant use of AI, it is not possible to neglect some of the components of this system, whether current or future. It is necessary to be able to take into account the human component, not only in terms of their current functions and roles, their future and joint development, but also in terms of new professions and roles.

3.5.3. *AI as a technical object above all and technology as the common denominator for all our social activities*

When talking about Big Data rather than AI, quite a short time ago, certain authors or futurologists had spoken of "the end of science": no further need for explanation, theory and model, because data are everywhere, and all we have to do is access the right ones, somewhere, to retrieve answers. This rather radical positioning nonetheless refers to a truth that goes beyond the digital framework, but fully concerns it: the observation that we inhabit systems and live according to the constraints of technology, not chosen systems of values or thoughts.

Overall, this is the positioning of J. Ellul (1988), who described the structuring, ubiquitous place of technology. The adoption of health-related AI follows the same logic, and would even close the loop: our conception and means of action in the health-field risk being strongly conditioned, not by the development of knowledge and the choice of social values, but by what is attainable by algorithms. For certain tasks, an artifact may be suitable, in the sense that it may be more efficient or reliable than a human being. The problem arises when the horizon of possibilities is reduced to what technology allows, and nothing else. In this sense, if we do not wish to abdicate, we must take care to maintain a broader ecosystem, not as favoring the emergence of AI, but rather as enhancing human activity, assisted or not, by tools like AI. In both cases, the usefulness of AI can be defined, but not in the same way, and it is up to us to make our choice, the choice for our living environment.

3.6. References

Apple (n.d.). App Santé. C'est tout vous [Online]. Available at: https://www.apple.com/fr/ios/health/ [Accessed 11 February 2023].

ATIH (n.d.). Agence technique de l'information sur l'hospitalisation [Online]. Available at: https://www.atih.sante.fr/plateforme/e-pmsi [Accessed 11 February 2023].

Baricco, A. (2019). *The Game*. Gallimard, Paris.

BBC (2021). DeepMind faces legal action over NHS data use [Online]. Available at: https://www.bbc.com/news/technology-58761324 [Accessed 11 February 2023].

Calico (n.d.). [Online]. Available at: https://www.calicolabs.com/ [Accessed 11 February 2023].

CNIL (2018). Le règlement général sur la protection des données – RGPD [Online]. Available at: https://www.cnil.fr/fr/reglement-europeen-protection-donnees [Accessed 11 February 2023].

CNIL (2021). La CNIL adopte un référentiel sur les entrepôts de données de santé [Online]. Available at: https://www.cnil.fr/fr/la-cnil-adopte-un-referentiel-sur-les-entrepots-de-donnees-de-sante [Accessed 11 February 2023].

Collins, G.S., Reitsma, J.B., Altman, D.G., Moons, K.G. (2015). Transparent reporting of a multivariable prediction model for individual prognosis or diagnosis (TRIPOD): The TRIPOD statement. *BMJ*, 7350–7594. doi: 10.1136/bmj.g7594.

Ellul, J. (1988). *Le bluff technologique*. Hachette, Paris.

Errard, G. (2021). Locations illégales : Airbnb condamnée à verser 8 millions à la Ville de Paris. *Le Figaro* [Online]. Available at: https://immobilier.lefigaro.fr/article/a-paris-airbnb-interdit-enfin-les-locations-non-enregistrees_0b0ac054-d978-11eb-a871-9928079feda7/ [Accessed 11 February 2023].

FDA (2022). Artificial intelligence and machine learning (AI/ML) enabled medical devices [Online]. Available at: https://www.fda.gov/medical-devices/software-medical-device-samd/artificial-intelligence-and-machine-learning-aiml-enabled-medical-devices [Accessed 11 February 2023].

Fedele, E., Trousset, V., Schalk, T., Oliero, J., Fovet, T., Lefevre, T. (2023). Identification of psycho-socio-judicial trajectories and factors associated with posttraumatic stress disorder in people over 15 years of age who recently reported sexual assault to a forensic medical center: Protocol for a multicentric prospective study using mixed methods and artificial intelligence. *JMIR Res Protoc.*, 12, e46652. doi: 10.2196/46652.

HAS (2011). Victime de violence : faites établir un certificat médical initial pour vous protéger [Online]. Available at: https://www.has-sante.fr/jcms/r_1501548/fr/victime-de-violence-faites-etablir-un-certificat-medical-initial-pour-vous-proteger [Accessed 11 February 2023].

HAS (2022). Entrepôts de données de santé hospitaliers : la HAS publie un panorama inédit en France [Online]. Available at: https://www.has-sante.fr/jcms/p_3386076/en/entrepots-de-donnees-de-sante-hospitaliers-la-has-publie-un-panorama-inedit-en-france [Accessed 11 February 2023].

Le Point (2023). Lyon : Uber condamné à verser 17 millions d'euros à des chauffeurs [Online]. Available at: https://www.lepoint.fr/justice/lyon-uber-condamne-a-verser-17-millions-d-euros-a-des-chauffeurs-20-01-2023-2505578_2386.php#11 [Accessed 11 February 2023].

Lefèvre, T., Chariot, P., Laugier, V., Saas, C., Guez, S. (2021). Big Data et droit pénal : utilisation, compréhension et impacts des techniques prédictives (Drop IT) [Online]. Available at: http://www.gip-recherche-justice.fr/publication/big-data-drop-it-big-data-et-droit-penal-utilisation-comprehension-et-impact-des-techniques-predictives-etude-drop-it-exemple-de-levaluation-de-lincapacite-totale-de-travail-chez-les-victi/ [Accessed 11 February 2023].

McDonald, P.L., Phillips, J., Harwood, K., Maring, J., van der Wees, P.J. (2022). Identifying requisite learning health system competencies: A scoping review. *BMJ Open*, 23/12(8), e061124. doi: 10.1136/bmjopen-2022-061124.

Ministère de l'Enseignement supérieur et de la Recherche (2019). Lancement de 4 instituts interdisciplinaires d'intelligence artificielle (3IA) et ouverture de deux appels à projets complémentaires [Online]. Available at: https://www.enseignementsup-recherche.gouv.fr/fr/lancement-de-4-instituts-interdisciplinaires-d-intelligence-artificielle-3ia-et-ouverture-de-deux-47144 [Accessed 11 February 2023].

Moons, K.G., de Groot, J.A., Bouwmeester, W., Vergouwe, Y., Mallett, S., Altman, D.G., Reitsma, J.B., Collins, G.S. (2014). Critical appraisal and data extraction for systematic reviews of prediction modelling studies: The CHARMS checklist. *PLoS Med*, 11(10), e1001744. doi: 10.1371/journal.pmed.1001744.

Système national des données de santé (n.d.). Qu'est-ce que le SNDS ? [Online]. Available at: https://www.snds.gouv.fr/SNDS/Qu-est-ce-que-le-SNDS [Accessed 11 February 2023].

Tournois, L. and Lefèvre, T. (2021). AI in forensic medicine for the practicing doctor. In *Artificial Intelligence in Medicine*, Lidströmer, N. and Ashrafian, H. (eds). Springer, Cham. doi: 10.1007/978-3-030-58080-3_221-1.

Tournois, L., Trousset, V., Hatsch, D., Delabarde, T., Ludes, B., Lefèvre, T. (2023). Artificial intelligence in the practice of forensic medicine: A scoping review. *Int J Legal Med*. doi: 10.1007/s00414-023-03140-9.

Trousset, V. and Lefèvre, T. (2022). Artificial intelligence in medicine and PTSD. In *Artificial Intelligence in Medicine*, Lidströmer, N. and Ashrafian, H. (eds). Springer, Cham. doi: 10.1007/978-3-030-64573-1_208.

Trystram, D., Couillet, R., Ménissier, T. (2021). Apprentissage profond et consommation énergétique : la partie immergée de l'IA-ceberg. *The Conservation* [Online]. Available at: https://theconversation.com/apprentissage-profond-et-consommation-energetique-la-partie-immergee-de-lia-ceberg-172341 [Accessed 11 February 2023].

Vie publique (2022). Soins hospitaliers : T2A et autres modes de financement [Online]. Available at: https://www.vie-publique.fr/fiches/37927-financement-des-soins-lhopital-la-tarification-lactivite-t2a [Accessed 11 February 2023].

Vitard, A. (2022). IBM cède une partie de Watson Health au fonds Francisco Partners. *L'usine digitale* [Online]. Available at: https://www.usine-digitale.fr/editorial/ibm-cede-une-partie-de-watson-health-au-fonds-francisco-partners.N1776862 [Accessed 11 February 2023].

PART 2

Artificial Intelligence at the Service of Healthcare

4

Legal Liability of Companion Robots

Le progrès : trop robot pour être vrai.[1]

Jacques Prévert

4.1. Introduction

What will we discuss in this chapter? First and foremost, robots, and then liability.

The robots are multi-faceted and therefore difficult to define. In general, they are perceived as machines with a physical envelope, interacting with their environment and with humans. The robots are said to be intelligent when endowed with artificial intelligence (AI), something which favors its autonomy[2].

French lawmakers have defined AI as the "theoretical and practical interdisciplinary field aiming to understand cognition and reflection mechanisms, as well as their imitation by a hardware and software device, for the purpose of assisting or substituting human activities" (Journal officiel de la République française 2018).

Chapter written by Guilhem JULIA.

For a color version of all the figures in this chapter, see www.iste.co.uk/julia/aihealthcare.zip.

1 In English, "Progress: too robotic to be true".

2 This autonomy sets it free from the master–slave dialectic that characterizes, for example, the robot surgeon, piloted by the doctor.

For their part, European lawmakers envisage AI as "a system that is either software-based or embedded in hardware devices, and that displays behavior simulating intelligence by collecting and processing data, analyzing and interpreting its environment, and by taking action, with some degree of autonomy, to achieve specific goals"[3].

The concept of AI is too broad, inaccurate and "all-encompassing". It nonetheless conveys a global idea: progress, which frees humans from painful tasks and limits the damage associated with those tasks.

The intelligent robot embodies the Western fear of a highly developed AI which could eventually dominate humans. Far from science fiction, this robot is currently present in our daily lives. As such, it has drawn the attention of French and especially European lawmakers.

For seven years, the European Parliament launched several resolutions[4], studies[5], regulation proposals[6] and guidelines[7] in robotics and AI.

This chapter concerns a particular robot: the companion robot. It differs from the telepresence robot, which is also used in health. This robot has the essential function of communicating with people outside the place where it is

3 European Parliament resolution of January 20, 2021 "on artificial intelligence".

4 Between 2017 and 2021, four resolutions concerning robots and AI were adopted by the European Parliament: the resolution of February 16, 2017 "containing recommendations to the Commission regarding civil law rules on robotics"; the resolution of February 12, 2019, "a comprehensive European industrial policy on AI and robotics"; the resolution of October 20, 2020 "containing recommendations to the Commission on a civil liability regime for artificial intelligence" and the resolution of January 20, 2021 "on artificial intelligence".

5 "European civil law rules pertaining to robotics", study submitted in October 2016 to the Committee on Legal Affairs of the European Parliament.

6 Proposal for a regulation of the European Parliament and of the Council of April 21, 2021 "establishing harmonized rules on artificial intelligence (artificial intelligence legislation known as the AI Act) and amending certain Union legislative acts".

7 On September 28, 2022, the European Commission published two directive proposals: the directive proposal by the European Parliament and by the Council "on the adaptation of rules on extra-contractual civil liability in the field of artificial intelligence (AI Liability Directive)" and the directive proposal by the European Parliament and by the Council "on liability caused by defective products".

located. Depending on the model, it can also detect obstacles present in a room and anticipate the risk of the person it is assisting falling.

As an example of a telepresence robot, we can mention Beam[8].

Figure 4.1. *Beam, the telepresence robot (source: Awabot)*

More sophisticated, the companion robot is designed for therapeutic purposes. It mainly assists the elderly or impaired patients (e.g. those experiencing pathologies such as autism or Alzheimer's disease).

Since 2017, the use of a robot for therapeutic support has been considered by European lawmakers:

> Elder care robot research and development has, in time, become more mainstream and cheaper, producing products with greater functionality and broader consumer acceptance; notes the wide range of applications of such technologies providing prevention, assistance, monitoring, stimulation, and companionship to

8 Beam was created and developed by the Awabot company. See: www.telepresence.awabot.com/ [Accessed: March 22, 2023].

elderly people and people with disabilities as well as to people suffering from dementia, cognitive disorders, or memory loss[9].

The assistance provided by the robot can be physical, psychological or both. The companion robot takes on several roles: nurse, psychologist, educator, etc.

These robots include exoskeletons and orthoses. "As opposed to the prosthesis, which replaces a missing limb, the orthosis is a medical device that makes it possible to supplement, compensate, support or protect a part of the body"[10].

Figure 4.2. *Mechatronic device (source: iStock)*

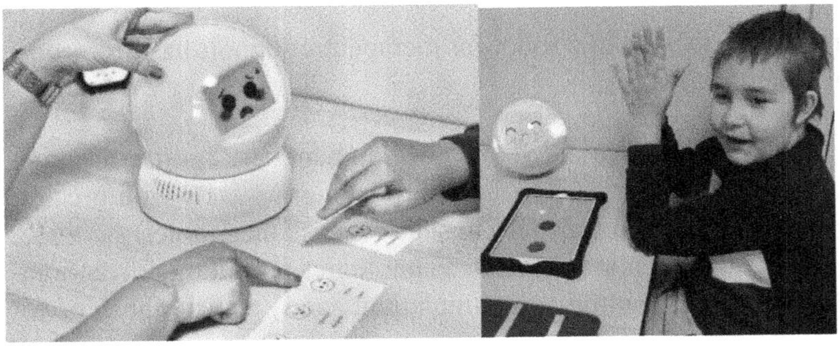

Figure 4.3. *Leka, the companion robot (source: Leka and AFP France handicap)*

9 Taking into account point 32 of the European Parliament resolution (February 16, 2017).

10 Definition appearing on the website: www.chabloz-ortho.com/ [Accessed: June 17, 2023].

As we can see, this is a mechatronic device worn by an individual, enabling artificial articulation. While the added physical envelope does not have the autonomy of an intelligent robot, it can still be used for medical purposes. Originally used for relieving employees'[11] workloads, the physical assistance function of these robots was then extended to the medical field so that paralyzed patients could learn to walk[12] again.

At present, companion robots – also referred to as social robots – are mainly used for dependent persons. Among the best known are Leka[13], Paro[14], Zora[15], Buddy[16] and Pepper[17].

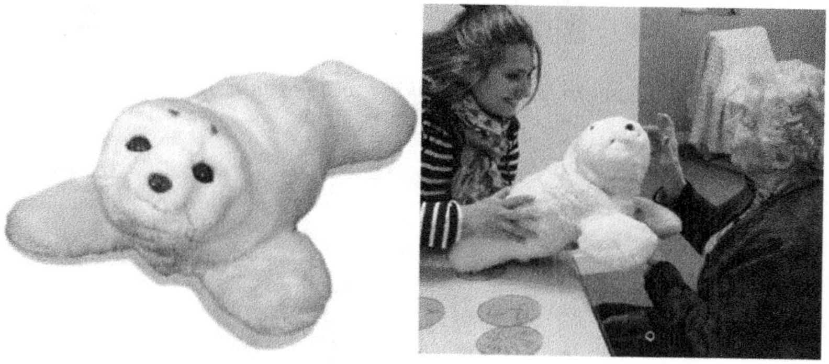

Figure 4.4. *Paro, the companion robot (source: Ilena Lescaut)*

11 This function proves to be in line with the etymology of the word robot, "robota", which means "chore" in Czech. The term "robot" first appeared in 1920 in the drama play *R.U.R. (Rossum's Universal Robots)* by the Czech writer Karl Capeck.

12 Since 2021, paraplegic and hemiplegic patients at the Renée-Sabran hospital in the region of Lyon have benefited from the services of Indego, an exoskeleton created by the Parker company.

13 Developed by the Leka company, this educational round robot assists autistic children in managing their emotions. See: www.leka.io/ [Accessed: June 17, 2023].

14 Developed by the Aist company, this robot has the appearance of a baby seal. See: www.phoque-paro.fr/ [Accessed: June 17, 2023]. Intended in particular for Alzheimer's patients, to whom this robot reminds of a pet.

15 Zora is a software solution developed by the Belgian company Zorabots, implanted in the famous robot Nao, created by Aldebaran Robotics. See: www.aldebaran.com/fr [Accessed: June 17, 2023].

16 This robot was developed by the company Blue Frog Robotics. See: www.bluefrog robotics.com/ [Accessed: June 17, 2023].

17 This robot is marketed by SoftBank Robotics and was designed by French teams from Aldebaran Robotics.

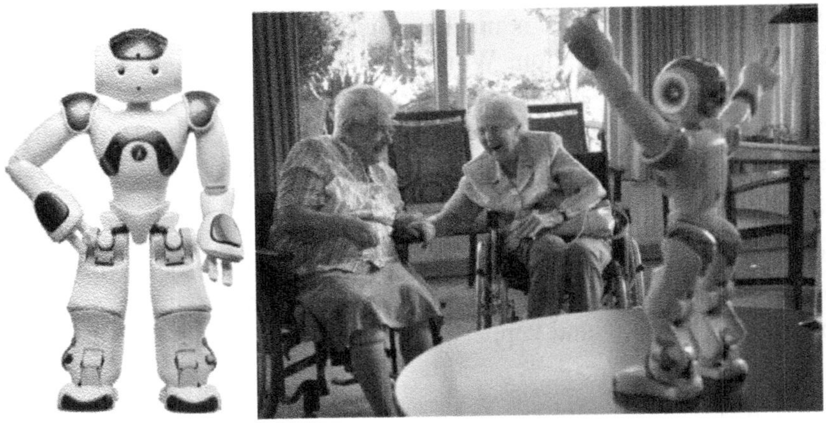

Figure 4.5. *Zora, the companion robot (source: Aldebaran)*

Figure 4.6. *Buddy, the companion robot (source: Blue Frog Robotics)*

Zora, Buddy and Pepper are mainly present in establishments for the elderly[18]. So far, these robots have fulfilled the role of a social companion; as such, they fall within the so-called field of affective robotics (Devillers 2020, 2022).

18 To see Zora at work as an animator for the elderly, see: www.youtube.com/watch?v=r2cFBktgY2g [Accessed: June 17, 2023].

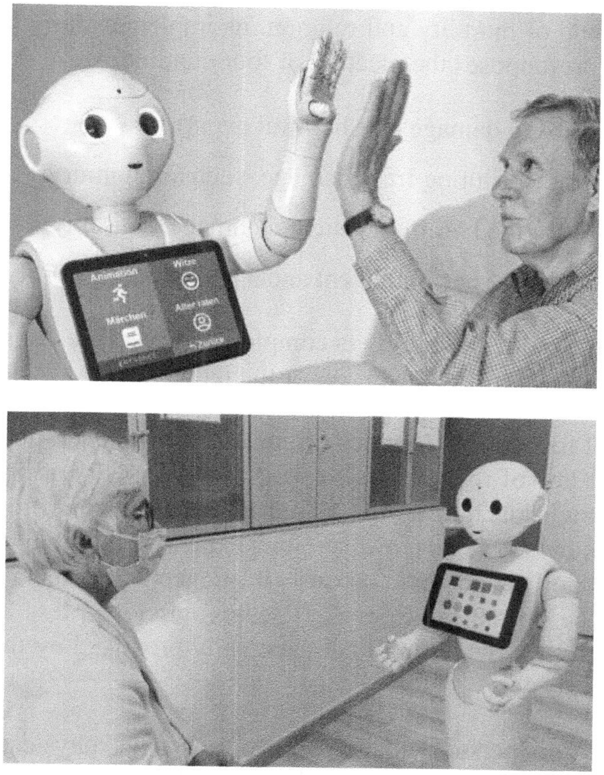

Figure 4.7. *Pepper, the companion robot (source: SoftBank Robotics)*

According to the United Nations, by 2050, the global number of people aged 65+ will have doubled. This is due, among other factors, to the aging of the generation born during the post-World War II birth peak, the famous baby boom[19]. The market for companion robots promises to thrive.

We will now move on to discuss liability, which is defined as the "obligation or duty of a person to account for their actions (or those of others), and to bear the consequences"[20]. Even though the concept of liability

19 Ined (2021). "The aging of the population is accelerating in France and in most developed countries", 15 September [online]. Available at: www.ined.fr [Accessed: June 17, 2023]. The French lawmaker reiterated its concern on how to adapt to the increasing aging population. This was translated by Law No. 2015-1776 from December 28, 2015 "relating to the adaptation of society to aging".

20 Larousse and French Academy dictionaries.

exists in the field of morality and religion, its implementation in the field of law generally presupposes the meeting of four conditions:

– an event causing damage (the harmful event);

– a consequence resulting from damage, such as an injury;

– a link between the harmful event and damage, causality;

– a link between the harmful event and a person, imputability.

Although the scope of liability is complex, in several cases, reparation for damage is facilitated by the lawmaker or the judge[21].

The idea of responsible robotics originated with science fiction. In 1942, Asimov's first law of robotics stated that: "a robot may not injure a human being or, through inaction, allow a human being to come to harm" (first stated in Asimov (1942)). However, the expression "liable robot" seems unsuitable (if not dangerous), because it suggests that the robot and the human could be on the same level. It seems fairer and less ambiguous to speak of liability for the harmful act eventually provoked by the companion robot.

Two types of personal damages are possible: physical injury and intellectual harm. These include the violation of privacy due to the status of the "observer of the lives of those around"[22] (Mendoza-Caminade 2016).

In the context of this contribution, we will predominantly consider the possibility of physical injuries, for example, a wrong move from the companion robot, which could shake the hand of the person it is assisting too tightly. Currently, this type of damage is extremely rare, which is a good thing. However, in the near future, liability is likely to be increasingly engaged due to the progress and growing autonomy of intelligent robots.

What is this autonomy all about? According to the European Parliament, it is the "ability to take decisions and to implement them in the outside

21 This facilitation operates via presumptions of causality, as will be shown later.

22 As Alexandra Mendoza-Caminade has stated: "Social robots can be observers of the lives of people around them. As part of the robot's operation, data will be collected for further analysis and processing by the robot. However, such data may be personal data belonging to persons located within the robot's range of action."

world, independently of external control or influence"[23]. This results in an increased risk of damage for the user of the companion robot, who is, let us recall, in a situation of "weakness" due to infirmity or a pathology.

The law has to face the dilemma of regulating technological progress and managing the risks associated with such progress. The European Parliament identified this dilemma when it stated that "civil liability rules for AI should seek to strike a balance between the protection of the public, on the one hand, and business incentives to invest in innovation, especially AI systems, on the other"[24].

Is the civil liability law suitable for addressing the damage caused by a companion robot ?

This question is not new. Each past technological change has given rise to new risks (Borghetti 2017). We may think, for example, of work industrialization and the accidents caused by the automation of repetitive tasks. However, the question of liability in the field of companion robots challenges the way in which the law apprehends AI and its social acceptability.

In the collective imagination, the machine is allegedly infallible; the damage it entails is therefore difficult to accept. Public opinion is moved more so by the damage caused by AI than the damage incurred by the human.

Poorly accepted because it is barely acceptable, the damage caused by a machine must be repaired. While the need for repair arises no doubt, it is still necessary to identify what type of liability to favor[25].

The question is pertinent, in the light of a (soon to come) reform of French law on civil[26] liability; whereas, the European Commission published

23 Aforementioned European Parliament resolution of February 16, 2017.

24 Appendix to the aforementioned European Parliament resolution of October 20, 2020.

25 On the general application of liability law to AI, see, in particular, Bensamoun and Loiseau (2022).

26 Bill "reforming civil liability", registered with the Senate on July 29, 2020.

on September 28, 2022 two directive proposals relating to civil liability in matters of AI[27].

In order to consider the current and future legal tools in French law and in EU law, a distinction should be made between common law liability (section 4.2) and special liability regimes (section 4.3).

4.2. Common law liability

Common law liability is the one that applies in the absence of no other, more specific, form of liability relating to a certain hypothesis. The articulation between the two laws obeys the famous adage "specialia generalibus derogant".

Traditionally, common law includes two types of liability: that caused by human activity (section 4.2.1) or that caused by a thing (section 4.2.2).

4.2.1. *The result of human activity*

A distinction should be made here between French positive law (section 4.2.1.1) and European prospective law (section 4.2.1.2).

4.2.1.1. *French positive law*

The famous Article 1240 from the French Civil Code states that: "Any act of a person which causes damage to another obliges him by whose fault the damage occurred to make reparation for it". This liability is caused by personal acts, stated in a more modern way by the 2020 reform proposal: "Everyone is responsible for the damage caused by their fault"[28].

The terms are clear. Only the result of human activity is targeted. Can robot activity be considered? This would amount to admitting liability due to

27 Directive proposal by the European Parliament and by the Council "on the adaptation of rules on extra-contractual civil liability in the field of artificial intelligence (AI Liability Directive)" and the directive proposal by the European Parliament and by the Council pertaining to the "liability caused by defective products". On these two texts, see, in particular: Bensamoun, A. (2023). Maîtriser les risques de l'intelligence artificielle: entre éthique, responsabilisation et responsabilité, *JCPG*, 5, 280.

28 Article 1240 of the 2020 reform proposal.

the robot's fault. We may very well object that the robot is not a physical person. Indeed, but thanks to an artifice by the lawmaker, a legal person can engage its liability. Another objection could be that there is a major difference between the robot and the legal person: the latter has legal personality, unlike the robot. Certainly, in order to remedy this, would it not suffice for the lawmaker to enshrine the robot's legal personality?

The whole French doctrine strongly opposes this recognition (Loiseau and Bourgeois 2014; Borghetti 2017; Szuskin 2018; Bensamoun and Loiseau 2022). For a less critical approach, refer to Choné-Grimaldi and Glaser (2018) in particular. One author even considers it to be a "crazy idea" (Loiseau 2022), a "legal monstrosity" (Loiseau 2018). Two main criticisms are expressed.

The first criticism concerns the risk of lowering the "status" of humans. Acknowledging robot rights as if they were humans is tantamount to denying the superiority of humans over machines, and more generally, of life over the absence of life.

The second criticism relates to the risk of non-accountability from robot manufacturers. In fact, recognizing robots having legal autonomy may induce them not to fulfill their contractual information obligations or – even worse – to exonerate themselves from their own liability in relation to a possibly defective robot[29].

For these reasons, the recognition of a new robotic legal personality is not to be welcomed. In other words, the robot is a thing and the thing, an object of law, must not become a subject of law.

4.2.1.2. *European prospective law*

In 2017, the European Parliament considered the possibility of endowing the robot with a legal personality[30]. This recognition sought to enable the robot to pay from its assets the reparation for the damage caused to a person. Since then, the European Parliament has abandoned this idea[31], but not that

29 Refer to section 4.3.2 for further development on liability caused by a defective product.

30 European Parliament resolution of February 16, 2017 "containing recommendations to the Commission regarding civil law rules on robotics".

31 The idea was not taken up in the resolutions and directive proposal after 2017.

of a liability for a fault caused by the human being bound a legal relationship with the robot.

The "AI liability" directive proposal of September 28, 2022[32] implemented a fault-based liability caused by the manufacturer of the AI system.

The notion of the "artificial intelligence system" was inspired in the 2021 draft regulation[33], which defines this system as "any software […] that can, for a given set of human-defined objectives, generate outputs, such as content, predictions, recommendations, or decisions influencing the environments they interact with"[34].

As one author pointed out, the expression "artificial intelligence system" has the merit of "denoting the plurality of mechanisms and components contributing to the functioning of these particular algorithms and closes the door to any anthropomorphic comparison" (Bensamoun 2023). Remember that, in this respect, the expression "artificial intelligence" is a misuse of language and AI is above all "advanced computing"[35].

The decision to opt for liability caused by the manufacturer's fault is not insignificant. It testifies to the will of the European lawmaker to preserve the interests of the manufacturer, not to excessively slow down the course of innovation.

Clearly, the interests of the victim would have been better respected with a no-fault liability regime. Indeed, in a no-fault liability regime, the victim does not need to prove fault, but only needs to prove a fact at the origin of damage, which is not the same thing.

By choosing fault liability, the Parliament singularly complicated the victim's task. In order to obtain reparation for damage, the victim will have

32 Directive proposal of the European Parliament and of the Council of September 28, 2022 "on adapting noncontractual civil liability rules in the field of artificial intelligence".

33 Proposal for a regulation of the European Parliament and of the Council of April 21, 2021 "establishing harmonized rules on artificial intelligence (legislation on artificial intelligence) and amending certain Union legislative acts".

34 Article 3 (1) of the 2021 proposed regulations.

35 According to the formula by Younès Bennani, Professor of machine learning and data science at Sorbonne Paris Nord University. Regarding the question of the expression "artificial intelligence" as a misuse of language, see, in particular, Julia (2018, 2020).

to prove the manufacturer fault, the harm caused by the AI system and the causal link between fault and harm. This triple proof is certainly difficult, especially given the complex technology at work within the robot.

In order to ease the burden of proof for the victim, the 2022 directive proposal formulated two rules.

The first rule concerns the access to information on the part of the victim. It obliges the supplier[36] to disclose certain information. More specifically, Article 3 of the text provides that at the request of the national court, the supplier must communicate "any proof it may hold regarding a specific high-risk AI system suspected of causing damage".

The reference to the "high-risk system" points to a distinction made by the proposed regulation of April 21, 2021[37] in function of the importance of the risk generated by AI systems. "Medical devices" belong to high-risk systems, of which companion robots are certainly part[38].

The rule of disclosure of information related to the AI system aims to facilitate the proof of fault weighing on the victim. However, the text subjects this obligation to conditions. The claimant (i.e. the victim) must have already requested this information from the provider[39]. In other words, a refusal must have already taken place before reiterating the request before the judge.

---

36 The concept of supplier stems from the proposed regulation of April 21, 2021, defined in Article 3 (2) as the natural or legal person who "develops or has developed an AI system with a view to putting it on the market or putting it into service under its own name or brand, against payment or free of charge".

37 Article 6 of the 2021 proposed regulation: "Irrespective of whether an AI system is placed on the market or put into service independently from the products referred to in points (a) and (b), that AI system shall be considered high-risk where both of the following conditions are fulfilled: a) the AI system is intended to be used as a safety component of a product, or is itself a product, covered by the Union harmonization legislation listed in Annex II; b) the product whose safety component is the AI system, or the AI system itself as a product, is required to undergo a third-party conformity assessment with a view to the placing on the market or putting into service of that product pursuant to the Union harmonization legislation listed in Annex II. b2. In addition to the high-risk AI systems referred to in paragraph 1, AI systems referred to in Annex III shall also be considered high-risk."

38 See section 4.3.2.1.1 on the notion of defective product.

39 Article 3-1 Par.1 of the 2022 directive proposal.

This prior request strongly recalls the requirement relating to the notification made to an Internet host in the event of illegal content. What is it about?

Committed to establishing a general framework for the obligations weighing on Internet companies, the so-called "electronic commerce" directive of June 8, 2000[40] inaugurated a quasi-immunity from liability in favor of the host. This is the natural or legal person who makes content available online[41]. It should not be confused with the publisher, who creates this content.

Neutral and purely technical, the host's role justifies the virtual absence of liability. This will only be implemented if the host does not quickly remove the illegal content once notified about the existence of such content[42].

During the transposition of the 2000 directive, the French lawmaker was perhaps too scrupulously attached to formalities concerning this notification[43]. In particular, claimants must prove that they first contacted or tried to contact the publisher before contacting the host. These requirements are justified by the lawmaker's desire to protect the host by preventing liability from being too easily invoked.

This desire for protection is justified by the fear that the major Internet companies will refuse to provide their services, or increase their cost in the presence of excessively heavy legal obligations. It is for this reason that the Internet service provider benefits from the same favor[44].

40 Directive 2000/31/EC of the European Parliament and of the Council of June 8, 2000 "on certain legal aspects of information society services, in particular electronic commerce, in the internal market", transposed into French law by Law No. 2004-575 of June 21, 2004 "for confidence in the digital economy".

41 Article 6 I-2 of Law No. 2004-575 of June 21, 2004 "for confidence in the digital economy".

42 Article 14 1 of the 2000 Directive.

43 Article 6 I-5 of the 2004 law.

44 Article 12 1 of the 2000 Directive.

These reasons explain why the recent European regulation on digital services[45] did not call into question the favorable liability regime for the host.

The lawmaker's position in the 2022 directive proposal is reminiscent of the one adopted in the 2004 law. However, the protection imperative is not present in the same way. Unlike the host (who is not the author of the illegal content), the robot's manufacturer is related to the damage caused to the victim. Therefore, it seems less legitimate to protect its interests than those of the host.

The 2022 directive proposal further specifies that "in support of that request, the potential claimant must present facts and sufficient evidence to support the plausibility of a claim for damages"[46]. This requirement gives the judge a great deal of latitude in assessing the elements of proof produced by the claimant. Such leeway can be a source of unpredictability and legal uncertainty for the victim, who will never know beforehand whether or not the judge will grant the request for information.

The second rule formulated by the directive proposal presupposes causality between the manufacturer's fault and the harm caused by the AI system[47]. This rule is intended to lighten the burden of proof weighing on victims, insofar as the presumption exempts them from providing proof of the causal link (which would otherwise weigh on them). In this respect, the rule seems favorable to the interests of the victim. However, the text postulates three conditions for the implementation of this presumption.

The victim must first prove that the fault was caused by the manufacturer. This is understandable: the causality presumption concerns the link between the manufacturer's fault and the harm suffered, but does not concern the fault itself. Fault is "a lack of compliance with a duty of care under Union or national law aimed directly at protecting against the damage provoked"[48].

45 Articles 4-1 and 6-1 of Regulation (EU) 2022/2065 "on digital services (known as DSA, Digital Services Act)", published in the OJEU on October 27, 2022.

46 Article 3-1 Par.2 of the 2022 directive proposal.

47 Article 4 of the 2022 directive proposal.

48 Article 4-1 (b) of the 2022 directive proposal.

The victim must then demonstrate that "the output of the AI system or its inability to produce a result gave rise to the relevant damage"[49]. Here too, we understand that the presumption does not exempt the victim from proving that the damage results from the AI system; in other words, that the damage has undoubtedly been caused by an act of the companion robot.

On the contrary, the text states that "it can be considered reasonably likely, based on the circumstances of the case, that the fault [for example, by the manufacturer] has influenced the output produced by the AI system or the failure of the AI system to produce an output"[50].

This condition is quite challenging. In order to benefit from the causality presumption between the manufacturer's fault and attribution to the AI system, namely to be exempted from proof of such causality, the victim must establish a "reasonably probable" link between the manufacturer's fault and the result of the AI system. Is this not the very negation of the principle of causality presumption? In principle, a presumption benefits its beneficiary without the need for an "active approach" (Bensamoun 2023) on its part.

Even more astonishingly, the text provides that, in the event of damage caused by a high-risk AI system (i.e. damage caused by an companion robot), the judge will not apply the causality presumption when the defendant, that is, the manufacturer of the AI system, "demonstrates that the claimant can reasonably access expertise and sufficient evidence to prove the causal link"[51]!

As one author pointed out: "Reading these limits is breathtaking, so easy it seems to refuse the victim or the patient the benefit of presumption, forcing them to resort to costly expertise" (Bernelin 2022).

While at first glance, the principle of causality presumption appears to be favorable to the interests of the victim, the concrete conditions for its implementation leave much to be desired. The hypotheses where the causality presumption actually comes into play are likely to be marginal as the legal obstacles are numerous.

49 Article 4-1 (d) of the 2022 directive proposal.

50 Article 4-1 (c) of the 2022 directive proposal.

51 Article 4-4 of the 2022 directive proposal.

In addition, even though the victim managed to obtain the implementation of the causality presumption, the defendant would always be able to overturn it, insofar as this presumption is endowed with a rebuttable character[52].

Behind the glaring difficulties in implementing the rules intended to lighten the burden of proof for the victim, we suspect – and deplore – the will of the European Commission to protect the interests of the manufacturers of AI systems.

4.2.2. *Caused by the thing*

The French Civil Code states that: "A party is liable for any damage caused by things that are in its custody". The 2020 reform proposal provides that: "A party is responsible in *full right* for the damage caused by the *physical* things in its custody"[53].

Both texts are based on the idea of objective liability, that is, no-fault (or strict) liability. Furthermore, the texts do not target human action, but that of the thing – a priori – the companion robot. The robot's envelope may very well be physical, but its operation is based on algorithms, that is, mathematical formulae and computer codes intrinsic in nature[54].

Therefore, the same physical envelope can be equipped with different AI software. This is what happens with the Nao robot: it does not have the same name and is not programmed in the same way, depending on whether it designed to assist an autistic child or a dependent elderly person.

The companion robot therefore constitutes as much a physical thing as an incorporeal thing. Positive law does not make a distinction depending on the nature of the thing (unlike the 2020 reform proposal, which requires a

---

52 Article 4-7 of the 2022 directive proposal provides that "the defendant has the right to rebut the causality presumption stated in Paragraph 1".

53 Article 1242 of the bill "reforming civil liability" of July 29, 2020. Our emphasis in italics.

54 An algorithm can be defined as "a series of instructions intended to carry out an operation or to obtain a result, a general method for solving a type of problem, a systematic process, which can be applied mechanically by simply following a specific set of instructions". *Lexique du numérique* [Online]. Available at: www.cours-appel.justice.fr/ [Accessed: June 17, 2023].

physical thing to implement liability). This requirement does not seem problematic because the AI system is inseparable from the companion robot's material envelope.

The seductive prospect of liability caused by the thing nonetheless raises two questions: can the companion robot be subject to custody (see section 4.2.2.1)? Also, how can we establish the link between the damage and the liability of the companion robot (see section 4.2.2.2)?

4.2.2.1. *The companion robot's custody*

Classically, custody designates the use, direction and control of the thing[55]. Is it applicable to the companion robot? What is more, is not the vocation of the robot to look after a person, rather than to be looked after by such a person?[56]

Furthermore, is the notion of custody compatible with the learning logic of this robot? Endowed with initial programming, the companion robot is an intelligent robot, that is, it learns progressively as it is used[57]. Robot learning works differently, depending on whether this learning process is supervised by a human being or not. This is the case of so-called reinforcement learning, which most intelligent robots are equipped with[58].

Is not the companion robot's gain of autonomy incompatible with the notion of custody? In this sense, one of the resolutions of the European

55 Article 1242 of the 2020 reform proposal: "The custodian (of the thing) is the one who has the power to use, control and direct such thing and is presumed to be responsible for any damage caused thereby". The article codifies the famous definition of material custody taken from the Franck jurisprudence.

56 As one author pointed out: "[…] the more this type of device [the companion robot] is supposed to adapt to the weaknesses of its user, the less will the latter's liability be justified on the grounds of the custody criterion. The empowerment of these connected objects could even reverse the relationship: the robot's effectiveness would in fact partly depend on its ability to exercise authority over the person it serves […]". C. Coulon (2021). *Lamy droit de la responsabilité*, 350-60 "Liability caused by connected objects", "custody and autonomy", Lamy, March 2021.

57 On the consequences of autonomous robot learning in terms of liability, see, in particular, the study "Règles européennes de droit civil en robotique", submitted in October 2016 to the Committee on Legal Affairs of the European Parliament, p. 18.

58 For a presentation of the different types of machine learning and their legal implications, see, in particular, Migayron (2018).

Parliament has pointed out that “the more autonomous is a robot, the less it can be considered as a simple tool controlled by other actors (such as the manufacturer, the operator, the owner, the user, etc.)”[59].

In the same vein, a French author (Szuskin 2018) quotes a thesis from American law that proposes drawing an analogy between AI and liability caused by animals. For instance, in the presence of a domesticated dog, liability is invoked in the name of the owner’s fault. On the contrary, in the presence of a wild dog, liability is engaged without a fault needing to be proven; liability is then objective (strict), as in the case of the thing.

To be applicable to a companion robot, the concept of custody should be relaxed. For example, we could consider that the possibility of cutting off the robot’s power supply suffices to confer custody of the robot.

It has yet to be determined who would be the robot’s guardian, who the obligation to repair the damage would fall upon.

Classically, the guardian is the user of the thing at the time of an occurrence of the damage. Therefore, the user of the companion robot is usually the victim. Of course, the robot cannot be held responsible for repairing its own damage.

An alternative would be to designate the owner and not the user as the robot’s guardian.

The 2020 reform proposal provides precisely that: “The owner is the presumed custodian”[60]. In the case of companion robots, it would be advisable to ensure that this presumption cannot be overturned, that is, it is irrefutable. This would prevent the user victim of the robot from being considered as the guardian.

Another solution would be to reawaken the doctrinal distinction between guardian of the structure/guardian of behavior. Jurisprudence[61] had reserved it for certain particularly dangerous objects animated by “their own

59 European Parliament resolution of 16 February 2017 “containing recommendations to the Commission regarding civil law rules on robotics”.

60 Article 1242 of the bill “reforming civil liability” of July 29, 2020.

61 Civ. nd, January 5, 1956, No. 56-02.126 and No. 56-02.138, case known as “Liquid oxygen”.

dynamism". The user is then considered the guardian of the object's behavior, while the manufacturer remains guardian of the structure.

The advantage of this distinction would be to place custody of the thing's structure – and therefore the burden of repair – on the manufacturer of the companion robot, rather than on its user, when the damage results from a design fault and not from a fault of use[62].

The hypothesis appeals but raises a difficulty. As the companion robot learns, it gradually adapts to the needs of its user. Does the guardian of behavior not then become the guardian of structure?

Moreover, it is not certain that the distinction between the two custodies survived the entry into force of the law relating to a defective product[63]. A judgment delivered by the Court of Justice of the European Union[64] specifies that this special liability regime excludes competing common law regimes. Moreover, in French law, the distinction was not taken up by the 2020 reform proposal.

4.2.2.2. *The link between damage and liability caused by the companion robot*

While there is no need to prove the companion robot's fault, it is still necessary to show that the damage suffered by the victim was caused by the robot.

This task is certainly not easy insofar as the operation of AI is often similar to a black box, especially in the presence of deep neural networks (deep learning). Fortunately, this proof is facilitated. The 2020 reform proposal relies on existing jurisprudence and provides that: "Caused by the thing is presumed when, in motion, (the thing) has come into contact with the recipient of damage"[65].

The existence of contact is frequent in the presence of a companion robot; for example, if the Buddy robot rolls over the feet of the elderly person it assists. This differs from the case of damage caused in the absence of

62 "Misusing the robot would entail liability on the part of its user, the design defect would target its designer" (Nevejans 2017).

63 Law No. 98-389 of May 19, 1998 "on liability caused by defective products".

64 CJEU, April 25, 2002, Aff. C-183/00.

65 This presumption was first established by case law, but is now codified.

contact. Is this possible in terms of companion robots? Yes, this could be the case of the Nao robot in the event of misunderstanding what the autistic child said to it, or, worse, insulting a minor. The damage suffered by the victim would be of a moral nature.

However, the damage suffered can also be of a physical nature, even in the absence of contact with the companion robot. Imagine that, in the near future, the robot Romeo is serving up a meal and spills a bowl of hot soup over the assisted person's hand. There would be no contact between the thing, the robot, and the recipient of damage, the user's hand. The damage caused, a burn, is nevertheless of a physical nature.

In the absence of contact with the robot, the victim has no causality presumption. It must prove "the inherent defect in the thing" or "the abnormality of its position, its state or its behavior"[66]. We may suspect this proof to be difficult to report for the non-expert in AI systems. In terms of deep learning computer programs, for example, it is almost impossible to explain how algorithms process data and deliver their result. The creators of the algorithms in these computer programs are themselves sometimes surprised by their performance: "what intrigues me the most is that it works so well!", one of them said[67].

Liability caused by the thing seems especially adapted to the damage provoked during the contact between the companion robot and its user. However, this liability requires designating the owner of the robot as guardian in order to preserve the victim's right to reparation.

This liability regime is of major interest to the victim of damage caused by the robot: it is not based on proof of fault, contrary to EU law, resulting from the 2022 directive proposal.

Aware of the difficulties inherent in proving this type of fault in terms of AI, the European lawmaker is attempting to facilitate its production by the victim. Unfortunately, both the conditions for the disclosure of information related to the high-risk AI system and those for the causality presumption undermine this facilitation in practice.

66 Article 1242 Par. 3 of the bill "reforming civil liability" of July 29, 2020.

67 Phrase by Jason Yosinki, AI researcher at Uber, quoted in Nouyrigat (2017).

4.3. Special liability regimes

These are the cases in which the legislator, whether French and European, has considered that common law was not suitable for certain types of damage. In particular, the "classic" provisions of liability law were criticized for not guaranteeing full reparation for the harm suffered by certain victims.

To remedy this injustice, two special liability regimes were created: that relating to traffic accidents (section 4.3.1) and the one dedicated to defective products (section 4.3.1).

4.3.1. *Caused by road accidents*

This special compensation scheme for victims of traffic accidents was born with the famous law known as "Badinter law"[68]. By definition, it is not applicable to the companion robot because the text requires a motorized land vehicle, which the companion robot is not[69].

In a similar register, the Court of Cassation recently ruled that "an electric wheelchair, a medical device intended for the transport of a person with a disability, is not a land motor vehicle in the sense of the law of July 5, 1985"[70].

Although unsuited to our subject, the liability regime relating to traffic accidents includes two elements which could be profitably used: the insurance obligation (section 4.3.1.1) and the notion of involvement (section 4.3.1.2).

4.3.1.1. *The insurance obligation*

The law of 1985 imposes on the owner of a land motor vehicle an obligation to take out liability insurance for damages that may be caused by

68 Law No. 85-677 of July 5, 1985 "to improve the situation of victims of traffic accidents and to speed up compensation procedures".

69 The land motor vehicle is defined by Article L. 211-1, 1st Par. of the Insurance Code as "any self-propelled vehicle intended to circulate on the ground and which can be actuated by mechanical force without being linked to a railway line, as well as any trailer, even uncoupled".

70 Civ 2nd, May 6, 2021, No. 20-14.551.

said vehicle[71]. It would be appropriate to oblige the manufacturers of the companion robot to take out insurance to cover the risk presented by their self-learning robot (in this sense, see Szuskin (2018)). In addition, the institution of a common compensation fund would help to repair the damage caused without slowing down manufacturer innovation.

However, this compensation scheme should not totally exempt the manufacturer from liability. In this sense, the producer could be obliged to provide relevant information on the risk inherent in the companion robot. This risk-related obligation already exists in consumer law for the risks that a product may present[72].

This obligation should be extended to the manufacturer of the companion robot. In the event of a breach of this obligation to inform, the robot's manufacturer could be rendered liable.

4.3.1.2. *The concept of involvement*

The regime provided for by the 1985 law is based on the involvement of a vehicle in the occurrence of a traffic accident[73]. Involvement is the material link that unites the vehicle to the accident. It differs from causality, which links the generating event to the damage. However, neither the lawmaker nor the judge has defined involvement. According to Professor Philippe Brun, the difference with causality seems to lie in "degree rather than in nature".

In this sense, implication is more easily proven than causality. Indeed, the involvement of the vehicle in an accident requires the vehicle to be related to

---

71 Article L. 211-1 of the Insurance Code states that: "Any natural person or any legal person other than the state, whose civil liability may be engaged for damage suffered by third parties resulting from harm to persons or property in which a vehicle is involved, must, in order to circulate, be covered by insurance guaranteeing this liability [...]."

72 Article L. 423-2 Par. 1, 2 and 3 of the Consumer Code provides that: "Manufacturers adopt the measures which, taking into account the characteristics of the products they supply, enable them: 1st to be kept informed about the risks that the products they market may present; 2nd to take the necessary actions to control these risks, including withdrawal from the market, adequate and effective warning of consumers and reminding consumers about the products placed on the market."

73 According to the first article of the law of 1985: "The provisions of this chapter apply, even when carried under contract, to victims of a traffic accident in which a land motor vehicle and its trailers or semi-trailers are *involved*, with the exception of railways and trams running on their own tracks." Our emphasis is shown in italics.

such an accident, not necessarily having caused it (Carval 2015). It suffices for the vehicle to have been engaged "in whatever way" in the accident.

Understood in this manner, the notion of involvement could be used outside the 1985 law. It would facilitate proof of the link between the companion robot and the damage caused. Similarly, the notion of accident, on which the Badinter law of 1985 is based, would make it possible "not to have to pass judgment on the functioning of this intelligence [artificial intelligence], a judgment inherent in the concepts of fault and default" (Borghetti 2017).

4.3.2. *Caused by a defective product*

This liability regime stems from a law of 1998[74], transposing a European directive of 1985[75]. In addition, the 2022 directive proposal[76] intends to adapt this regime to the damage caused by AI.

Again, a distinction should be made between French positive law (section 4.3.2.1) and European prospective law (section 4.3.2.2).

4.3.2.1. *French positive law*

This appears in Articles 1245 and subsequent articles of the French Civil Code. These provisions were not called into question by the 2020 reform proposal intended to modify liability law.

The French Civil Code states that: "the manufacturer is responsible for the damage caused by a defect in its product, whether or not it is bound by a contract with the victim". This regimes proves to be adapted to the damage caused by the companion robot because it provides for objective (strict, no-fault) liability, of the manufacturer in the event of a defect in the product.

The manufacturer is defined by law as "the manufacturer of a finished product, the producer of raw materials, the manufacturer of a component

74 Law No. 98-389 of May 19, 1998 "on liability caused by defective products".

75 Council Directive 85/374/EEC of July 25, 1985 "on the approximation of the laws, regulations and administrative provisions of the Member States concerning liability caused by products".

76 Directive proposal of the European Parliament and of the Council of September 28, 2022 "on liability caused by defective products".

part"[77]. This definition seems consistent with the complexity of the elements present within the companion robot. Manufacturers in the sense of the law are in fact: the manufacturer of the material medium, the manufacturer of the connected part, the algorithm designer, and the software programmer.

In addition, in the event of "damage caused by the defect of a product incorporated into another", the law provides for the solidarity of the "manufacturer of the component part and of the person who carried out the incorporation"[78]. This provision facilitates the reparation for the damage suffered by the victim of the defective product.

A priori adequate, the application of this regime to the companion robot raises two questions: the definition of the defective product (section 4.3.2.1.1) and exoneration from liability (section 4.3.2.1.2).

4.3.2.1.1. The concept of defective product

For liability to apply, damage must have been caused by a defective product. Is the companion robot a product in the legal sense?

In 1998, a ministerial response[79] clarified that the product causing the damage could be software. It can therefore be the software embedded into a companion robot.

To engage the liability of its manufacturer, the product must have a defect. On the contrary, this means that in case of damage caused by a decision made on the basis of a non-faulty algorithm, damage compensation can only take place under a regime attributing liability to the thing, as studied previously[80].

As for the concept of defect, the law provides that "a product is defective when it does not offer the security that can legitimately be expected"[81]. The legitimate expectation is particularly strong in the field of AI because the so-called intelligent machine is reputed to be infallible.

77 Article 1245-5 of the French Civil Code.

78 Article 1245-7 of the French Civil Code.

79 Question asked on June 15, 1998, No. 15677, JOAN, p. 3230; response published August 24, 1998, p. 4728.

80 See section 4.2.2 on acts caused by the thing.

81 Article 1245-3 Par. 1 of the French Civil Code.

The difficulty lies in proving the safety defect. This proof weighs on the victim[82]. Instead, and contrary to the regime attributing liability to the thing, there is no presumption of a defective product at the origin of damage. If the victim fails to prove the defect, they will be deprived of reparation. How do we simplify the burden of proof falling upon the victim?

The companion robot can be assimilated to a medical device[83] in the sense of the French Public Health Code, that is: "Any instrument, device, equipment, software, implant […] intended by the manufacturer to be used […] in humans for one or more medical purposes [such as]; 1° diagnosis, prevention, monitoring, prediction, prognosis, treatment or alleviation of a disease; 2° diagnosis, control, treatment, alleviation of an injury or disability […]"[84].

What is the point of this qualification? The law provides that "medical devices are designed and manufactured in such a way that, when used for their intended purpose and under the conditions intended for that purpose, they do not compromise […] the health and safety of users or other persons"[85].

In addition, the placing on the market of a medical device is subject to obtaining a "CE-marking" that certifies the safety it allegedly offers[86]. We could imagine that the absence of this marking on a companion robot leads to the presumption of a safety defect. It would no longer be up to the victim to prove the safety defect but up to the manufacturer to prove the absence of a safety defect. Such a reversal of the burden of proof would result in favoring the interests of the victim over those of the manufacturer of the defective robot.

We still have to identify which part of the companion robot caused the damage: was it the material part or its connected part? The person responsible will not be determined in the same way. Consider the seal robot,

82 Article 1245-8 of the French Civil Code: "The claimant must prove the damage, the defect and the causal link between defect and damage."

83 The Paro seal robot received the medical device certification in April 2021, Class 1.

84 Article L. 5211-1 of the French Public Health Code, resulting from Ordinance No. 2022-1086 of July 29, 2022 "adapting French law to Regulation (EU) 2017/746 of the European Parliament and of the Council of 5 April 2017 on in vitro diagnostic medical devices".

85 Article R. 5211-21 of the French Public Health Code.

86 This marking has been applied to the Hal exoskeleton, certified as a medical device.

Paro, for example. Its battery can experience overheating, which could cause its user burns. The connectivity of the robotic companion may also fail and lead to certain personal data being mistakenly sent to unauthorized third parties. The first damage – the physical one – is certainly imputable to the manufacturer of the medium, while the second harm – of a moral nature – is rather imputable to the designer of the AI software.

4.3.2.1.2. Exoneration from liability

The French Civil Code provides that: "The manufacturer is automatically liable for the damage caused by the defect of its product unless it proves [...] that the state of scientific and technical knowledge, at the time it put the product into circulation, did not make it possible to detect the existence of the defect"[87].

This cause of exoneration known as "risk of development" is not favorable to the victim of a companion robot because it perfectly corresponds to liability caused by learning AI: a software program which evolves of its own accord between the moment of its circulation and the occurrence of damage. If this reason for exoneration is maintained, it risks leading to the systematic exclusion of manufacturer liability, and therefore, to a lack of reparation for damage under these grounds.

Would it be possible to remove this cause of exoneration in terms of damage caused by the intelligent robot? This seems possible insofar as, at the time of the adoption of the directive, the European Commission had left the choice to the Member States of the European Union to include (or not) this ground for exemption in their internal law.

The French lawmaker had chosen to retain it so as not to curb the technological progress of companies. A dilemma arose between repairing the damage caused and encouraging innovation. When the law was passed, the French government had considered excluding this cause of exoneration in the presence of a health product, but the hostility of the pharmaceutical industry led to it being maintained.

Since the companion robot can be assimilated to a medical device, it would be appropriate to reduce or even remove this cause of exemption, at least in the presence of physical damage caused by this robot. Favorable to

87 Article 1245-10 4 of the French Civil Code.

the interests of the victim, the approach would also be in line with the spirit of the 2020 reform proposal, which prohibits reparation limiting clauses for bodily damage[88].

4.3.2.2. *European prospective law*

Unlike the other directive proposal published on the same day[89], the one relating to defective products[90] was based on the absence of fault. It aimed to correct the shortcomings of the initial text of 1985 relating to damage (non-existent at the time), caused by AI.

The European lawmaker emphasizes two important goals[91]: on the one hand, adapting the concepts of the initial text to the products born of the digital economy, among which are robots; on the other hand, facilitating the burden of proof weighing on the victim of the damage caused by an intelligent object.

The text does not call into question the concepts and principles established by the 1985 directive. Therefore, the definition for the product[92], the default[93], the manufacturer[94], the no-fault[95] liability principle and exoneration cases[96] are not substantially changed.

These definitions are rather adjusted to the time of our digital world. As such, the definition of product now includes "digital manufacturing files and software"[97]. There is no doubt that both the companion robot's physical envelope and its AI system fall within the scope of the text. Furthermore, it

88 Article 1284 Par.2 of the 2020 directive proposal: "However, no one may limit or exclude their liability due to physical damage."

89 Directive proposal of the European Parliament and of the Council of September 28, 2022 "on adapting non-contractual civil liability rules in the field of artificial intelligence".

90 Directive proposal of the European Parliament and of the Council of September 28, 2022 "on liability caused by defective products".

91 Explanatory memorandum to the 2022 directive proposal.

92 Article 4-1 of the 2022 directive proposal.

93 Article 6 of the 2022 directive proposal.

94 Article 7-4 of the 2022 directive proposal.

95 Article 7-1 of the 2022 directive proposal.

96 Article 10 of the 2022 directive proposal.

97 Article 4-1 of the 2022 directive proposal.

emphasized that the product security defect could be related to the product's ability to "continue learning after deployment"[98].

This precision is welcome; it makes it possible to include the damage caused by autonomous learning programs, such as those used by intelligent robots. This means that manufacturer liability will be implemented for systems that learn autonomously. It will not be possible for them to claim an exemption caused by the autonomous learning of the intelligent robot, which is the case of the companion robot.

The major contribution of the text lies in the facilitation of the burden of proof for the victim wishing to obtain reparation for damage. It echoes the content of the other directive proposal, published on the same day.

Indeed, Article 8 of the directive proposal relating to defective products establishes an obligation for the defendant (in this case, the manufacturer) to disclose pertinent information. The obligation is strongly reminiscent of the one provided for in the other directive proposal "on liability in matters of AI", except that here, the disclosure obligation is not confined to high-risk systems and the claimant does not have to provide proof of prior failure in the request made to the manufacturer.

On the contrary, the claimant is required to "present facts and sufficient elements of proof to support the plausibility of the claim for damages"[99].

The reserves previously made can be reiterated here. The text leaves the judge ample space to decide whether or not to grant the request for information made by the victim.

Similarly, the text establishes two presumptions: a defectiveness presumption of the product causing the damage and a presumption of the causal link between the product's defect and the damage[100].

Remember that while the liability system caused by a defective product does not require proof of fault for the product's manufacturer, it nonetheless requires proof of the defect of the said product and of the causal link

98 Article 6-1 c of the 2022 directive proposal.

99 Article 8-1 of the 2022 directive proposal relating to defective products and Article 3-1 of the one relating to fault liability.

100 Article 9 of the 2022 directive proposal.

between such a defect and the damage suffered by the victim. The presumptions proposed here are intended to dispense the victim from providing these two elements of proof. The mechanism recalls, of course, the causality presumption discussed in the other directive proposal.

The text has the advantage of considering the probative difficulties encountered by the victim "due to a certain technical or scientific complexity"[101], which will often be the case in terms of damage caused by an intelligent robot, such as the companion robot.

In this case, Article 9-4 of the text provides that the product's defect and its link with damage will be proven when the claimant demonstrates that "the product has contributed to the damage" and "that it is probable for the product to have been defective, or that its defect was a probable cause of damage, or both". The text further provides that the victim must act on "the basis of sufficiently relevant evidence.".

Once again, the conditions imposed on the recognition of presumptions contradict, in practice, the openly stated purpose: to relieve the victim's burden of proof. Does not proving the product's contribution to the damage and the probability of the product's defect amount to proving the product's defectiveness and the causal link between this defect and the damage? In other words, do not the conditions for implementing presumptions contradict their function? We would rather think so insofar as presumptions are endowed with a rebuttable character, that is, they can be reversed by the defendant[102].

Within special liability regimes, the one relating to defective products deserves attention. It has the advantage of being applicable in the absence of fault from the manufacturer of the companion robot. It also makes it possible to take into account the autonomous learning of the intelligent robot and to consider that damage may result for its user.

However, the implementation of this regime is not automatic. The victim of damage caused by the defective robot must prove the defect of this robot and the link of this defect with the damage suffered. In concrete terms, it is not at all certain that the probationary relief provided for by the 2022

101 Article 9-4 of the 2022 directive proposal.

102 Article 9-5 of the 2022 directive proposal.

directive proposal will apply, considering that their implementation seems to be compromised by the conditions imposed.

To truly facilitate the reparation for the damage suffered by the victim, it would be more appropriate to remove the cause of exoneration from the risk of development. This cause enables the manufacturer to take refuge behind the increasing autonomy of intelligent products so as not to be liable for possible malfunctions. This ground for exoneration therefore seems too favorable to the interests of the manufacturer to be upheld with regards to damage caused by companion robots. In this respect, it is regrettable that the 2022 directive proposal retained this cause for exoneration[103].

4.4. Conclusion

Throughout this chapter, we have tried to identify the ways in which liability law could apprehend the damage caused by an intelligent companion robot. More specifically, we have focused on French and European rights, present and future.

The future of French liability law does not really care about AI. In this area, as in others, the impetus will certainly come from the European Community[104].

At this stage, French law does not legislate in terms of damage caused by AI. However, its "traditional" instruments prove to be adaptable, in particular, liability caused by the thing and liability caused by the defective product.

We agree with one author that "technological modernity does not necessarily call for a renewal of legal rules, and that, at least initially, it may be sufficient to adapt what already exists" (Loiseau 2022).

---

103 Article 10-1 e of the directive proposal of the European Parliament and of the Council of September 28, 2022 "on liability caused by defective products". "An economic operator […] is not liable for the damage caused by a defective product if he/she provides one of the following proofs: […] if it is a manufacturer, the objective state of scientific and technical knowledge at the time the product was placed on the market or put into service or during the period during which the product was under the control of the manufacturer, did not make it possible to detect the defect […]."

104 Existing French legislation in personal data, e-commerce, intellectual property and consumer law is largely derived from European Union directives and regulations.

While prospective European law may seem more daring, its texts do not propose creations ex nihilo. Rather, they are based on adaptations of existing regimes. Therefore, liability regimes are adapted to match fault liability and defective product liability.

Aware of the uncertainties related to the development of AI, the European lawmaker is cautious. It stipulates that the directive proposal on fault liability will have to be reviewed by the end of the five years, following its transposition[105].

In particular, the reconsideration will focus on "the risks likely to affect important legal values such as [...] health [...]". This naturally includes the harmful actions of companion robots caused by their growing autonomy.

French and European law seem equipped to cope with the damage that increasingly efficient companion robots will cause in the future. We can only hope that the future of these robots does not resemble the world dreaded by: "a world won for technology" but "lost for freedom" (Bernanos 1946).

4.5. References

Asimov, I. (1942). Runaround. In *Astounding Science Fiction*. Street & Smith Publications Inc., New York.

Bensamoun, A. (2023). Maîtriser les risques de l'intelligence artificielle : entre éthique, responsabilisation et responsabilité. *JCPG*, 5, 280.

Bensamoun, A. and Loiseau, G. (eds) (2022). *Droit de l'intelligence artificielle*, 2nd edition. LGDJ, Paris.

Bernanos, G. (1946). *La France contre les robots*. Editions France libre, Rio de Janeiro.

Bernelin, M. (2022). Intelligence artificielle : une proposition de directive sur la responsabilité civile extracontractuelle. *Dalloz actualité*, 22 November.

Borghetti, J.-S. (2017). L'accident généré par l'intelligence artificielle autonome. *JCPG*, 3, 23.

Carval, S. (2015). L'implication et la causalité. *RCA*, 21.

105 Recital No. 31 of the directive proposal on the adaptation of non-contractual civil liability rules in the field of AI of September 28, 2022.

Choné-Grimaldi, A.-S. and Glaser, P. (2018). Responsabilité civile du fait d'un robot doué d'intelligence artificielle : faut-il créer une personnalité robotique ? *Contrats – Concurrence – Consommation*, 1.

Devillers, L. (2020). *Les robots émotionnels. Santé, surveillance, sexualité... : et l'éthique dans tout ça ?* L'Observatoire, Paris.

Devillers, L. (2022). L'éthique de la robotique sociale. Conference, Blue Frog Robotics, Paris.

Journal officiel de la République française (2018). Vocabulaire de l'intelligence artificiel. *JORF*, 9 December.

Julia, G. (2018). L'illusion de l'intelligence artificielle. In *Lex robotica – Le droit à l'épreuve de la robotique*, Guével, D. and Depadt, V. (eds). LGDJ, Paris.

Julia, G. (2020). L'intelligence peut-elle être artificielle ? In *Sciences et sens de l'intelligence artificielle*, Julia, G. (ed.). Dalloz, Paris.

Loiseau, G. (2018). La personnalité juridique des robots : une monstruosité juridique. *JCPG*, 22, 1039.

Loiseau, G. (2022). Le droit de la responsabilité civile s'adapte aux systèmes d'intelligence artificielle. *Communication, commerce électronique*, 11.

Loiseau, G. and Bourgeois, M. (2014). Du robot en droit à un droit des robots. *JCPG*, 48, 2162.

Mendoza-Caminade, A. (2016). *Le droit confronté à l'intelligence artificielle des robots ; vers l'émergence de nouveaux concepts juridiques ?* Recueil Dalloz, Paris.

Migayron, S. (2018). Pratique contentieuse. Intelligence artificielle : qui sera responsable ? *Communication – Commerce électronique*, 4.

Nevejans, N. (2017). *Traité de droit et d'éthique de la robotique civile.* LEH Édition, Bordeaux.

Nouyrigat, V. (2017). Algorithmes : une nouvelle intelligence est née. *Sciences & Vie*, 1198, 49.

Szuskin, L. (2018). Intelligence artificielle et responsabilité. *Communication – Commerce électronique*, 6.

5

From Computer-assisted Surgery to AI-guided Surgery

5.1. Computer-assisted surgery

For over 20 years, surgical computer assistance has been booming in orthopedic surgery: frequent tools include navigation, 3D printing and the robotic arm. These technologies carry with them the promise of standardized surgery, in which the surgeon, assisted by the machine, gains further accuracy (Grégory et al. 2019a).

A few years ago, a new system appeared: mixed reality. This is a computer headset that the surgeon can interact with at the surgical theater, without risking errors such as asepsis, thanks to artificial intelligence (AI) sensors, through voice control or by tapping a virtual keyboard. Mixed reality was initially perceived as the newcomer to computer-assisted surgery (Grégory et al. 2018). This system seems relevant to us in that it opens up a new era: AI-assisted surgery, which will be addressed in this chapter.

5.2. Mixed reality, a computer-assisted surgery tool and a key element of AI-guided surgery

First of all, it is pertinent to define the terms mixed reality, virtual reality and augmented reality:

Chapter written by Thomas GRÉGORY, Younès BENNANI and Charles DACHEUX.
For a color version of all the figures in this chapter, see www.iste.co.uk/julia/aihealthcare.zip.

– Virtual reality (VR) designates the set of devices enabling the digital simulation of an environment via a computer. Depending on the different technologies used, VR immerses the person into a virtual universe, stimulating different senses. So far, VR has not found a direct application for surgery. However, its immersive properties make this technology interesting for training (Grégory et al. 2019b).

– Augmented reality is "the superposition of reality and other elements (sounds, 2D and 3D images, videos, etc.) calculated by a computer system in real time" (Wikipedia definition). These are often alphanumeric data. For example, a combat helicopter pilot can access flight data displayed on the helmet's visor thanks to "heads-up" devices.

– Mixed reality (MR) is a form of augmented reality. The concept of MR was developed by Microsoft, who launched the HoloLens glasses 1 in 2015. These have been gradually marketed in the United States (since February 2016) and in France (since October 2016). In 2019, the updated version of this headset (HoloLens 2) was released. What sets MR apart is that the HoloLens are actually real computers equipped with lasers and sensors using AI algorithms. These sensors make it possible to interact with the glasses by means of an oral command or by performing gestures in front of the glasses (the glasses being equipped with two cameras). Through photogrammetry software working with the "3D face mesh" method, the embedded laser enables glasses to model the forms of the surrounding environment (e.g. the floor, the ceiling, a desk). Therefore, a virtual 3D object (a hologram) can be placed in the real environment known by the computer.

Each of these technologies can be reduced to one word: immersion (in the case of virtual reality), integration (for augmented reality) and interaction (for mixed reality)

In December 2017, after several months of research and study in collaboration with Microsoft, Terarecon and Evolutis, the first surgery using MR with the HoloLens headset was performed by our team, at the University Hospital of Avicenne in France[1] (Grégory et al. 2018) (Figure 5.1). It was a reverse shoulder prosthesis. During the operation, the surgeon had access to three interfaces, on demand: 1) 3D imaging of the patient using Terarecon's Holoportal interface that grants access to the hospital's PACS (Picture Archiving and Communication System). This

1 See: www.youtube.com/watch?v=xUVMeib0qek&t=24s.

enabled the surgeon to manually superimpose the visible part of the scapula glenoid with the corresponding part of the scapula hologram, thereby reaching the hidden part of the bone under the soft parts. 2) The operating technique developed by Evolutis (HeadOp Interface) in holographic form over the patient's 3D imaging, based on preoperative planning. The surgeon was thus able to compare step by step what he was doing with what he had to do in order to achieve the proper positioning of the prosthesis planned before the operation. 3) The Skype interface enabling the surgeon to communicate with surgeons in the United States and England (these surgeons could follow the operation behind their computer, seeing what Professor Grégory was seeing thanks to the two HoloLens cameras, and also visualizing the holograms displayed by the surgeon) (Figure 5.2) (Grégory et al. 2019c). The surgeon's assistant was also equipped with HoloLens glasses and the holograms were simultaneously shared by the surgeon and his assistant in real time.

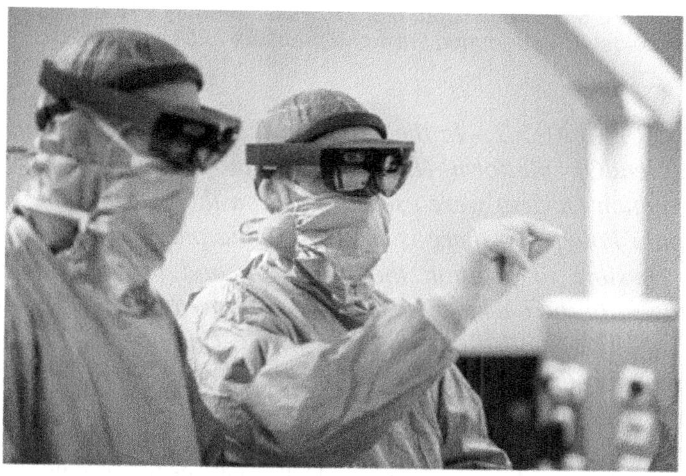

Figure 5.1. *Professor Grégory simultaneously using Microsoft's HoloLens mixed reality headset with his assistant (source: Raphaël de Bengy)*

This world premiere led to experimentation with the use of MR in other areas of orthopedic surgery (Grégory et al. 2021, 2022) and specialties other than orthopedic surgery (maxillofacial surgery, plastic surgery, oncological surgery, neurosurgery, etc.) (Germain et al. 2010; Koulalis et al. 2011; Clark and Schmidt 2013; Stübig et al. 2013; Badiali et al. 2014; Tabrizi and Mahvash 2015; Theopold et al. 2016; Tepper et al. 2017; Vávra et al. 2017).

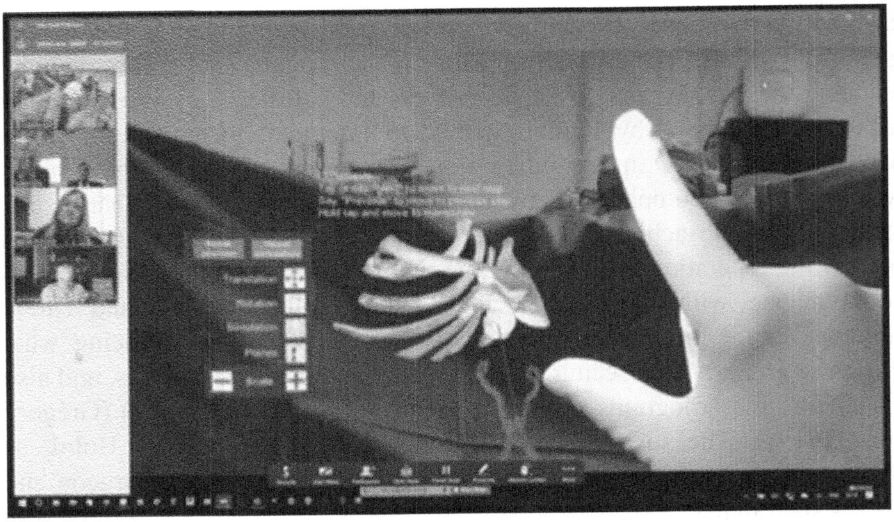

Figure 5.2. *Image capture of Professor Grégory's HoloLens (Microsoft) visor during the world premiere in December 2017*

COMMENT ON FIGURE 5.2.– *In the center of the image, we see the shoulder prosthesis HeadOp platform (Evolutis): at the stage when the glenoid forceps (Aventum Device) were used to position the guiding pin. To the left of the scapula hologram, there is a holographic platform of this platform, making it possible to position the hologram and to scroll through the surgical stages. In the background, there is an operating field. To the left of the visor, we can visualize the surgeons in the United States and England remotely assisting the surgery. On the right, we see the surgeon's gestures enabling him to manipulate the hologram.*

The prospects are of several kinds: 1) the possibility for the surgeon to use a computer during surgery while remaining sterile, by interacting with the computer not via a keyboard or a mouse but by voice command and/or gestures; 2) the possibility of having the intervention supervised by observers outside the operating theater; 3) the use of advanced digital technology at an affordable price to democratize its use (the price of HoloLens 2 oscillates around $3,500); and 4) with later versions of the HoloLens, the possibility of using the MR laser (i.e. the HoloLens "3D face mesh" method) for the continuous automatic calibration of the patient's preoperative imaging at the operating theater, in real time, without the need for the sensors to be positioned on the patient. Navigation could dispense with the need for positional sensors on the bone structures and instruments and free itself from the registration stage, which is currently a source of inaccuracy. Let us give an example: the scanner makes it possible to reconstruct the contours of a patient's skin and bone. The HoloLens laser would allow the HoloLens computer to locate the contour of the patient's skin. Therefore, the HoloLens could automatically calibrate the scanner's skin hologram according to the contours of the patient's skin, and infer the bone's position in real time. Developed in a field other than medicine (and a fortiori, orthopedic surgery), this technology has the potential to free navigation from obstacles and to foster its widespread use.

5.3. The concept of AI-guided surgery

AI is currently used in everyday practice in diagnostic procedures.

The advent and development of machine learning and deep learning enable the study of medical imaging in a diagnostic framework with AI decision-making algorithms in order to best personalize patient care (Grégory et al. 2019b, 2019c). Regarding this diagnostic approach, Olczak et al. (2017), for example, showed that the analysis of bone X-rays by AI was at least as good as the one performed by a senior orthopedic surgeon.

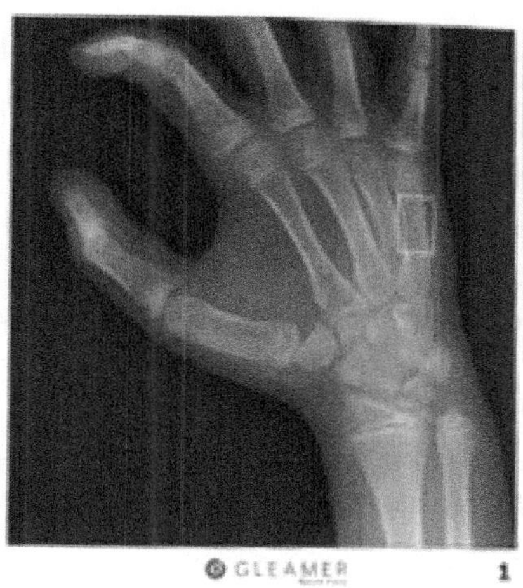

Figure 5.3. *AI algorithm (GLEAMER) framing the area of interest corresponding to a fracture on an X-ray*

This solution has made it possible to drastically minimize diagnostic errors (fractures having gone unnoticed) in traumatological emergency centers (Figure 5.3).

The concept of AI-guided surgery emerged in our team following an observation during the use of MR in the operating theater: the MR computer headset has the capacity to collect surgical images, thanks to its cameras. It can host an application, making it possible for an AI algorithm to analyze these surgical images and retrieve this information to the surgeon in real time (Figure 5.4).

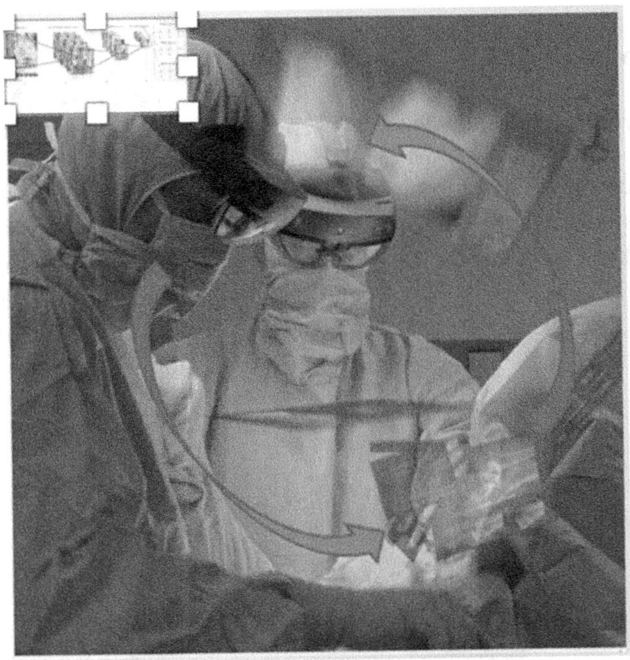

Figure 5.4. *Illustration of the concept of AI-guided surgery: the computer headset has the ability to collect surgical images thanks to its cameras, in order to host an application that makes it possible for an AI algorithm to analyze these surgical images and retrieve this information to the surgeon in real time*

Therefore, the massification of surgical data, recorded during the routine use of MR glasses by multiple surgeons, could be analyzed by AI algorithms to provide orthopedics with the surgical applications of the future. We could imagine, for example, that an AI algorithm warns the surgeon of the presence of a nervous structure to be respected, even before the surgeon has visualized this structure. We could also imagine a head of department being warned by another algorithm of a difficulty encountered by a junior surgeon at an operating room within their department, long before the junior surgeon has made the decision to call a senior for help.

It is rather challenging at this stage to imagine what these AI algorithms could find. It is likely that we do not know yet what we will be looking for, but everyone working around AI and Big Data knows that the promise is immense. The faster transmission of data thanks to 5G will accelerate this aspect of surgical data massification (Grégory and Bennani 2019).

5.4. Conclusion

Since then, we have undertaken several pioneering studies as part of research work in our laboratory.

Two of these studies illustrating the concept of AI-guided surgery are presented further in this book: the detection of anatomical structures and lesions in hand surgery by AI (Chapter 6) and surgical diagnosis augmented by AI (Chapter 7).

5.5. References

Badiali, G., Ferrari, V., Cutolo, F., Freschi, C., Caramella, D., Bianchi, A., Marchetti, C. (2014). Augmented reality as an aid in maxillofacial surgery: Validation of a wearable system allowing maxillary repositioning. *J. Cranio-Maxillofac. Surg.*, 42, 1970–1976.

Clark, T.C. and Schmidt, F.H. (2013). Robot-assisted navigation versus computer-assisted navigation in primary total knee arthroplasty: Efficiency and accuracy. *ISRN Orthop.*, 1–6.

Germain, M.A., Liverneaux, P., Missana, M.-C. (2010). Microchirurgie avec le robot Da Vinci S. La télémicrochirurgie : l'essor imminent. *e-mémoires de l'Académie Nationale de Chirurgie*, 74–77.

Grégory, T. and Bennani, Y. (2019). Qu'est-ce que l'intelligence artificielle et quel sera son impact en santé ? Et pourquoi avoir créé l'institut MOVEO au sein de la Maison des sciences numériques de l'Université Paris 13 ? *Maîtrise orthopédique*, 288, 2.

Grégory, T., Grégory, J., Sledge, J., Allard, R., Mir, O. (2018). A surgery guided by mixed reality: Presentation of a proof of concept. *Acta Orthop.*, 89(5), 480–483.

Grégory, T., Wunenburger, P.E., Dufournier, B., Boukhentiche, A., Dacheux, C. (2019a). La réalité mixte, l'intelligence artificielle et le chirurgien augmenté. *Maîtrise orthopédique*, 288, 2.

Grégory, T., Thumser, J., Guetari, C., De Clermont Tonnerre, E., Dacheux, C. (2019b). La simulation en chirurgie orthopédique à l'heure du numérique. *Maîtrise orthopédique*, 288, 1.

Grégory, T., Merlini, L., Prenaud, C., Louis, E., Eskiizmirliler, S., Pierrart, J. (2019c). Intelligence artificielle, Big Data et médecine personnalisée. *Maîtrise orthopédique*, 288, 2.

Grégory, T., Mosmemi, A., Hurst, S., Dacheux, C. (2021). Mixed reality assisted percutaneous scaphoid fixation: A proposed new surgical technique. *Tech. Hand Up Extrem. Surg.*, 26(1), 32–36.

Grégory, T., Grégory, J., Dacheux, C., Hurst, S. (2022). Surgeon experience of mixed reality headset technology during the Covid-19 pandemic: A multicenter international case series in orthopedic surgery. *BMJ Surg. Interv. Health Technologies*, 4(1).

Koulalis, D., O'Loughlin, P.F., Plaskos, C., Kendoff, D., Cross, M.B., Pearle, A.D. (2011). Sequential versus automated cutting guides in computer-assisted total knee arthroplasty. *The Knee*, 18, 436–442.

Olczak, J., Fahlberg, N., Maki, A., Razavian, A.S., Jilert, A., Stark, A., Sköldenberg, O., Gordon, M. (2017). Artificial intelligence for analyzing orthopedic trauma radiographs. *Acta Orthop.*, 88, 581–586.

Stübig, T., Petri, M., Zeckey, C., Hawi, N., Krettek, C., Citak, M., Meller, R. (2013). 3D navigated implantation of the glenoid component in reversed shoulder arthroplasty. Feasibility and results in an anatomic study. *Int. J. Med. Robot. Comput. Assist. Surg. MRCAS*, 9, 480–485.

Tabrizi, L.B. and Mahvash, M. (2015). Augmented reality-guided neurosurgery: Accuracy and intraoperative application of an image projection technique. *J. Neurosurg.*, 123, 206–211.

Tepper, O.M.M.D., Rudy, H.L., Lefkowitz, A., Weimer, K.A., Marks, S.M., Stern, C.S., Garfein, E.S. (2017). Mixed reality with HoloLens: Where virtual reality meets augmented reality in the operating room. *Plast. Reconstr. Surg.*, 140, 1066–1070.

Theopold, J., Pieroh, P., Scharge, M.L., Marqua, B., Hohmann, T., Josten, C., Hepp, P. (2016). Improved accuracy of K-wire positioning into the glenoid vault by intraoperative 3D image intensifier-based navigation for the glenoid component in shoulder arthroplasty. *Orthop. Traumatol. Surg. Res.*, 102, 575–581.

Vávra, P., Roman, J., Zonča, P., Ihnát, P., Němec, M., Kumar, J., Habib, N., El-Gendi, A. (2017). Recent development of augmented reality in surgery: A review. *J. Healthc. Eng.*

6

Detection of Anatomical Structures and Lesions in Hand Surgery Through the Use of Artificial Intelligence

The hand is a formidable, highly complex organ. Each anatomical structure, even the smallest one, can play a crucial role: arteries, tendons and nerves work together to generate a wide range of movements. For this reason, hand surgery is a complex operation, requiring a wide range of skills and experience. This chapter will explore two object detection problems related to hand surgery: the detection of anatomical structures and lesions (relying on modular learning) and endoscopic carpal tunnel release (using self-supervised learning). Object detection will be used to detect anatomical structures and lesions. We will also show the ways in which modular machine learning and self-supervised learning can be used to improve results, even with only a small amount of labeled data.

6.1. Introduction

In recent years, machine learning applications in the medical field have become very popular. However (especially in the field of computer vision), the lack of labeled data is a recurring problem, because labeling is time consuming and sometimes requires advanced knowledge. As a result, there is a need to reduce decision complexity or to introduce unlabeled data into

Chapter written by Léo DÉCHAUMET, Younès BENNANI, Joseph KARKAZAN, Nosseiba BEN SALEM, Abir BARBARA, Charles DACHEUX and Thomas GRÉGORY.
For a color version of all of the figures in this chapter, see www.iste.co.uk/julia/aihealthcare.zip.

the training flow. This chapter will look into the use of modular learning to reduce decision complexity in the detection of anatomical structures and lesions. At a later stage, it will use contrastive learning to perform an encoder using unlabeled data.

Self-supervised learning has gained popularity in recent years because large amounts of unlabeled data can be used to learn useful data representations. In fact, this method uses a pretext task extracted from the data themselves, in order to generate pseudo-labels and train a supervised model. In computer vision, almost all pretext tasks rely on the transformation of images. Different pretext discriminative tasks have been proposed, such as predicting the relative position of two patches within an image (Doersch et al. 2015), predicting the degree of rotation (Gidaris et al. 2018) or solving a puzzle (Noroozi and Favaro 2016). Nevertheless, most recent methods rely on contrastive learning (He et al. 2019; Misra and van der Maaten 2019; Caron et al. 2020; Chen et al. 2020; Dwibedi et al. 2021). In contrastive learning, an image and its transformation are considered as a positive pair, while other images in the dataset/batch are considered as negative samples. A model is trained to group the positive pairs together, while discarding the negative samples. In other words, the representation is trained to be invariant to a set of transformations. The choice of transformations is therefore a crucial parameter. In the second part of this work, we will use self-supervised contrastive learning in order to learn the proper representation of an image from a carpal tunnel endoscopy.

6.2. Context

6.2.1. *Object detection*

Object detection algorithms can be sorted into two categories: one-step detectors and two-step detectors. In two-step detection (e.g. Faster R-CNN (Ren et al. 2015) and Cascade R-CNN (Cai and Vasconcelos 2017)), the region proposal (regression task) and the classification task are performed separately. In one-step detection (e.g. YOLO (Redmon et al. 2015) and RetinaNet (Lin et al. 2017)), both tasks are performed simultaneously.

Although two-step detectors generally perform better than one-step detectors, they are slower.

We have chosen the Faster R-CNN architecture, a famous two-step object detection algorithm, for its simplicity, efficiency and performance, especially on small objects.

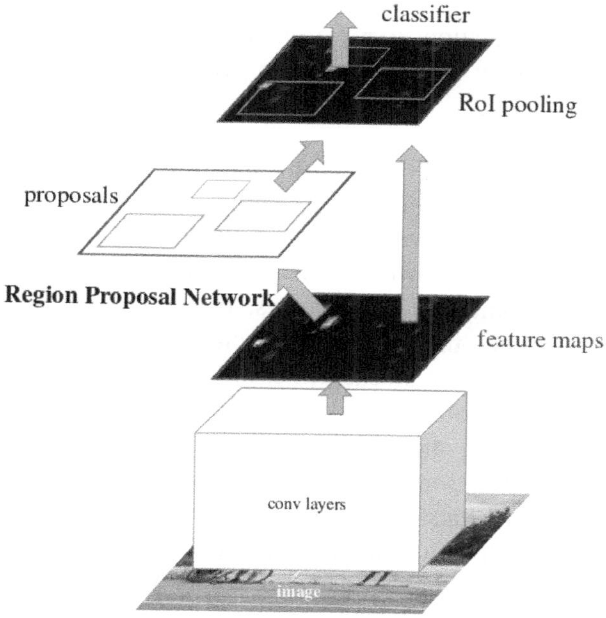

Figure 6.1. *Faster R-CNN architecture, drawn from Ren et al. (2015). The features extracted by the coder are fed into a region proposal network and then all regions are classified*

6.2.2. *Contrastive self-supervised learning*

Contrastive learning aims to find a suitable representation by bringing together similar images within the representation space and by moving dissimilar images further apart. In a self-supervising configuration, we do not have access to labels. Therefore, positive and negative pairs have to be created from the data themselves. Very often, a positive sample $\delta+$ is created by applying a set of transformations T to an image x from the dataset or batch. The rest of the images in the dataset or batch are considered negative samples ($\delta-$). We will define below the following loss function, called InfoNCE loss (van den Oord et al. 2018):

$$1!L_{infoNCE} = -log\left(\frac{exp(sim(q,k_+)/\theta)}{exp(sim(q,k_+)/\theta) + \sum_{i=0}^{K} exp(sim(q,k_i)/\theta)}\right)$$

As similarity function, we use cosine similarity. q is a vector obtained with the following operation, $q = f_\theta(x)$, where f_θ is an encoder. k_+ is the coded positive sample; whereas, $(k_+ = f_\theta(x))$ and $k_0, k_1, ... k_n$ are the coded negative samples.

In contrastive learning, this set of transformations is often chosen manually by an expert, depending on a specific downstream task. The choice of these transformations is crucial, because it defines the invariance of the model. For example, if we wish to classify species of flowers, the coder should not be invariant to color changes, because this information gives important details about the species. The classification of furniture relies more on shape than color: a black, white, blue or purple chair always looks like a chair. For more complex tasks, it can be difficult to know to which transformation the model should be invariant. The article by Purushwalkam and Gupta (2020) offers some interesting leads on contrastive learning and provides some explanations of the impressive results of this approach. The authors show that the transformations used in SOTA (e.g. MoCo, SIMCLR) work well on common and clean datasets, where a single object is centered in the image (e.g. ImageNet). However, images from more realistic datasets usually contain multiple objects. An aggressive transformation, such as random cropping may not be suitable for this type of dataset.

6.3. Problem 1: anatomical structure and lesion detection

Microsurgery, which was developed in the 1970s, is a specialty in its own right. It is now an integral part of the curriculum of several surgical specialties, including plastic surgery, neurosurgery, and orthopedic surgery, among which hand and upper limb surgeries stand out. The difficulty of access to the laboratory, the cost of training and the use of animal models are all criteria having led to the development of new materials and training techniques to continue to provide quality education, more easily accessible.

Artificial intelligence (AI) could be particularly beneficial to the learning and practice of microsurgery, thanks to two types of recently developed algorithms: object detection and super-resolution.

The purpose of this study is to explore the contribution of machine learning (in particular, object detection), to image processing in hand surgery, and more specifically, to microsurgery. In this chapter, we will use object detection to detect anatomical structures and lesions. We will explore three different approaches.

6.3.1. *Overview of the problem*

The dataset is made up of images and shows the palmar surface of the long fingers. We divide the classes into three families:

– healthy anatomical structure: tendon, artery, nerve;

– damaged anatomical structure: damaged tendon, damaged artery, damaged nerve;

– others: muscle, pulley.

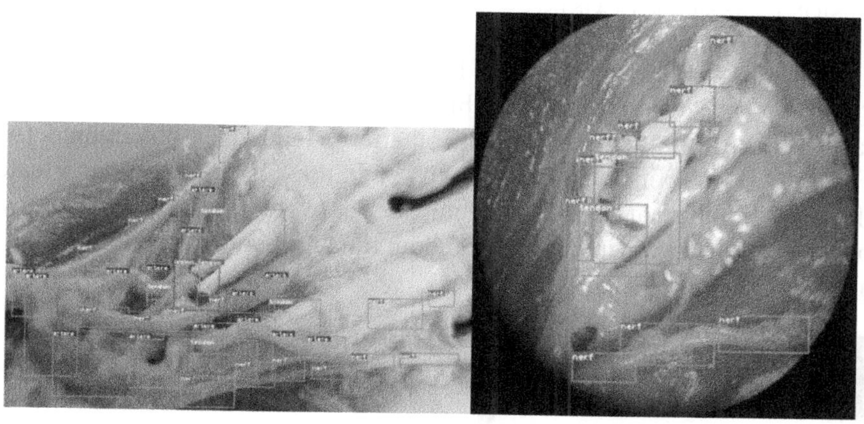

a) b)

Figure 6.2. *The dataset comprises two types of images: a) pictures without zoom and b) pictures taken using a microscope. Nerves are shown in blue, tendons in orange and arteries in purple*

Earlier works (e.g. Grégory et al. 2021) showed good results in the detection of healthy anatomical structures. Our study focuses on the detection of damaged structures. In sections 6.3.2 and 6.3.3, we will present two approaches. In the modular approach, the anatomical structures are detected before being introduced into a binary classifier, to decide whether they are damaged or not. In the second approach, we train two distinct object detection models: one to detect healthy structures and the other to detect injured structures.

6.3.2. *Modular approach*

Healthy structures and injured structures are semantically similar. In fact, an injured tendon is still a tendon (the same goes for nerves and arteries). Following this idea, we train our object detection algorithm (Faster R-CNN) by replacing injured anatomical structures with healthy anatomical structures. In other words, healthy structures and all of their "wounded versions" are considered under one class. Then, we use a simple classifier, which takes the structure's image as input and predicts whether there is a lesion or not.

LESION CLASSIFIER TRAINING.–

To train the lesion classifier, we build a lesion dataset with two classes, "injured" and "healthy". To do this, we crop the structures around each label representing a nerve, tendon or artery, injured or not injured (see Figure 6.3). We find that the number of injured structures is far greater than the number of healthy structures. To overcome this problem, we balance the dataset using a set of random transformations (see Figures 6.15 and 6.16).

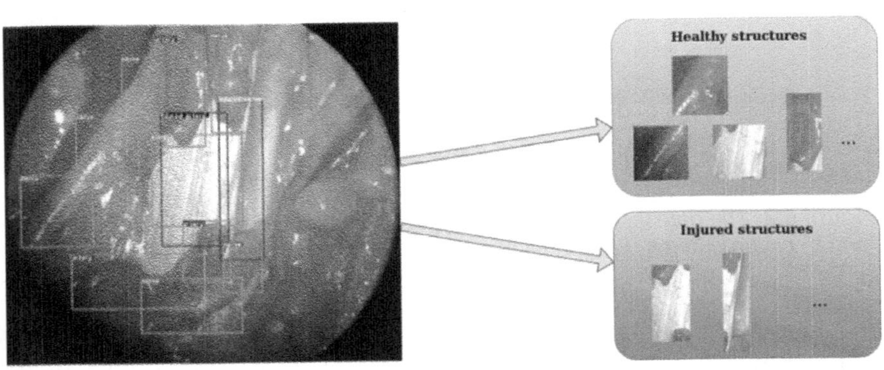

Figure 6.3. *We construct the lesion dataset by cropping around the boxes. The dataset contains two classes: healthy structures (in green) and injured structures (in red). Nerves are shown in blue, tendons in orange and arteries in purple*

We construct a binary classifier, which takes an image as input and returns 0 if the anatomical structure is healthy, and 1 if it is injured. We use a ResNet50 as encoder and an MLP as classifier. We use the binary cross-entropy loss function, the SGD (Stochastic Gradient Descent) optimizer, with a learning rate of 0.005, a weight decay of 5*e-6 and a momentum of 0.9. The batch size is 64.

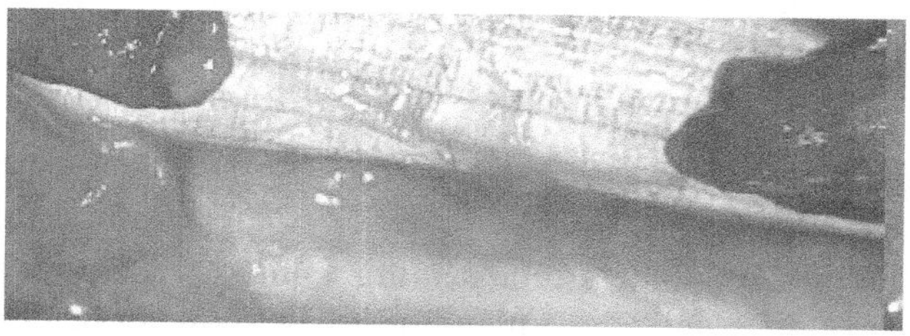

Figure 6.4. *The image contains two structures, a healthy tendon and an injured artery. The label is therefore ambiguous. We must include information about the structure to be observed to disambiguate the decision*

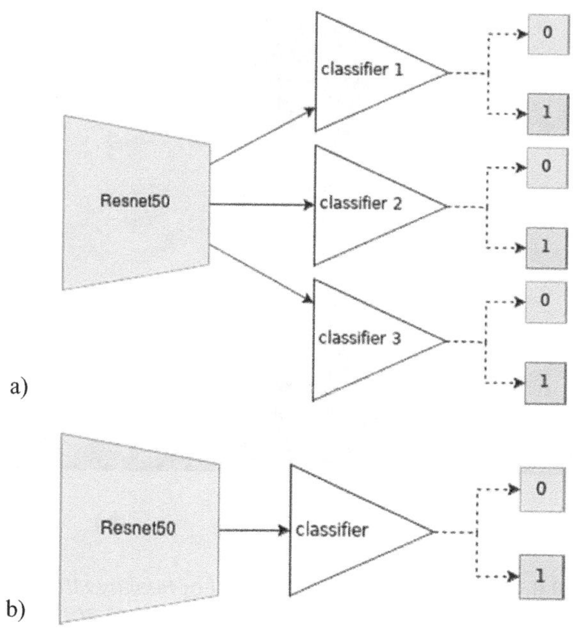

Figure 6.5. *Two classifier architectures for lesion detection. a) Images are fed into an encoder before being classified using a single MLP. b) On the contrary, the architecture contains three heads (one for each structure) with a shared encoder. The encoder is a ResNet50 for both architectures*

However, we have found that the ground truth can sometimes be ambiguous. As we can see in Figure 6.4, several anatomical structures can be represented in a single image. Thus, the label may be different depending on the structure we are looking at. Therefore, it makes sense to build three binary classifiers (one for each structure). In this way, we improve our dataset to introduce information about the structure. Each classifier shares the same skeleton, which is a ResNet50, but has different heads (see Figure 6.5).

6.3.3. *Separate approach*

The distribution of objects representing injured structures and healthy structures is very different. The amount of boxes showing healthy objects is significant, because these closely follow the anatomical structure. In this section, we will study the relevance of separating the detection of dense objects (healthy structures) from small and "weakly distributed" objects (damaged structures).

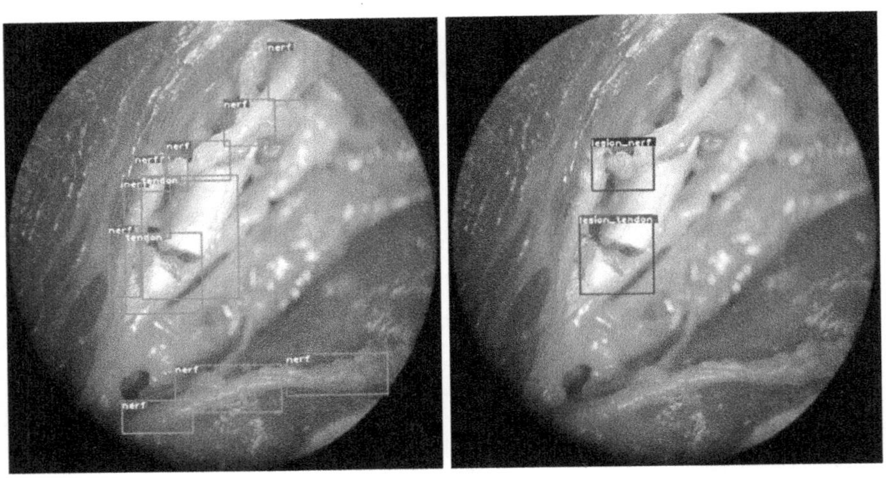

a) b)

Figure 6.6. *We separate the formation of a) healthy structures (in green) and b) injured structures (in red). Nerves are shown in blue, tendons in orange and arteries in purple*

IMPLEMENTATION.–

We trained two distinct object detection models: one for healthy structures and the other for injured structures. We used the SGD (Stochastic Gradient Descent) optimizer, with a learning rate of 0.1 and a weight decay of 0.0005. We decreased the learning rate using a program called "cosine annealing" (Loshchilov and Hutter 2016) for 60 iterations.

During the training, we noted a relevant fact: the model specializing on healthy structures seemed to perform better when trained on a smaller batch size. However, this was not the case for the specialized model on damaged structures. This behavior can legitimize this separate training and account for the performance improvement of this approach (see Figure 6.7).

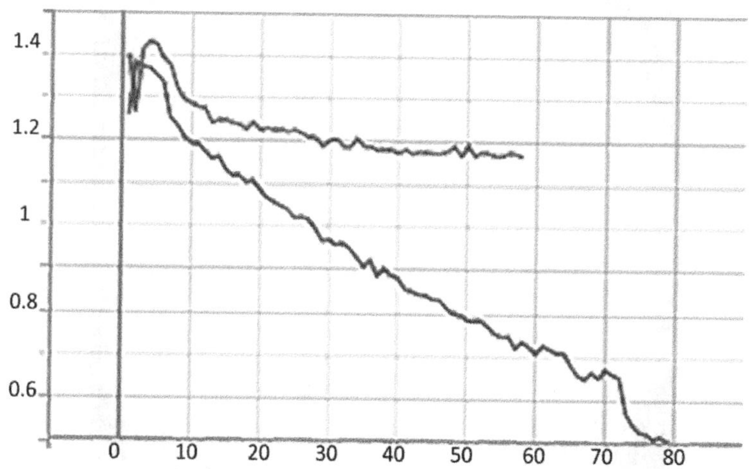

Figure 6.7. *The evolution of model learning loss, trained with healthy structures. The red curve represents training with a batch size of 8, the green curve with a batch size of 2. We see that training benefits from a smaller batch size. This behavior is not observed when training only damaged structures*

OBJECT DETECTION TRAINING.–

The object detection algorithm is trained to detect anatomical structures, regardless of whether these are injured or not. We use the ResNet50 as an encoder and the SGD optimizer. The batch size is 2.

6.3.4. *Evaluation method*

The common way to evaluate an object detection algorithm is to calculate precision and recall for each class, as well as average precision. However, in our data (and particularly in the case of healthy structures), the bounding boxes do not represent the entire object but only a fraction of the structure. In that sense, a prediction can be correct, and also incorrect according to validation, because the prediction and the label do not match (see Figure 6.8). Therefore, the use of conventional evaluation methods can lead to an underestimation of performance. To mitigate this issue, we evaluate precision and recall using different IoU (Intersection over Union) thresholds. We also analyze the sources of error in this model.

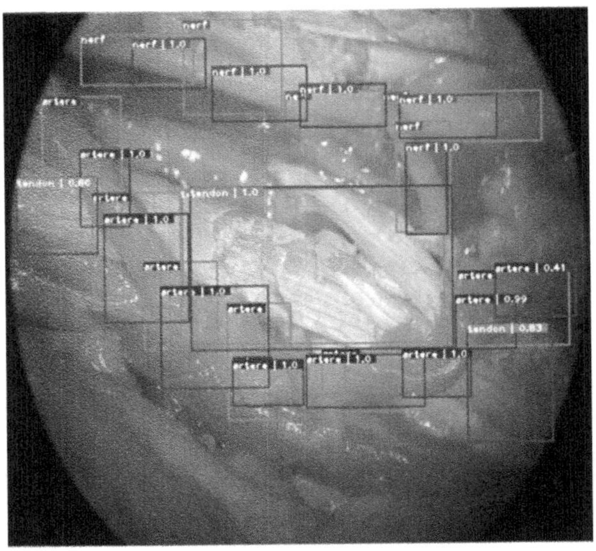

Figure 6.8. *Due to the nature of labeling, model evaluation is challenging*

COMMENT ON FIGURE 6.8.– *In this example, the nerves are represented in blue, the tendons in orange and the arteries in purple. Labels are represented by green boxes and predictions in red. As a single anatomical structure is labeled using several bounding boxes, some predictions are valid (they are on the structure), but are considered false positives because they do not match any ground truth.*

An object detection algorithm can have multiple sources of error: the object was misclassified, the bounding box position does not correspond to the ground truth, etc.

Current evaluation methods have a major drawback: they do not explain what kinds of errors are made by the algorithm. We used the free software TIDE (Bolya et al. 2020) to analyze the causes of error in our model (see Figure 6.9).

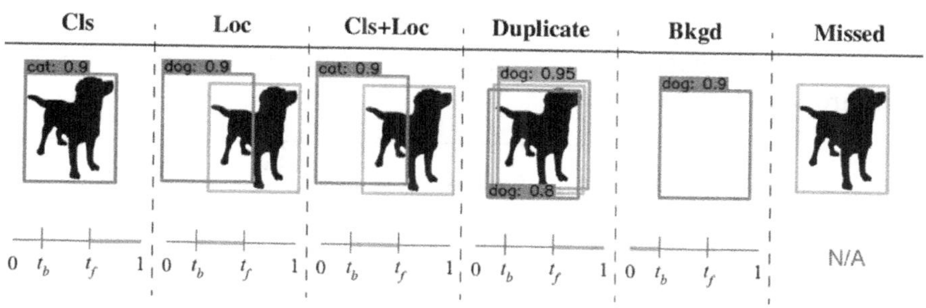

Figure 6.9. *Six types of errors, image drawn from Bolya et al. (2020). Red corresponds to false positive detection, orange denotes ground truth and green designates true positive detection*

Before the validation step, we removed all the predicted boxes with a score of below 0.3 (less than 30% confidence). We then applied the non-maximum removal algorithm to our data, so as to remove any duplicates.

6.3.5. *Results and opening*

We grouped the results by type of structure:

– lesions, which contain injured tendons, injured arteries and injured nerves;

– healthy structures, which contain healthy tendons, healthy arteries and healthy nerves;

– others, which contain muscles and pulleys.

The three approaches were evaluated:

– naive (all-in-one) approach: a detector is trained using all eight classes;

– modular approach: the detection of lesions is carried out by a specific module;

– separate approach: lesions and healthy structures are trained separately.

Each column contains the average results for the three class groups. The results are shown in Table 6.1.

	Approach	**Lesions**	**Healthy structures**	**Others**
Recall	**Naive approach**	56.1	51.8	77.0
	Modular approach	66.8	57.7	–
	Separate approach	79.1	57.9	–
Precision	**Naive approach**	80.1	51.1	57.9
	Modular approach	66.0	51.5	–
	Separate approach	76.2	51.5	–

Table 6.1. *Comparison of all approaches*

We have mixed results regarding healthy structures. Figure 6.10 shows that this is mainly due to a poor localization of the predicted object, depending on the labels chosen (as explained in section 6.3.4).

We succeeded in obtaining interesting results, especially for the main purpose of this problem (lesion detection). However, our method presented two main drawbacks:

– As shown in Figure 6.8, model evaluation was underestimated, especially for healthy structures. It is really difficult, not to say impossible, to obtain a correct and significant result for healthy structures. Fortunately, we did not come across this problem for injured structures.

– We have finally demonstrated that the best approach would involve using one model for damaged structures and another one for healthy structures. However, in practice, using two models to solve a single problem may not be suitable, because power consumption, processing time, computational resources, etc., are almost multiplied by 2. In practical terms, this can be a problem in itself when computational resources are limited and the object detection task must be performed in real time.

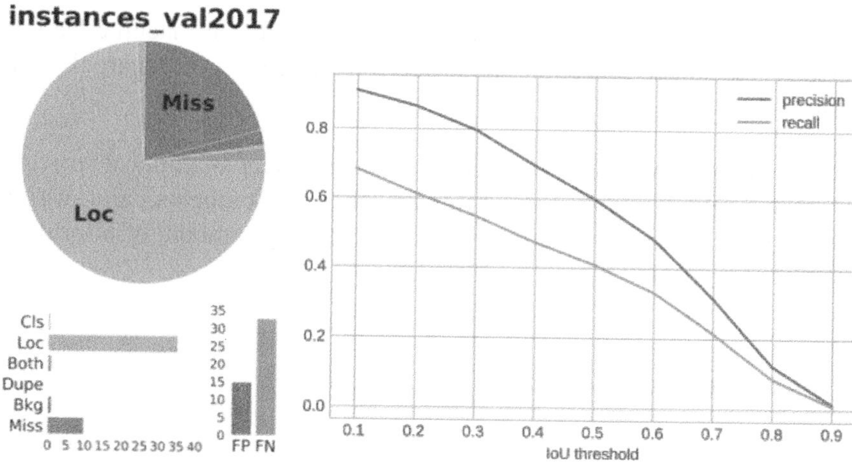

a) b)

Figure 6.10. *Result analysis of a model trained only on healthy structures*

COMMENT ON FIGURE 6.10.– *a) This figure shows that the main source of error is the poor location of the predicted object in relation to the label. This can be explained by the labeling strategy. In fact, a single object can contain several bounding boxes. So there are several correct solutions. b) We verified that the performance of our algorithm was correlated with the chosen IoU threshold.*

6.4. Problem 2: endoscopic carpal tunnel release

Carpal tunnel syndrome is a compression of the median nerve inside the carpal tunnel. Due to complications in the absence of appropriate care, complications inherent in its surgical management – as well as its high frequency in the general population – this syndrome represents a major challenge.

There are multiple methods to treat the symptoms of this syndrome. One of these techniques, called endoscopic carpal tunnel release, is performed by indirect vision (a camera is inserted inside the carpal tunnel and the video is displayed on the screen).

The goal of this study is to explore the contribution of machine learning, especially of object detection, to proceed with endoscopic carpal tunnel release.

In this chapter, we rely on object detection to detect anatomical structures and lesions. We explore two different labeling strategies, and we use self-supervised contrastive learning to exploit the large amount of information contained in unlabeled data.

6.4.1. *Classic approach to object detection*

Labeling has a major drawback: the bounding boxes are small and represent only a fraction of the object. This can adversely affect the performance of an algorithm. Therefore, we chose to modify the label by merging all the bounding boxes touching one another, in order to obtain a large bounding box surrounding the entire object (see Figure 6.11). This approach brought us back to a more classic object detection problem, where the entire object is contained in a bounding box.

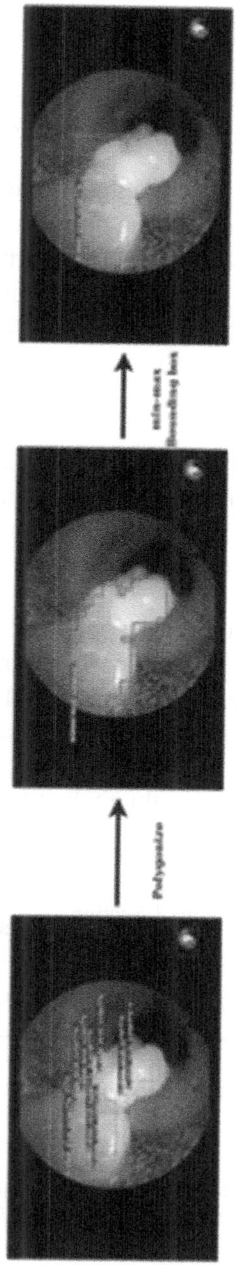

Figure 6.11. *All bounding boxes that overlap or are close to one another are merged to form a polygon (polygonization). Then, the minimum and maximum values for the X and Y axes were taken into account to create a new bounding box, surrounding the polygon (min–max bounding box)*

COMMENT ON FIGURE 6.11.– *In this example, the green boxes represent subcutaneous fat fragments; whereas, the pink box represents the fusion of subcutaneous fat fragments.*

To compare the quality of the two labels, we trained two object detection models: one with small boxes and another one with large boxes.

We used the Faster R-CNN architecture for both approaches, with a pretrained ResNet50 on ImageNet. The optimizer is SGD, with a momentum of 0.9 and a weight decay of 0.0005. The learning rate was initially set at 0.01 and started to decrease by 0.9 after 10 epochs. In our experience, the batch size was the only hyperparameter that differed: we used a batch size of 8 for training with the merged boxes, but a batch size of 2 for training on the original labels.

We used the IoU method to calculate precision and recall, with an IoU threshold of 0.5. The labels in the two approaches do not represent the same thing. Using the original labels, there are several overlapping boxes representing a single anatomical structure.

In the "big boxes" configuration, a single box represents each object. To evaluate the performance of the algorithm trained on small boxes, we "polygonized" the ground truth and the model predictions (as depicted in Figure 6.11). We then computed the IoU on these polygons.

We used the classical IoU to evaluate the model trained on large boxes.

	Recall			**Precision**		
Classes	**Ligament**	**Subcutaneous fat**	**Section slice**	**Ligament**	**Subcutaneous fat**	**Section slice**
Initial boxes	45.1	66.0	23.6	38.6	57.4	30.9
Weighted boxes fusion	61.9	78.3	44.1	38.2	66.7	34.9

Table 6.2. *Comparison of the two labeling strategies. Precision and recall, for all three classes, are calculated using a 0.5 IoU error threshold*

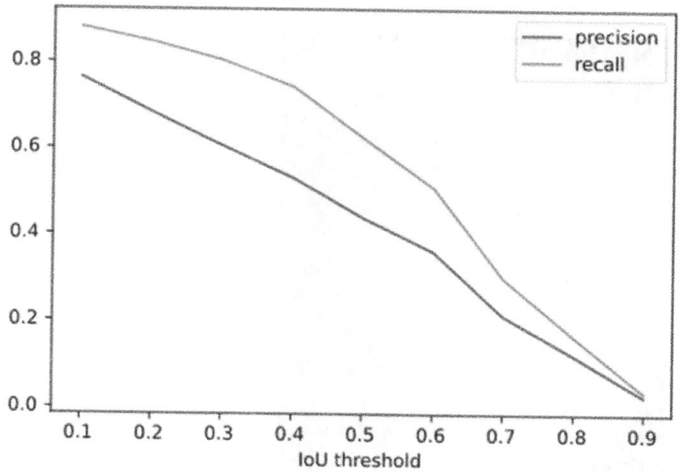

Figure 6.12. *Evolution of the average precision and recall of the model trained on large boxes, depending on the choice of IoU threshold. There was a strong correlation between the IoU threshold and algorithm performance, which confirms that the main source of error stemmed from the bad localization of predicted objects*

6.4.2. *Self-supervised learning approach*

The standard way to learn proper data representation is to train an encoder on a large amount of labeled data. For example, Pytorch's pretrained ResNet50 was trained on the ImageNet dataset. When working with medical data, gaining a large amount of labeled data is very difficult (sometimes even impossible), because labeling requires advanced skills and is time consuming.

In the field of unsupervised representation learning, self-supervised learning has received increasing attention over the years. In particular, methods based on contrastive learning showed impressive results in closing the gap between supervised methods, sometimes outperforming them on some tasks at the final stages.

In this section, we will explore the relevance of self-supervised learning for surgical images. We pretrained a ResNet50 on over 65,000 images drawn from carpal tunnel release videos and fine-tuned our encoder on the object detection task. We proved that SSL can improve performance on medical data.

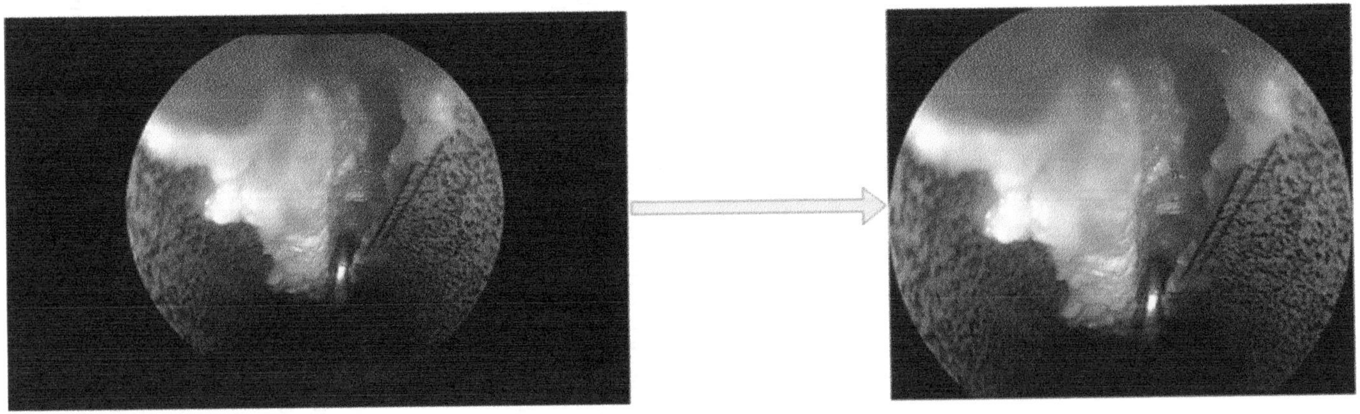

Figure 6.13. *We cropped the unnecessary black margin around the circle. This had two advantages: a) image width was halved, so less computation was needed for training and b) this harnessed image distortion when resizing to 224 x 224, because the image was already square*

The raw dataset contained 32 videos of endoscopic carpal tunnel release.

Our videos were not perfectly clean. In that sense, we identified two problems:

– Some parts of the video were irrelevant, notably at the beginning and end of the video, when the camera was not on the wrist.

– A black filling was present on both sides of the image. Self-supervised learning is a computationally expensive operation, which is why it is appropriate to discard irrelevant parts when training data.

To clean our dataset, we used Kdenlive, a video editor. We resized all videos to a resolution of 512 x 512 pixels.

There are many methods for performing self-supervised learning directly on videos (see Wang and Gupta 2015; Huang et al. 2021; Cao et al. 2022). However, we chose to use a self-supervised method based on images, in order to have a more generic method. We extracted every image from the videos to generate a dataset of over 65,000 images.

NNCLR (Nearest-Neighbor Contrastive Learning of Visual Representations).–

Self-supervised contrastive learning of visual representation is a thriving area of research. Chen et al. (2020) have shown that an end-to-end architecture can be very efficient, provided that the batch size is large enough. However, using a large batch size requires a lot of computing power. He et al. (2019) used a memory bank to store the representation of negative samples, thus avoiding the use of large batches. Chen and He (2020) and Assran et al. (2022) approached the question using Siamese networks. Caron et al. (2018), and its natural evolution Caron et al. (2020), assigned the input data to a cluster and used the cluster's index as a pseudo-label.

We can refer to Jaiswal et al. (2020) for further explanations on contrastive learning.

NNCLR (Dwibedi et al. 2021) is a recent method that has reached the state of the art in contrastive learning. Most contrastive methods treat two views of the same image as a positive pair. In NNCLR, the nearest neighbor of an image is treated as a positive sample. We think this method is well suited to our case because our unlabeled dataset is created from videos, and contains many similar images.

We used NNCLR to train the encoder. We replaced the classic contrastive cross-entropy loss with the decoupled contrastive loss (Yeh et al. 2021), since it makes it possible to use a smaller batch size while maintaining an adequate performance. The optimizer is SGD, with an initial learning rate of 0.1. The learning rate was updated using a cosine annealing program for 20 epochs. The batch size is 90. We trained the model using mixed precision.

The transformation policy used in SimCLR (Simple Framework for Contrastive Learning of Representations) (Chen et al. 2020) did not work properly on our data, so we created a custom transformation policy: Random Cropping, Horizontal Flip, Random Brightness Contrast, Hue Saturation Value, Posterize and Gaussian Blur. We found that this sequence of transformations was a suitable pretext task, because the learned representation focused more on shape than on color or fine grain.

To test our encoder, we used it for the detection task on the carpal tunnel release data. We froze all layers except the last one and compared our results against the pretrained ResNet50 provided by Pytorch (pretrained on ImageNet).

6.4.3. *Results*

	Recall			Precision		
Classes	**Ligament**	**Subcutaneous fat**	**Section slice**	**Ligament**	**Subcutaneous fat**	**Section slice**
ResNet50	–	–	–	–	–	–
Initial boxes	45.1	66.0	23.6	38.6	57.4	30.9
Weighted boxes fusion	61.9	78.3	44.1	38.2	66.7	34.9
Our version of ResNet50	–	–	–	–	–	–
Weighted boxes fusion	55.6	80.4	52.9	57.4	66.1	52.2

Table 6.3. *Comparison of the result obtained using the pretrained coder on ImageNet (the first two lines), and the one pretrained on our unlabeled data*

We found that our ResNet trained with NNCLR significantly improved the accuracy of our detector (see Table 6.3).

6.5. Conclusion

In this chapter, we have worked on two object detection tasks: the detection of anatomical structures and lesions, and carpal tunnel endoscopy:

– We showed that object detection can be used to detect anatomical structures and lesions during microsurgery, as well as that labeling anatomical structures using multiple bounding boxes is a bad idea, as it makes it difficult to evaluate object detection patterns. Other works may focus on semantic segmentation, rather than object detection.

– We proved that unlabeled medical images, in the form of videos, can be used for a useful medical task, such as detecting objects in carpal tunnel endoscopy, in order to improve performance. We have found that transformation policies commonly used in self-supervised contrastive learning are too aggressive for our data. We have thus come up with a custom transformation policy, so that the encoder focused more on the overall shape, rather than on fine details.

We hope that this work will contribute to a better understanding of self-supervised contrastive learning and take advantage of unlabeled data in deep learning applied to the medical field.

6.6. Appendices

Many object detection algorithms, including Faster-RCNN, detect a large number of boxes for a single object. This behavior leads to a large amount of duplicates (lots of boxes overlapping). As a result, we used two methods to remove irrelevant predictions:

– A probability threshold was applied to keep only the "best prediction" (the prediction with the highest score). In most of our experiments, we used a probability threshold of 0.3, sometimes 0.2.

– We applied NMS (non-maximum suppression), which is a commonly used algorithm to remove duplicates (boxes that overlap too much).

Figure 6.14 summarizes this process.

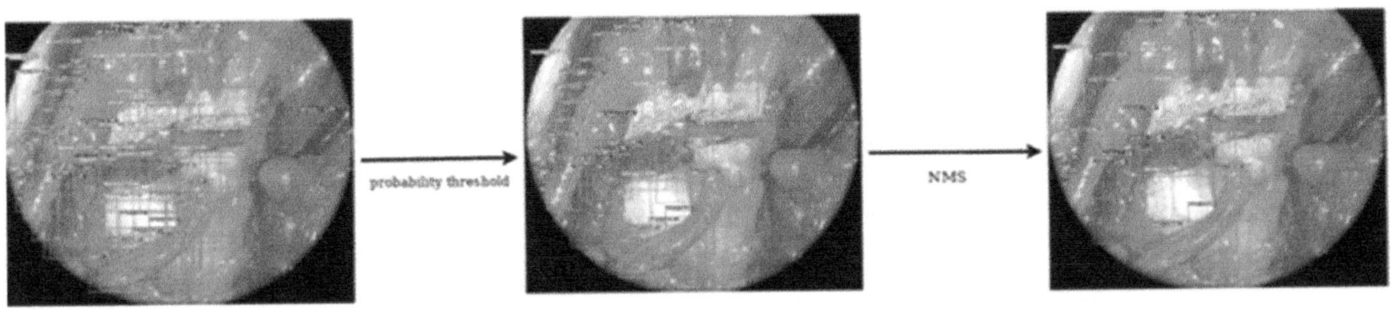

Figure 6.14. *We only kept predictions with a confidence score of 30%, and we applied the NMS to remove duplicate boxes. Nerves are shown in blue, tendons in orange and arteries in purple*

As the dataset contained many more healthy structures than injured ones, we balanced this by using a set of image transformations: Random Horizontal Flip, Random Vertical Flip, Color Jitters, Random Grayscale and Normalization. Each image was resized to 224 x 224.

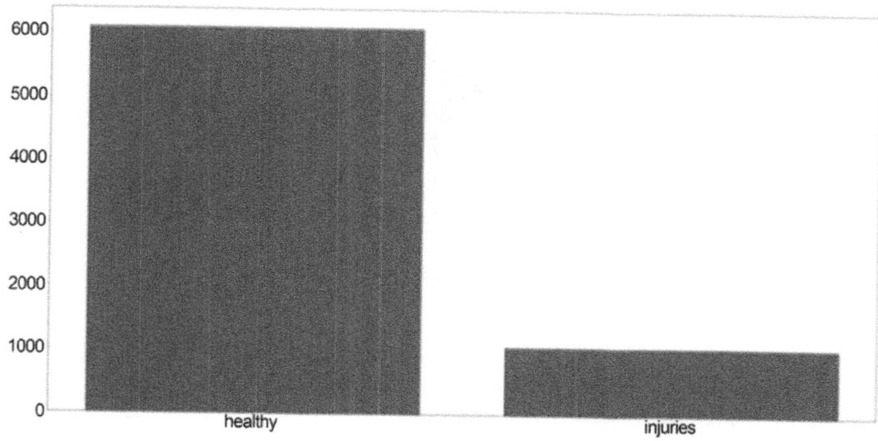

a)

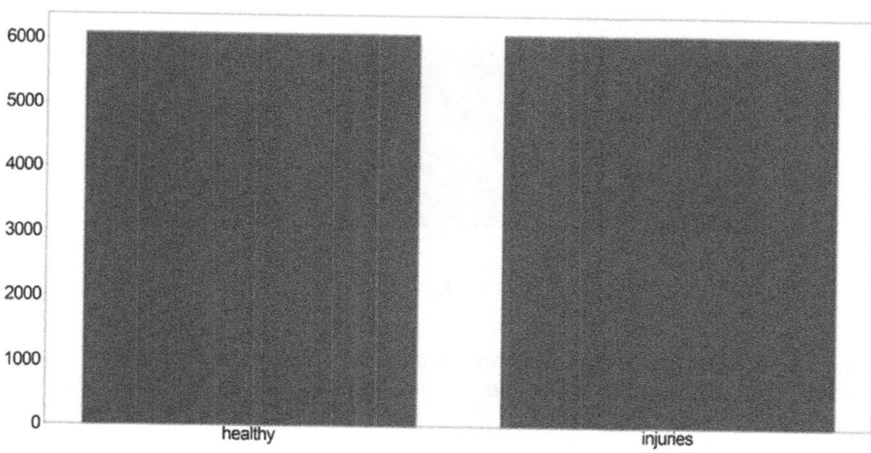

b)

Figure 6.15. *Dataset balancing for single-head classifier. Distribution of labels a) before data augmentation and b) after data augmentation*

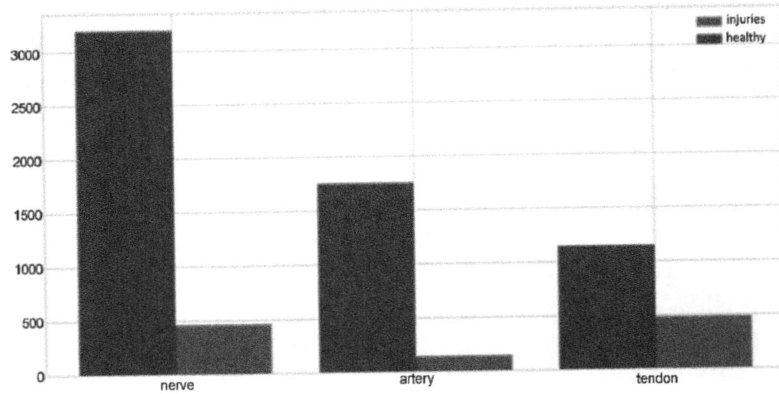

a)

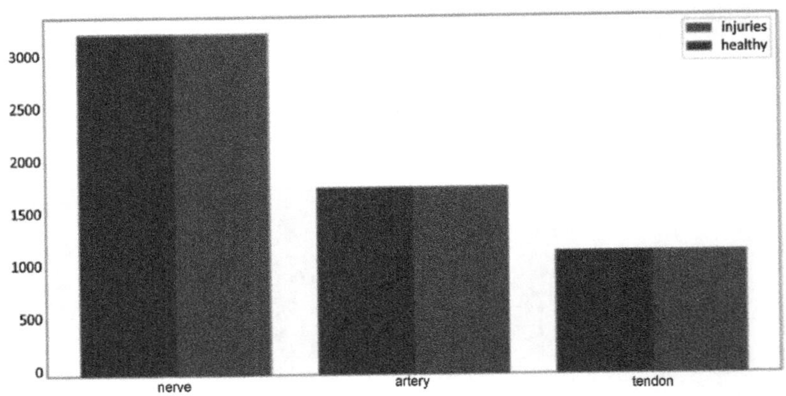

b)

Figure 6.16. *Dataset balancing for multi-head classifier. For each type of structure, we wished to have the same number of injured structures and healthy structures. Distribution of labels a) before data augmentation and b) after data augmentation*

Table 6.4 shows the results for the lesion classification module (single head and multi-head).

	Tendon	Artery	Nerve	Total
Simple	–	–	–	93
Multi-head	91	99	96	96

Table 6.4. *Accuracy measurement of the lesion classification module*

Table 6.5 shows the results by class for the modular approach, the separate approach and the all-in-one approach.

	All-in-one		Modular		Separate	
	Precision	Recall	Precision	Recall	Precision	Recall
Pulley	63.4	88.8	–	–	–	–
Nerve	44.3	49.4	44.5	53.1	44.7	53.2
Artery	46.4	48.4	49.7	51.3	49.3	51.6
Tendon	62.6	57.6	60.3	68.6	60.5	68.8
Injured tendon	80.1	39.1	61.7	88.5	86.0	82.7
Injured nerve	74.1	54.8	58.8	48.8	79.7	72.0
Muscle	52.5	65.3	–	–	–	–
Injured artery	86.1	48.3	59.5	63.0	71.4	74.1
Average	63.7	56.5	55.5	62.2	65.2	67.0

Table 6.5. *Precision and recall for each anatomical structure*

GRAD CAM.–

Grad Cam is a method that follows the gradient, in order to help understand how a neural network makes a decision. To understand the learned representation, we drew a heat map on the image (Figure 6.18). The areas in red are the most important ones for the encoder; whereas, the areas in blue are less important.

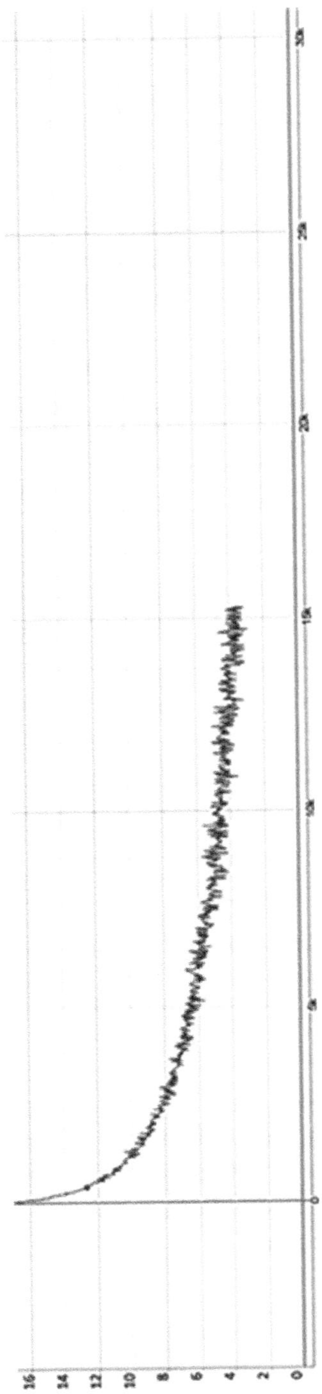

Figure 6.17. *The evolution of the NNCLR learning cost*

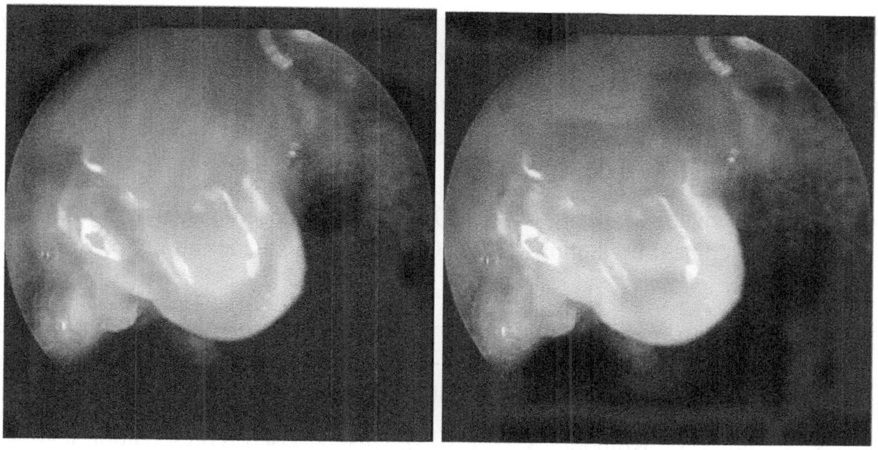

a) b)

Figure 6.18. *Grad Cam a) from our ResNet and b) from ImageNet's pretrained ResNet. In this example, our representation focuses more on the relevant data of the image than the one pretrained by ImageNet. However, we note that a lot of irrelevant areas are marked in red, which means our ResNet can be improved*

6.7. References

Assran, M., Caron, M., Misra, I., Bojanowski, P., Bordes, F., Vincent, P., Joulin, A., Rabbat, M., Ballas, N. (2022). Masked Siamese networks for label-efficient learning [Online]. Available at: https://arxiv.org/abs/2204.07141.

Bolya, D., Foley, S., Hays, J., Hoffman, J. (2020). TIDE: A general toolbox for identifying object detection errors. *CoRR* [Online]. Available at: https://arxiv.org/abs/2008.08115.

Cai, Z. and Vasconcelos, N. (2017). Cascade R-CNN: Delving into high quality object detection. *CoRR* [Online]. Available at: http://arxiv.org/abs/1712.00726.

Cao, Z., Huang, Z., Pan, L., Zhang, S., Liu, Z., Fu, C. (2022). TCTrack: Temporal contexts for aerial tracking. arXiv:2203.01885.

Caron, M., Bojanowski, P., Joulin, A., Douze, M. (2018). Deep clustering for unsupervised learning of visual features. *CoRR* [Online]. Available at: http://arxiv.org/abs/1807.05520.

Caron, M., Misra, I., Mairal, J., Goyal, P., Bojanowski, P., Joulin, A. (2020). Unsupervised learning of visual features by contrasting cluster assignments. *CoRR* [Online]. Available at: https://arxiv.org/abs/2006.09882.

Chen, X. and He, K. (2020). Exploring simple Siamese representation learning. *CoRR* [Online]. Available at: https://arxiv.org/abs/2011.10566.

Chen, T., Kornblith, S., Norouzi, M., Hinton, G.E. (2020). A simple framework for contrastive learning of visual representations. *CoRR* [Online]. Available at: https://arxiv.org/abs/2002.05709.

Doersch, C., Gupta, A., Efros, A.A. (2015). Unsupervised visual representation learning by context prediction. *CoRR* [Online]. Available at: http://arxiv.org/abs/1505.05192.

Dwibedi, D., Aytar, Y., Tompson, J., Sermanet, P., Zisserman, A. (2021). With a little help from my friends: Nearest-neighbor contrastive learning of visual representations. *CoRR* [Online]. Available at: https://arxiv.org/abs/2104.14548.

Gidaris, S., Singh, P., Komodakis, N. (2018). Unsupervised representation learning by predicting image rotations. *CoRR* [Online]. Available at: http://arxiv.org/abs/1803.07728.

Grégory, T., Karkazan, B., Dacheux, C., Nahri, I., Bennani, Y. (2021). La détection des structures anatomiques de la main est possible en réalité augmentée grâce à l'utilisation de l'intelligence artificielle. Étude cadavérique. *Hand Surgery and Rehabilitation*, 40, 899–900.

He, K., Fan, H., Wu, Y., Xie, S., Girshick, R.B. (2019). Momentum contrast for unsupervised visual representation learning. *CoRR* [Online]. Available at: http://arxiv.org/abs/1911.05722.

Huang, L., Liu, Y., Wang, B., Pan, P., Xu, Y., Jin, R. (2021). Self-supervised video representation learning by context and motion decoupling. *CoRR* [Online]. Available at: https://arxiv.org/abs/2104.00862.

Jaiswal, A., Ramesh Babu, A., Zadeh, M., Banerjee, D., Makedon, F. (2020). A survey on contrastive self-supervised learning. *Technologies*, 9(2).

Lin, T., Goyal, P., Girshick, R.B., He, K., Dollár, P. (2017). Focal loss for dense object detection. *CoRR* [Online]. Available at: http://arxiv.org/abs/1708.02002.

Loshchilov, I. and Hutter, F. (2016). SGDR: Stochastic gradient descent with restarts. *CoRR* [Online]. Available at: http://arxiv.org/abs/1608.03983.

Misra, I. and van der Maaten, L. (2019). Self-supervised learning of pretext-invariant representations. *CoRR* [Online]. Available at: http://arxiv.org/abs/1912.01991.

Noroozi, M. and Favaro, P. (2016). Unsupervised learning of visual representations by solving jigsaw puzzles. *CoRR* [Online]. Available at: http://arxiv.org/abs/1603.09246.

van den Oord, A., Li, Y., Vinyals, O. (2018). Representation learning with contrastive predictive coding. *CoRR* [Online]. Available at: http://arxiv.org/abs/1807.03748.

Purushwalkam, S. and Gupta, A. (2020). Demystifying contrastive self-supervised learning: Invariances, augmentations and dataset biases. *CoRR* [Online]. Available at: https://arxiv.org/abs/2007.13916.

Redmon, J., Divvala, S.K., Girshick, R.B., Farhadi, A. (2015). You only look once: Unified, real-time object detection. *CoRR* [Online]. Available at: http://arxiv.org/abs/1506.02640.

Ren, S., He, K., Girshick, R.B., Sun, J. (2015). Faster R-CNN: Towards real-time object detection with region proposal networks. *CoRR* [Online]. Available at: http://arxiv.org/abs/1506.01497.

Wang, X. and Gupta, A. (2015). Unsupervised learning of visual representations using videos. *CoRR* [Online]. Available at: http://arxiv.org/abs/1505.00687.

Yeh, C., Hong, C., Hsu, Y., Liu, T., Chen, Y., LeCun, Y. (2021). Decoupled contrastive learning. *CoRR* [Online]. Available at: https://arxiv.org/abs/2110.06848.

7

Surgical Diagnosis Augmented by Artificial Intelligence

Deep learning-based applications have been incredibly successful in recent years. Text, audio, image and video have all been explored with great success through deep learning approaches. In particular, the use of convolutional neural networks (CNN) in computer vision has led to reliable results. In order to obtain these results, large amounts of data are required. However, all data are not always accessible. Besides, annotating data can be difficult and time consuming. Self-learning is a semi-supervised approach, having proved its efficiency in mitigating this problem and achieving top performances. Theoretical analysis has even proven that it can lead to better generalization than a normal classifier. Another problem that neural networks may face is that problem complexity is usually higher these days, which requires high computational cost. Compared to dealing with a problem in a single block, breaking down a complex problem into several simple subtasks can offer various advantages, such as faster learning, better generalization, better interpretability, etc. The problem division procedure is called modular learning through task decomposition, and is inspired in human cognition. Section 7.3 of this chapter will present and evaluate different modular learning architectures for the classification of dorsal capsulo-scapholunate septum (DCSS) instability. Our experiments have shown that, compared to non-modular systems, modular learning improves performances. In addition, we discovered that weighted modular learning, which involves weighting the output using the probabilities of the trigger

---

Chapter written by Nosseiba BEN SALEM, Younès BENNANI, Joseph KARKAZAN, Léo DÉCHAUMET, Abir BARBARA, Charles DACHEUX and Thomas GRÉGORY.

module, achieves near-perfect classification. Section 7.4 will focus on our approach for the labeling and segmentation of self-learning data applied to shoulder arthroscopy images.

7.1. Introduction

Cognitive neuropsychology has been a great source of inspiration and key to the success of data science. Our brains are the most powerful machines. For this reason, experts have tried to replicate how the brain works and its problem-solving skills in machines. This is the underlying concept for neural networks and their ability to deal with complex problems. Continuing to explore the human mind, some researchers have turned their attention to how our brain is subdivided into independent components. Each semi-autonomous group of neurons specializes in a function and interacts with other subsets (Kelkar and Medaglia 2018). This is how modular architecture started being applied to learning. The main idea is to break down a complex task into simple and independent sub-tasks. Modular architecture was first introduced in Rueckl et al. (1989), when he and his team demonstrated that, under certain conditions, splitting processing led to better performances. Later, other researchers revealed that adding knowledge a priori helps the model and improves results (in comparison with the non-modular model). In recent research, Mittal et al. (2022) stated that modularity leads to better generalization, faster learning, has scaling properties and enhances interpretability. This explains its growing interest among researchers. Modular architecture is a concept, so there are several strategies to break down a problem. For example, models can compete with one another to accomplish the same task (Alpaydin 1993) or they can cooperate (Rashwan et al. 1994), etc. However, it is not always easy to determine how and where to subdivide.

Another concept that has shown remarkable results is the self-learning of semi-supervised algorithms. Due to the pressing need for massive amounts of data to train models and the difficulty or high cost of data labeling, semi-supervised learning has become an active research discipline. Self-learning mitigates this problem by relying on a small subset of labeled samples and a large subset of unlabeled samples, always achieving top results (Berthelot et al. 2019). It assumes that the decision must be placed in a low-density region in order to obtain better generalization (Chapelle and Zien 2005). Pseudo-labeling refers to the iterative annotation of unlabeled samples or "pseudo-labels", and their addition to the training subset (a common use of self-learning).

In this work, we built systems using modular learning and self-learning and applied them in two contexts. The first application aimed to classify the instability of a structure in the wrist, called dorsal capsulo-scapholunate septum (DCSS). We tested different modular learning strategies and compared them to non-modular architecture. In the second application, we tested pseudo-labeling on shoulder arthroscopy images for structure detection using image segmentation.

A brief background overview and review-related work on modular learning and self-learning will be presented in section 7.2. Section 7.3 will present the approach we propose to classify DCSS using modular learning as well as the results obtained. Finally, section 7.4 will present the self-learning approach for data labeling and segmentation.

7.2. Fundamental framework and state of the art

In this section, we will introduce some basic notions about modular learning. We will also provide an overview of previous approaches in the literature.

According to neuroscience, our brain is an amalgam of several independently functioning modules that cooperate and communicate with one another (Warren 2002). This decomposition inspired researchers to build a system made up of different simple modules and integrating their outputs. Each module is a neural network whose parameters can be learned and which produces a prediction probability. Modules are trained independently and controlled by a trigger module. The latter is responsible for activating the modules following a certain rule, either defined by the user or found automatically. There are several ways to define the interaction between the different modules. For example, a complex problem can be broken down into smaller subtasks. Each module is responsible for a fragment. Modules can cooperate with each other to create a complementary network, or can compete with each other, by learning to solve the same problem.

The use of modular learning offers major advantages over non-modular systems (Mittal et al. 2022). For example, using multiple simple networks can significantly reduce computation time, generally needed to train a complex model. Modular systems have proven to significantly improve the robustness of neural networks (Wang and Zhou 2012). Combining knowledge from different modules makes the model more robust. It also reduces the model's complexity, thus optimizing computation time during the learning process. In addition, modularity limits the propagation of biases, unlike non-modular models.

In 1989, Rueckl began to study the representation and location of objects ("what" and "where" to be separated). They used retinal images for classification and revealed that, under certain circumstances, modular learning is more computationally efficient and learns more easily (when compared to non-modular networks).

Depending on the type of interaction between structures, there are several strategies for building modular architecture.

For example, in Auda et al. (1995), decoupled modules are used: data are separated and each group is assigned to a module. The final prediction reflects the maximum probability of all modules. In the case of Rashwan et al. (1994), a hierarchical network is used.

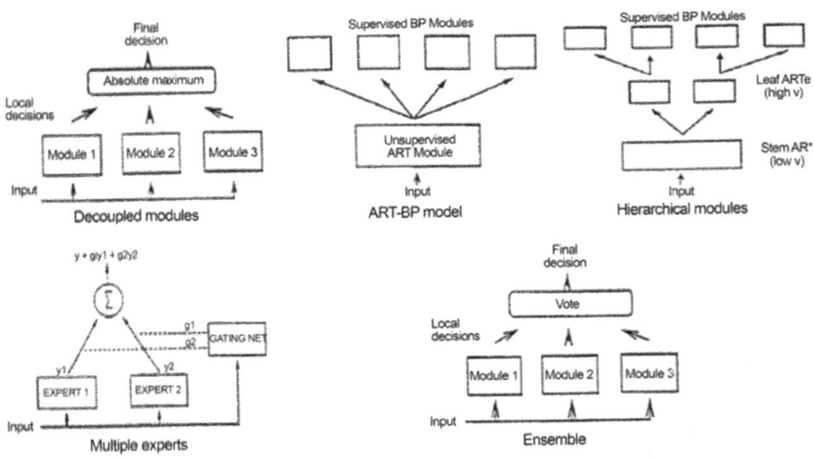

Figure 7.1. *Types of modular neural networks (Auda et al. 1996)*

Other authors, such as Alpaydin (1993) and Bartfai (1994) use ensemble networks where all the modules are identical and learn to perform the same task. The final prediction is a majority vote of the prediction probability from all networks. Figure 7.1 summarizes the different types of modular neural networks.

The most common structure is the multiple expert network (Jacobs et al. 1991). This comprises a trigger and an expert module. The trigger module controls network activation and task distribution. The networks need not be identical; there can be a hybrid system with a variety of techniques (Bennani 1995). In our case, we used several experts. Figure 7.2 shows the structure of multiple experts with one gating module and expert networks n.

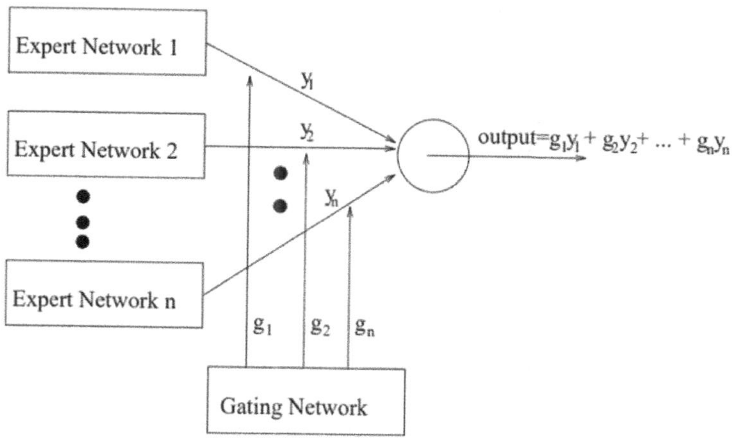

Figure 7.2. *Multiple expert network (Anderson et al. 2000)*

7.3. Modular learning for classification

7.3.1. *Methodology*

7.3.1.1. *Motivation*

The first goal of this work is to classify images of the DCSS in order to identify the stage of scapholunate instability, using modular architecture. The DCSS is a wrist structure that supports the scapholunate joint (Overstraeten et al. 2013). Scapholunate instability is a common disease in DCSS. It results in severe wrist dysfunction, making it difficult for the patient to perform daily activities (Kitay and Wolfe 2012). The identification of scapholunate instability requires an accurate diagnosis, ideally to prevent it in its early stages. We used wrist arthroscopy images, and the purpose was to determine whether the structure was healthy or if there was instability grade 1, 2 or 3. We exploited the nature of the problem to build a modular system. The problem could be divided into two parts: first, to predict whether the structure was healthy or pathological. Then, if the DCSS was pathological, we could use a second component to discriminate between the three grades.

7.3.1.2. *System architecture*

The system comprised two modules: the detection module and the discrimination module. The detection module was trained to detect whether the DCSS was healthy (or not) from the arthroscopy image. If the DCSS was healthy, we produced its prediction probability *P(y='healthy'|X)*. If the DCSS was pathological, we sent the image to the discriminating module. The latter could be designed in different ways, and the final output could be calculated differently. We chose to test three architectures (modular, modular 1 against 1, and weighted modular). The three different scenarios will be detailed as follows.

7.3.1.2.1. Modular approach (global)

Let H be the healthy event, $\bar{H}$ be the pathological one and $S_i, i \in \{1,2,3\}$ be the grades of instability. In this case, the discriminating module is trained to differentiate the three grades of instability. Given the image predicted by the trigger module as "pathological", the discriminating module calculates the prediction probability $P(S_i|X, \bar{H}), i = 1, \dots, 3$. The prediction of the discriminating module was as follows:

$$argmax_i\, P(S_i|X, \bar{H}) \qquad [7.1]$$

7.3.1.2.2. Modular approach (1 on 1)

In this case, we built three experts in competition with one another. The first module was intended to discriminate between grades 1 and 2, the second one between grades 1 and 3, and finally, one module for grades 2 and 3. The output was the maximum of each expert.

The first module calculated the following probability:

$$P_{m_1}(S_i|X, \bar{H}) \times P_{m_1}(\bar{H}|X) + P_{m_1}(S_i|X, H) \times P_{m_1}(H|X), \quad i = 1,2$$

the second module:

$$\mathrm{P}_{\mathrm{m}_2}(\mathrm{S_i}|\mathrm{X},\overline{\mathrm{H}}) \times \mathrm{P}_{\mathrm{m}_2}(\overline{\mathrm{H}}|\mathrm{X}) + \mathrm{P}_{\mathrm{m}_2}(\mathrm{S_i}|\mathrm{X},\mathrm{H}) \times \mathrm{P}_{\mathrm{m}_2}(\mathrm{H}|\mathrm{X}), \quad \mathrm{i} = 1{,}3$$

and the last module:

$$\mathrm{P}_{\mathrm{m}_3}(\mathrm{S_i}|\mathrm{X},\overline{\mathrm{H}}) \times \mathrm{P}_{\mathrm{m}_3}(\overline{\mathrm{H}}|\mathrm{X}) + \mathrm{P}_{\mathrm{m}_3}(\mathrm{S_i}|\mathrm{X},\mathrm{H}) \times \mathrm{P}_{\mathrm{m}_3}(\mathrm{H}|\mathrm{X}), \quad \mathrm{i} = 2{,}3$$

The prediction of the discriminating module was as follows:

$$argmax_{(i,k)}\, P_{m_k}(S_i|X), \quad i = 1, \dots ,3 \quad k = 1, \dots ,3 \qquad [7.2]$$

7.3.1.2.3. Weighted modular approach

This system is similar to the first modular case, except for the output calculation:

$$\mathrm{P}(\mathrm{S_i}|\mathrm{X},\overline{\mathrm{H}}) \times \mathrm{P}(\overline{\mathrm{H}}|\mathrm{X}) + \mathrm{P}(\mathrm{S_i}|\mathrm{X},\mathrm{H}) \times \mathrm{P}(\mathrm{H}|\mathrm{X}), \quad \mathrm{i} = 1, \dots ,3$$

In this case, the trigger module assigned a weight to each output, and chose the output giving the highest prediction probability. The advantage of this method is that it takes into account the error from the trigger module.

In the first system, we assumed that the trigger module was the exact opposite of this architecture. For example, if the difference between the prediction probabilities of the trigger expert was not significant, it meant that the module was not confident. By assigning weights to the outputs acknowledging the probabilities from the trigger module, we added this information to the prediction.

Figure 7.3 shows the weighted modular architecture. The prediction of the discriminating module was as follows:

$$argmax_i\, P(S_i|X), \quad i = 1, \dots ,3 \qquad [7.3]$$

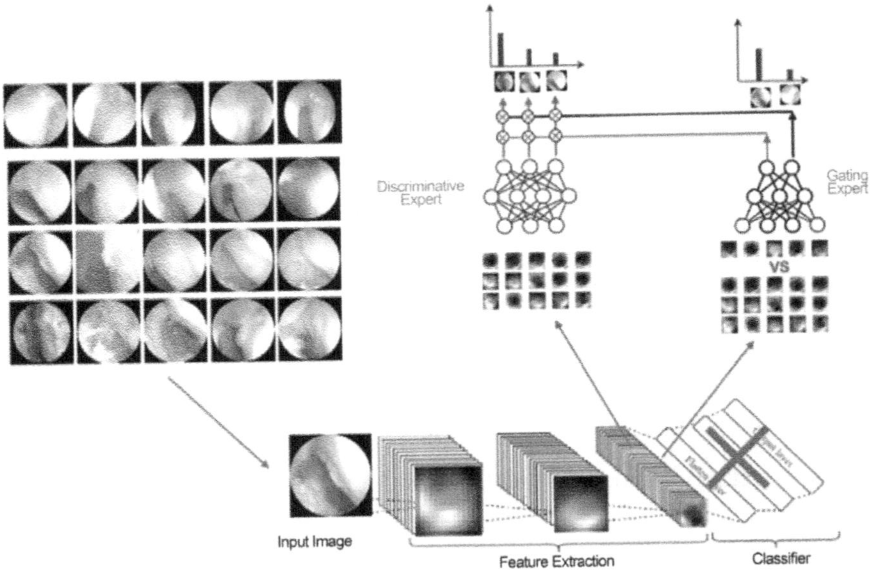

Figure 7.3. *Weighted modular learning architecture. For a color version of this figure, see www.iste.co.uk/julia/aihealthcare.zip*

7.3.1.3. *Learning phase*

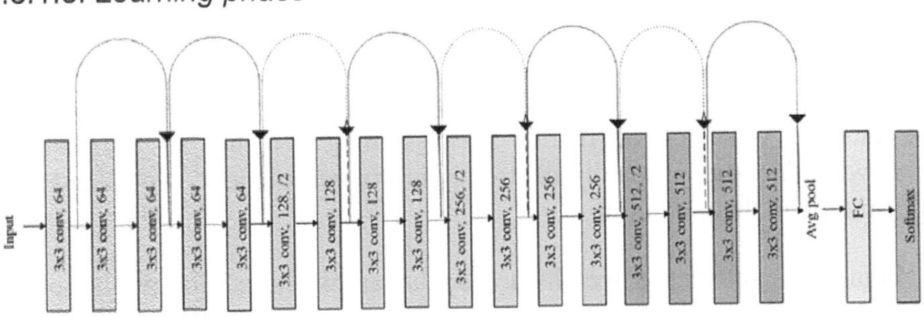

Figure 7.4. *ResNet18 architecture (Ramzan et al. 2019). For a color version of this figure, see www.iste.co.uk/julia/aihealthcare.zip*

In each module, the network was made up of a ResNet18 pretrained model and fully connected layer. The architecture of ResNet18 is shown in Figure 7.4. It is made of 18 deep layers. All four layers are similar, and each is composed of two deep residual network blocks. The residual network was characterized by the addition of an identity connection. This means that if the layer's output was $F(x)$, the block's output was $F(x) + x$ followed by the rectified linear unit (ReLU) activation function. The residual network attempts to solve the evanescent gradient problem, that is, when the gradient quickly reaches zero (He et al. 2015). The last layer was a grouping of averages followed by a fully connected layer and a Softmax.

7.3.2. *Results*

7.3.2.1. *Dataset*

The images used in this work were drawn from DCSS arthroscopic videos performed at Avicenne Hospital.

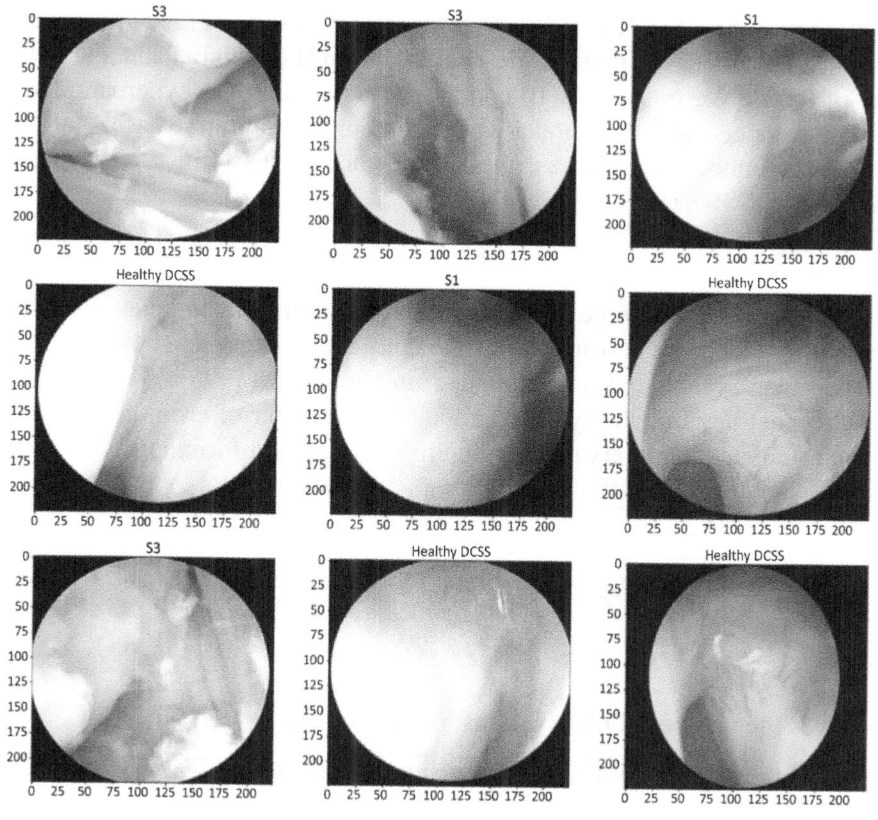

Figure 7.5. *Examples of visualization of DCSS images. For a color version of this figure, see www.iste.co.uk/julia/aihealthcare.zip*

The data collected comprises a total of 840 photos, including 105 healthy DCSS images (12.5%), 173 (20.6%) grade 1, 187 (22.2%) grade 2 and 375 (44.64%) grade 3 images.

In order to maintain a balance between the classes, we expanded the training set using image manipulations such as random rotations, brightness adjustment, image zoom, etc. After transformation, we were able to obtain 3,076 healthy DCSS images, 1,111 grade 1, 1,126 grade 2 and 1,279 grade 3 images. The image size was then resized to 224×224.

Figure 7.5 shows samples of the dataset.

7.3.2.2. *Setting*

We used 80% (6592) of the dataset for training and 20% (252) for testing. We used the stochastic gradient descent to optimize the model and a learning rate of 0.001. We trained for 10 epochs and used the same hyperparameters for both models. The first model was trained on all training datasets labeled healthy or unhealthy; whereas, the second model was trained only on the unhealthy DCSS cases.

7.3.2.3. *Results and discussions*

We evaluated the three types of modular learning techniques using the recognition rate with an estimate of the confidence interval. The confidence interval was calculated as explained in Bennani (1995). This interval assumes that the probability distribution of the number of errors is binomial, so we calculated the interval according to the following formula:

$$I_\alpha = \frac{P+\frac{Z_\pi^2}{2N}\pm Z_\alpha\sqrt{\frac{P(1-P)}{N}+\frac{Z_\alpha^2}{4N^2}}}{1+\frac{Z_N^2}{N}} \quad [7.4]$$

where:

– N is the number of observations in the test dataset;

– P is the probability for an observation to be an error;

– α is the confidence level, usually set at 95%, Z_α is a value given by the normalized centered Gaussian distribution ($Z_{95\%}$ = and $Z_{90\%}$ = 2.4).

Table 7.1 summarizes the results obtained. As can be seen in the table, modular learning has increased the recognition rate of 97.6% to 98.4% and a tighter confidence interval of [97.79%; 100%] with an almost perfect trigger module. These results demonstrate that adding knowledge a priori from the modular nature of the problem favored better generalization and a finer decision boundary than the non-modular architecture. Breaking down the task makes the problem less complex, which offers a higher probability of converging towards the fundamental truth function.

	Recognition rate (%)	Confidence interval (%)
Not modular	97.60	[96.52; 100]
Modular (global)	98.40	[97.79; 100]
Modular (1 on 1)	94.40	[91.10; 100]
Weighted modular	98.81	[98.40; 100]

Table 7.1. *Average recognition rate on different modular architectures*

		Predicted results				Recall (%)
		Healthy	**Grade 1**	**Grade 2**	**Grade 3**	
Basic truth	**Healthy**	30	0	0	0	100
	Grade 1	2	60	1	0	95.23
	Grade 2	0	0	62	0	100
	Grade 3	0	0	0	97	100
Precision (%)		93.75	100	98.41	100	–

Table 7.2. *Modular evaluation chart weighted on the test dataset*

The experiments reported in Tables 7.1 and 7.2 also showed that the weighted modular had better performances than the modular architecture of the first case, with a recognition rate of 98.81%. This indicates that adding the trigger module probabilities helps to calibrate results.

We studied the distribution of the difference between the prediction probability of the different classes in the discriminating module. In

Figure 7.6, we can see that the median difference is almost equal to 1, which proves that the discriminating module is confident in its decision. We can also note a high difference between the prediction probability of grades 2 and 3, which means that the model is able to confidently distinguish between the two grades. However, surprisingly, the probabilities between grades 1 and 3 are relatively low. When analyzing the images in further detail, we noted the presence of redness in both grades, which could be the reason for these results.

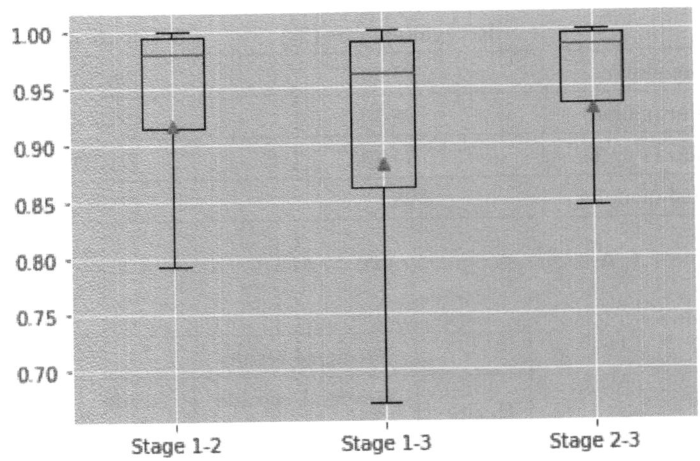

Figure 7.6. *Distribution of prediction deviation. For a color version of this figure, see www.iste.co.uk/julia/aihealthcare.zip*

Since the problem is of a medical nature, it is important to explain the choice made by the model. However, the neural network is a black box. We therefore attempted to evaluate two methods for interpreting the results using an image heat map. The pixels with the highest contribution to the prediction of the neural network are located in hotter areas. The first method is called GradCam (Gradient-weighted class activation mapping), which creates visual explanations (Selvaraju et al. 2019). GradCam creates a coarse location map, which highlights key areas of the image using the gradients of any target concept and routing them to the final convolutional layer. It is therefore possible to visualize the results of the different layers of the CNN model. Figure 7.7 provides an overview of the method's framework

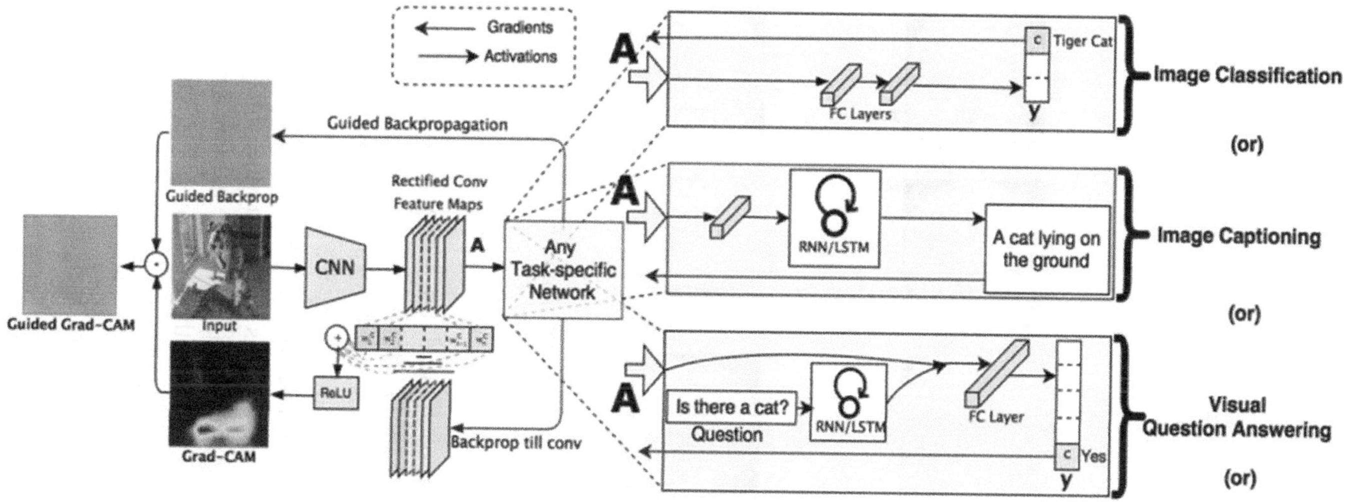

Figure 7.7. *Overview of the GradCam method (Selvaraju et al. 2019). For a color version of this figure, see www.iste.co.uk/julia/aihealthcare.zip*

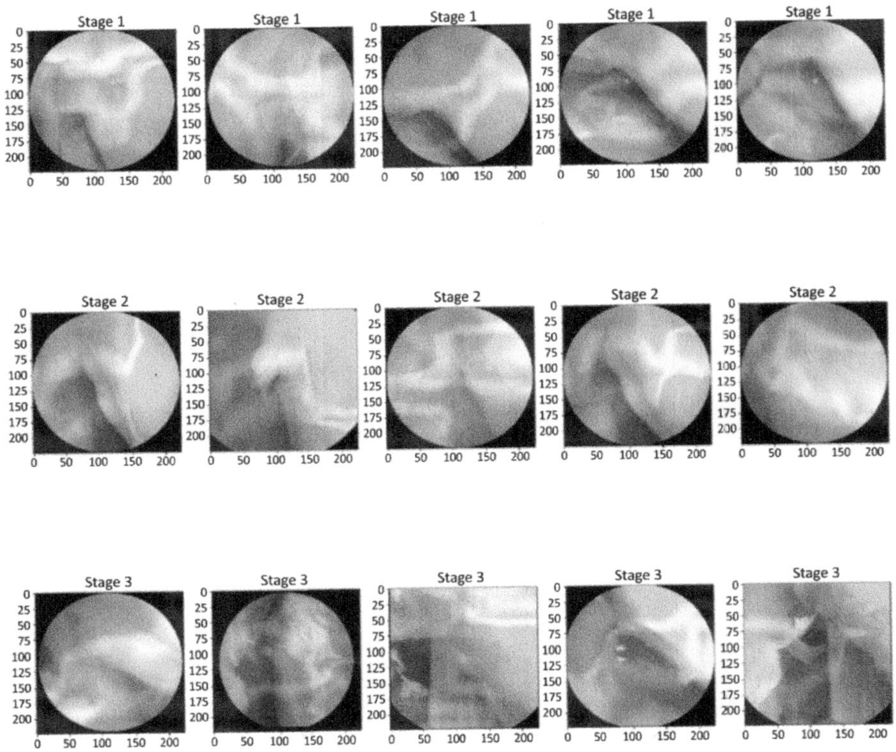

Figure 7.8. *Model interpretation with GradCam. For a color version of this figure, see www.iste.co.uk/julia/aihealthcare.zip*

The second approach used for explainability is the Sobol attribution method (Fel et al. 2021). It is based on sensitivity analysis techniques commonly used in physics and economics, in particular, the Sobol indices. Not only does this method identify the contribution of each image region to the decision of the neural network but Sobol indices are also able to estimate the higher order interactions between the image regions and their contributions. To estimate the indices, the authors used the Jansen estimator and the quasi-Monte Carlo method for sampling. They first sampled masks from the sequence, applied them to the image with a perturbation operator and then obtained prediction scores by transmitting the resulting image to the system. The explanations were then calculated using the masks and the prediction scores.

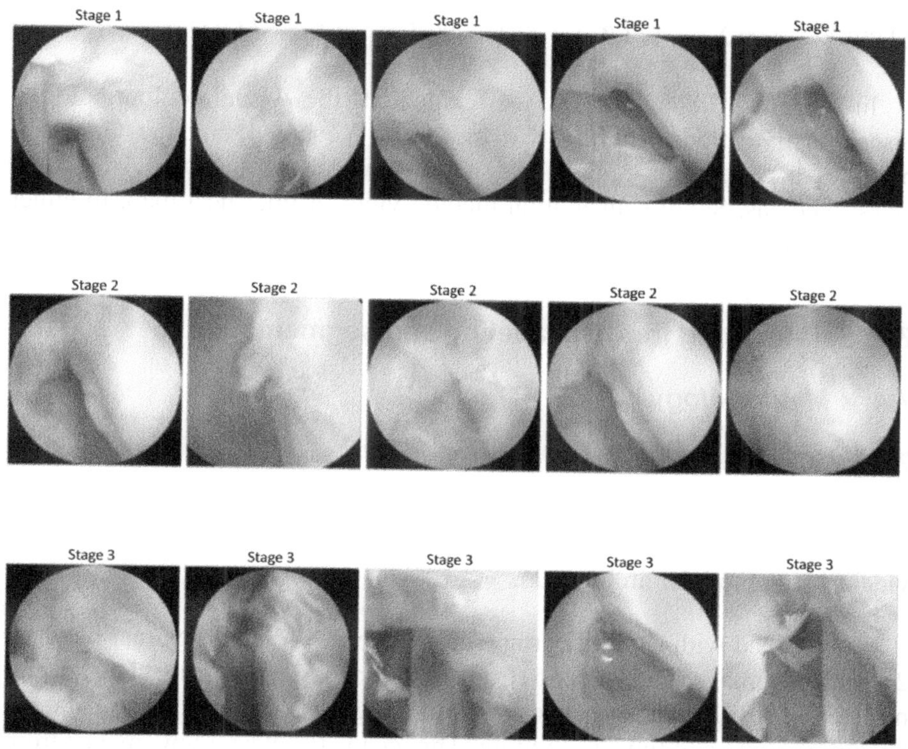

Figure 7.9. *Model interpretation via the Sobol attribution method. For a color version of this figure, see www.iste.co.uk/julia/aihealthcare.zip*

Let f be the decision function of the neural network, N be the number of planes, A and B be the matrices obtained after perturbation and $C^{(i)}$ be the same as A with the associated column of variable *(i)* replaced by a column of B. The estimator of the individual sensitivity index is then:

$$\hat{S}_i = \frac{\hat{V} - \frac{1}{2N}\sum_{j=1}^{N}\left(f(\mathbf{B}_j) - f\left(\mathbf{C}_j^{(i)}\right)\right)^2}{\hat{V}} \qquad [7.5]$$

and the total order is calculated as follows:

$$\hat{S}_{T_i} = \frac{\frac{1}{2N}\sum_{j=1}^{N}\left(f(\mathbf{A}_j) - f\left(\mathbf{C}_j^{(i)}\right)\right)^2}{\hat{V}} \qquad [7.6]$$

where $\hat{\mathbf{V}} = \frac{1}{N-1}\sum_{j=0}^{N} \left(f(\mathbf{A}_j) - f_{\phi}\right)^2$, and $f_{\varphi} = \frac{1}{N}\sum_{j=0}^{N} f(\mathbf{A}_j)$.

In Figures 7.8 and 7.9, we evaluated the visual output of the discriminative model for the two methods. We noted that the GradCam provides a continuous region, and we observed a certain model for each class; whereas, Sobol's attribution method yields a finer heat map. In either case, both methods were able to locate a grade 3 laceration in the DCSS.

7.4. Self-learning for data labeling and segmentation

7.4.1. *Methodology*

7.4.1.1. *Motivation*

The main goal of this section is to first label arthroscopy images using self-learning, and then to detect and identify structures from arthroscopy videos using modular architecture.

We worked with shoulder arthroscopy videos. We could extract between 25 and 30 images per second from one video. This means that several minutes in a video can produce multiple images, so labeling these data can be cumbersome and time consuming. The idea is to select a few images from each video and to apply the self-learning process for pseudo-labeling, that is, to produce predicted labels from a small set of labeled data and add them to the training dataset from the rest of the video. In this way, we can exploit all of the available data.

7.4.1.2. *System architecture*

The self-learning model (namely the pseudo-labeling) is built using a segmentation network. It takes an arthroscopic image as input and its basic truth mask with five classes (background, long biceps tendon, subscapularis tendon, supraspinatus tendon, glenoid and humeral cartilage), and it outputs a prediction mask.

When training the segmentation task, we found that the model was able to perform binary segmentation, that is, to identify structure against background. However, it failed to distinguish between the different classes. This is what motivated the use of modular architecture for learning.

The first network learned to differentiate the anatomical structure's background. Then, we removed the predicted background from the initial image and transferred it to the second network. The latter was trained to learn to discriminate between the four classes.

At first, the self-learning phase trains the two models with the available annotated images. Next, we predicted the mask for all of the images in the unlabeled set. Then, we kept only the images producing an average prediction probability above a threshold. We set another threshold to filter the selected outputs, pixel by pixel, following their prediction probability. Experiments have shown that adding the second filter to the predicted images increases the recognition rate.

$\widehat{y_m}$ being an image predicted by the model, $\widehat{y_{m_{i,j}}}$ represents the pixel at position (i, j). Let $T \in [0,1]$ be the threshold and function *softmax* be defined as $S: R^K \rightarrow (0,1)^K where\ K \geq 1$; $\mathrm{S(x_i)} = \frac{e^{x_i}}{\sum_{j=1}^{K} e^{x_j}}$ for $\mathrm{i} = 1, \ldots, \mathrm{K}$ and $\mathrm{x} = (\mathrm{x}_1, \ldots, \mathrm{x}_\mathrm{K}) \in \mathrm{R}^\mathrm{K}$. The image is filtered as follows:

$$\hat{y}_{mi,j} = \begin{cases} \hat{y}_{mi,j}, & \text{if} \arg \max_{(i,j)} S(\hat{y}_{mi,j}) \geq T \\ 0, & \text{otherwise} \end{cases} \qquad [7.7]$$

We added the final results to the training dataset and repeated the operation until we reached the stopping criterion; either all images being annotated or the algorithm reaching the maximum number of iterations.

When $\mathrm{P} \in [0,1]$ is a threshold, at each iteration, the dataset of selected images is as follows:

$$\hat{\mathrm{I}}\{\widehat{\mathrm{f}_{\mathrm{w}^{(l)}}}(\mathrm{x_m}) \mid \arg\max_{\mathrm{x_m}} \mathrm{S}\left(\widehat{\mathrm{f}_{\mathrm{w}^{(l)}}}(\mathrm{x_m})\right) \geq \mathrm{P}\} \qquad [7.8]$$

and the output prediction is defined as follows:

$$\widehat{\mathrm{y_m}} = \delta_{\arg\max_{(i,j)} \mathrm{S}\left(\mathrm{I}_{\mathrm{m}_{i,j}}\right) \geq \mathrm{T}} \widehat{\mathrm{I_m}}; \quad 0 \leq \mathrm{m} \leq \mathrm{n}(\hat{\mathrm{I}}) \qquad [7.9]$$

where $\mathrm{n}(\hat{\mathrm{I}})$ is the cardinality of the dataset $\hat{\mathrm{I}}$.

7.4.1.3. *Learning phase*

The architecture of each module is inspired in UNet (Ronneberger et al. 2015). The choice of this particular pretrained model is primarily motivated by its common use in medical applications. The second key is its ability to perform well with few labeled images (Ronneberger et al. 2015). The architecture of UNet is U-shaped and comprises an encoder (contraction path) and a symmetric decoder (expansion path). The contraction path is made of two convolution blocks 3 × 3, followed by the ReLU activation function and then a max pooling 2 × 2. These operations were repeated five times. The number of channels doubled each time (64, 128, 256, 512, 1024). The expansion path was made of the same blocks and the ReLU, and used 2 × 2 for the upward convolution. The final layer was a convolution of 1 × 1. Figure 7.10 shows the UNet architecture.

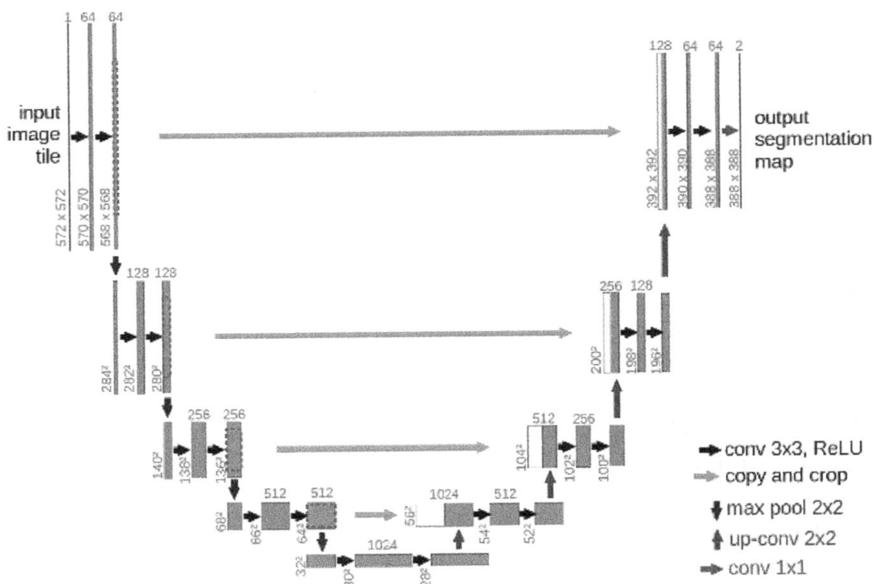

Figure 7.10. *UNet architecture (Ronneberger et al. 2015). For a color version of this figure, see www.iste.co.uk/julia/aihealthcare.zip*

7.4.2. *Results*

7.4.2.1. *Dataset*

The data for our second study were collected by video recording of shoulder arthroscopies performed at Avicenne Hospital between November 2021 and June 2022. The videos of these arthroscopies could be retrieved directly from the video arthroscopy console in mp4 format. From these arthroscopies, a total of 459 images were extracted (121 from the long biceps tendon, 41 from the supraspinatus tendon, 181 from the subscapularis tendon and 116 from the glenoid or humeral cartilage), and registered in png format.

Images were annotated by a surgeon using LabelStudio software. Labeling was done using polygonal annotation. This technique provides a more accurate annotation for irregular shapes. Figure 7.11 shows examples of shoulder arthroscopy images and their segmentation.

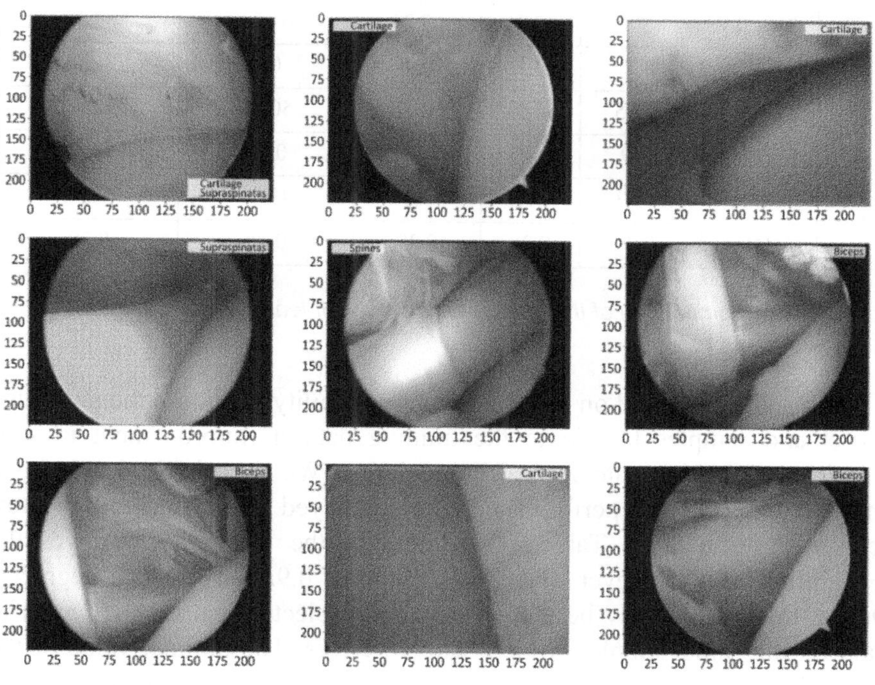

Figure 7.11. *Segmentation visualization examples of a shoulder arthroscopy image. Each color designates the corresponding classes: red, biceps; blue, cartilage; green, subscapularis; and yellow, supraspinatus. For a color version of this figure, see www.iste.co.uk/julia/aihealthcare.zip*

7.4.2.2. *Setting*

The data were split into a 70% training set (321 images) and a 30% test dataset (138 images). We used 10% of the training dataset (32 images) as labeled data to train the first self-training model and we assumed that 90% of the training dataset (289 images) were unlabeled data. The final evaluation was performed on the test dataset. Images were resized to 224 × 224. We used an Adam optimizer and an epoch number of 15. After the experiments, we set the threshold at 0.7.

7.4.2.3. *Results and discussions*

Threshold		Average value	Classes			
			Biceps	**Cartilage**	**Subscapularis**	**Supraspinatus**
0.6	**SR (%)**	71.2	64.48	37.25	25.95	84.35
	IOU	0.31	0.47	0.29	0.15	0.34
0.7	**SR (%)**	80	70.76	65.25	64.21	85.73
	IOU	0.3	0.3	0.4	0.4	0.11
0.8	**SR (%)**	79.55	44.91	62.35	50.83	92.32
	IOU	0.39	0.35	0.29	0.29	0.61
0.9	**SR (%)**	76.73	43.66	73.17	43.03	88.64
	IOU	0.3	0.38	0.39	0.16	0.39

Table 7.3. *Comparison of the threshold value in self-learning (SR: success rate)*

We used a threshold on the prediction probability to choose the unlabeled subset and samples to add to the training dataset (improvement in self-learning recognition rate from 76% to 80%). We varied the threshold to analyze its effect on performance. We displayed the results on the test dataset. As shown in Table 7.3, increasing the threshold improves the recognition rate. However, for the threshold of 0.9, performance degrades. One of the reasons may be that strict sample selection causes the model to train on the same samples, which leads to errors. The optimal value of the threshold is 0.7, with a recognition rate of 80%. We also showed that the supraspinatus class, identified in yellow in Figure 7.11, obtained the highest recognition rate compared to the other classes. We found that adding the pixel-by-pixel threshold improved the recognition rate (from 76% to 80%). We observed the effect of the labeled data ratio on performances during the first iteration, as shown in Figure 7.12. We noted that the higher the percentage, the higher the accuracy rate. We chose the 10% ratio. Samples of segmentation predictions on the test dataset are shown in Figure 7.13.

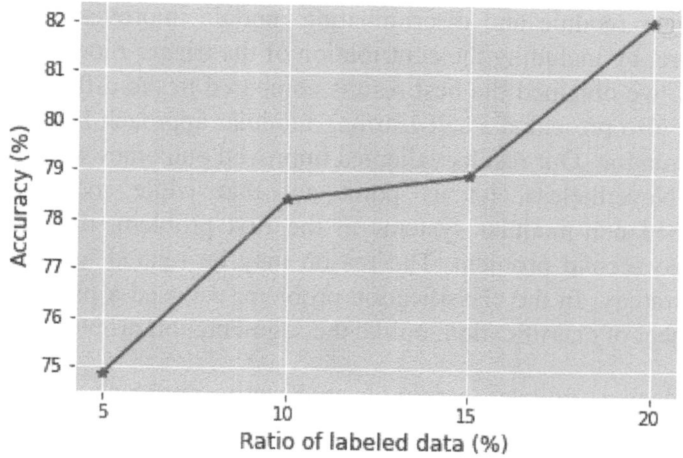

Figure 7.12. *Comparison of the relationship between labeled data and recognition accuracy rate. For a color version of this figure, see www.iste.co.uk/julia/aihealthcare.zip*

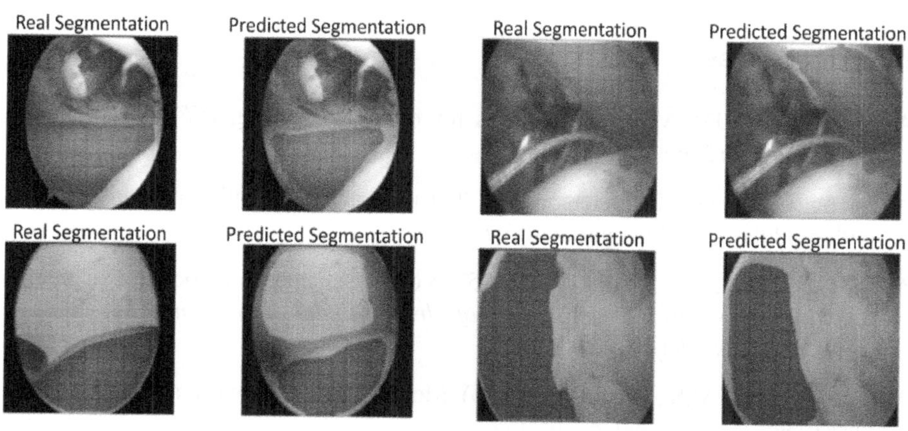

Figure 7.13. *Examples of segmentation results predicted with self-training. Each color designates the corresponding classes: red, biceps; blue, cartilage; green, subscapularis; and yellow, supraspinatus. For a color version of this figure, see www.iste.co.uk/julia/aihealthcare.zip*

7.5. Conclusion

In this chapter, we first presented a modular framework for the classification of the DCSS. We showed that breaking down the problem into a trigger module and discriminating module improves performances. Furthermore, by including the contribution of the trigger module in the form of weights, we obtained the best results compared to the different strategies tested. We also presented a self-learning modular approach for data labeling and segmentation. Our results validated improved outcomes when using self-learning. Nevertheless, let us point out that while modular learning outperformed non-modular systems in the first problem, this was not the case for the second problem. The reason may be related to the problem's dividing strategy. In the classification problem, we used a priori knowledge on the subject of classification, unlike the segmentation problem.

In conclusion, modular learning is an effective approach to reduce model complexity and to improve model generalization. However, managing when and where to divide a problem is crucial. In future work, a different strategy should be developed and analyzed in further detail for modular segmentation by self-learning. In addition, we propose a new feature selection measure for interpretability on convolutional neural networks.

7.6. References

Alpaydin, E. (1993). Multiple networks for function learning. *IEEE International Conference on Neural Networks*, 1, 9–14.

Anderson, C., Draper, B., Peterson, D. (2000). Behavioral cloning of student pilots with modular neural networks. *ICML*.

Auda, G., Kamel, M., Raafat, H. (1995). Voting schemes for cooperative neural network classifiers. *Proceedings of International Conference on Neural Networks (ICNN'95)*, 3, 1240–1243.

Auda, G., Kamel, M.S., Raafat, H. (1996). Modular neural network architectures for classification. *Proceedings of International Conference on Neural Networks (ICNN'96)*, 2, 1279–1284.

Bartfai, G. (1994). Hierarchical clustering with art neural networks. *Proceedings of International Conference on Neural Networks (ICNN'94)*, 2, 940–944.

Bennani, Y. (1995). A modular and hybrid connectionist system for speaker identification. *Neural Computation*, 7, 791–798.

Berthelot, D., Carlini, N., Goodfellow, I., Papernot, N., Oliver, A., Raffel, C. (2019). Mixmatch: A holistic approach to semi-supervised learning [Online]. Available at: https://arxiv.org/abs/1905.02249.

Chapelle, O. and Zien, A. (2005). Semi-supervised classification by low density separation. In *Proceedings of the Tenth International Workshop on Artificial Intelligence and Statistics, Proceedings of Machine Learning Research*, 6–8 January, 57–64 [Online]. Available at: https://proceedings.mlr.press/r5/chapelle05b.html.

Fel, T., Cadene, R., Chalvidal, M., Cord, M., Vigouroux, D., Serre, T. (2021). Look at the variance! Efficient black-box explanations with sobol-based sensitivity analysis [Online]. Available at: https://arxiv.org/abs/2111.04138.

He, K., Zhang, X., Ren, S., Sun, J. (2015). Deep residual learning for image recognition [Online]. Available at: https://arxiv.org/abs/1512.03385.

Jacobs, R., Jordan, M., Nowlan, S., Hinton, G. (1991). Adaptive mixture of local expert. *Neural Computation*, 3, 78–88.

Kelkar, A. and Medaglia, J.D. (2018). *Evidence of Brain Modularity*. Springer International Publishing, Cham. doi: 10.1007/978-3-319-16999-62422-1.

Kitay, A. and Wolfe, S.W. (2012). Scapholunate instability: Current concepts in diagnosis and management. *The Journal of Hand Surgery*, 37(10), 2175–2196 [Online]. Available at: https://www.sciencedirect.com/science/article/pii/S036350231201101X.

Mittal, S., Bengio, Y., Lajoie, G. (2022). Is a modular architecture enough? [Online]. Available at: https://arxiv.org/abs/2206.02713.

Overstraeten, L., Camus, E., Wahegaonkar, A., Messina, J., Tandara, A., Cambon-Binder, A., Mathoulin, C. (2013). Anatomical description of the dorsal capsule scapholunate septum (dcss) – Arthroscopic staging of scapholunate instability after DCSS sectioning. *Journal of Wrist Surgery*, 2, 284.

Ramzan, F., Khan, M.U., Rehmat, A., Iqbal, S., Saba, T., Rehman, A., Mehmood, Z. (2019). A deep learning approach for automated diagnosis and multi-class classification of Alzheimer's disease stages using resting-state fMRI and residual neural networks. *Journal of Medical Systems*, 44.

Rashwan, M., Raafat, H., Ismail, A., Shahein, H. (1994). Improving classification using a tree structured neural network. *Journal of Intelligent and Fuzzy Systems*, 2, 101–114.

Ronneberger, O., Fischer, P., Brox, T. (2015). U-net: Convolutional networks for biomedical image segmentation. *CoRR* [Online]. Available at: http://arxiv.org/abs/1505.04597.

Rueckl, J., Cave, K., Kosslyn, S. (1989). Why are "what" and "where" processed by separate cortical visual systems? A computational investigation. *Journal of Cognitive Neuroscience*, 1, 171–186.

Selvaraju, R.R., Cogswell, M., Das, A., Vedantam, R., Parikh, D., Batra, D. (2019). Grad-CAM: Visual explanations from deep networks via gradient-based localization. *International Journal of Computer Vision*, 128(2), 336–359. doi: 10.1007%2Fs11263-019-01228-7.

Wang, S.-J. and Zhou, C. (2012). Hierarchical modular structure enhances the robustness of self-organized criticality in neural networks. *New Journal of Physics*, 14, 023005.

Warren, J. (2002). Synaptic self: How our brains become who we are. *Journal of the Royal Society of Medicine*, 95(7), 373–374.

Conclusion[1]

Nowadays, quite unfairly condemned[2], Alexis Carrel is sometimes quoted as having coined the phrase: “it takes more [imagination, judgment and] intelligence to become a great physician than to become a great chemist” (Carrel 1935). The question posed here is whether this intelligence can be external to the professional.

We owe a big thank you to our colleague, Guilhem Julia, for organizing these rich successive meetings devoted to the topic of AI. Along with most of the authors of these interventions, we have long been convinced that multidisciplinarity (within universities and beyond) constitutes the future of research, and Mr. Julia demonstrates this to us on every occasion. We would also like to sincerely thank the faculty deans of the Sorbonne Paris Nord University and its president, as well as the president of the Condorcet campus, for their support.

As Julien Ducerf wrote some time ago, “the majority of AI technologies are several years old, even decades for some. Yet we treat them as recent innovations. Innovation [more likely] stems from its uses” (Ducerf 2022). These are some of the new uses we have been introduced to. It is above all, AI and medicine, AI and therapeutics, AI and healthcare that were brilliantly discussed during these exchanges. While the topic has already been the

---

Conclusion written by Didier GUÉVEL.

1 Text completed on November 23, 2022.

2 A few unfortunate and decontextualized phrases can, on some occasions, determine an individual’s posterity.

subject of reflections (see, for example, Kuhn and Pomart (2022)), speakers have developed the subject in great depth.

– As for health: health, Hygieia or Salus, the daughter of Aesculapius, was a beautiful goddess of antiquity. We lack a deity dedicated to AI, which could perhaps be chosen among the universes of contemporary science fiction, where we count around 50. We will come back to the definitions of health below.

– As for intelligence: we will not repeat here all of the possible definitions of multiple intelligences, but instead just recall, as concluded during a previous conference devoted to AI and organized by Mr. Julia ("*Sciences & sens de l'intelligence artificielle*" (Guével 2020), symposium to which we will refer further below), that the expression "artificial intelligence" is probably inappropriate and we should rather say "algorithmic process"; this being only an immaterial instrument.

Contrary to what is customary in the legal world, we will summarize the present works, not in two, but in three parts. We witnessed a chronological presentation of treatments, together with legal analyses (in a certain way, a regulatory apprehension of processes). However, perhaps (some may have suggested this) we should go further in terms of health, going beyond what is understood in the broader sense.

Chronology of treatments

As much as law is confused with its pathology (trial), health is frequently equated with illness and its treatment. In both cases, we confuse the sea foam of dysfunction with the ocean of normal physiology and the good organization it covers. In this spirit, the many fascinating presentations we have attended have mainly focused on chronology with regards to pathologies.

Prevention begins with the fight against medical isolation, as Professor Cammilleri cleverly reminded us. The issue of disease prevention (the issue of predictive analyses) was addressed; thanks to Rushed Kanawati in particular, we were able to learn everything that the analysis of complex networks can bring (predictive tasks in network medicine), even in genetic matters. On this last point, we will also refer to the conclusions of our previous symposium devoted to genetics ("*Le génome en mal de Droit(s)?*" (Cheynet de Beaupré et al. 2019)).

However, as with any new method, the process may involve some worrying aspects. Nicolas Da Silva and Philippe Batifoulier revealed the extent to which the apparent good intentions of commercial insurance companies in terms of "appropriate behavior" and the use of connected objects can still be ambiguous (the pretext of public health could actually serve purely financial interests). For her part, Anne Cammilleri explained how certain applications could promote care in a hospital environment, while also showing the dangers others could conceal.

Diagnosis assistance is probably the most valuable service that AI can provide, as long as it is used as an aid, as an instrument, and does not replace the therapist. Everything must work to build trust in algorithmic processes. Younès Bennani and Thomas Grégory showed how, thanks to deep neural networks and multinodal data, we can detect anomalies in certain parts of the human body (in particular, tiny fractures likely to go otherwise unnoticed). They discussed the examples of the hand, the shoulder and the wrist (these processes can help the preparation of surgical interventions).

Drug treatments can also rely on AI. We know that, recently, a large pharmaceutical laboratory concluded an agreement with a company specializing in AI, with a view to developing new molecules[3].

Follow-up care was also covered, thanks to the beautiful presentation by Guilhem Julia, on the subject of companion robots equipped with an AI (and exoskeletons) and the legal problems they risk causing. These remarks constitute the brilliant extension of a previous symposium organized around the topic of robotics (*Lex robotica*[4]). Having ourselves, in the past, presented

3 Sanofi and Exscientia. See *Le Monde* January 8, 2022, Économie & entreprise, p. 15.

4 Also refer to *Lex Robotica. Aux frontières du Droit et de la robotique*. Minutes of the *Lex Robotica* symposium (on the boundaries between technology and law; pondering the humanoid of 2017) held on Thursday, September 21, 2017 organized by the National Conservatory of Arts and Crafts (Faculty of Law, Political and Social Sciences from Paris 13 University, Sorbonne Paris Cité, HT2S Laboratories (History of Technosciences and Society) and IRDA (Research Institute for Attractive Law), CNIL (Ethics and the Digital), ICCA (Cultural Industries and Artistic Creations), Lextenso, 2018).

a show with a humanoid robot[5] and various projects, particularly abroad, on this same topic (Guével 2016, 2018; Gautrais and Mekki 2018), we believe we can attest to the great relevance of Guilhem Julia's remarks and the interest of his suggestions (particularly with regards to the notion of "involvement"[6]). Implicitly, there is not only the all too famous legal distinction between structural and behavioral custody, but also the question of the "uncanny valley[7]", describing the human being's uneasiness, and the anguish at discovering that the humanoid or animaloid are no more than a robot resembling a robot. Lawyers would probably benefit from finding a way to take this disarray or collapse into account.

Anne Cammilleri added that follow-ups could be provided by various apps.

In the end, a place was alternately reserved for an overall assessment and lessons to be learned from the algorithmic analyses of collected data.

Regulatory apprehension

At the same time, several participants recalled that a framework for these different processes was essential. Here, as elsewhere, caution should be implemented, if only by virtue of the precautionary principle.

Especially, as Mr. Julia said, it is "almost impossible to explain how algorithms process data and deliver their result". It is often said that the reasoning mechanism of AI frequently eludes whoever programmed it. There is digital magic[8].

We know all too well about the perverse effects of AI embedded into cars[9] or planes[10]. Obeying AI can lead to disaster. It has also been asserted

5 On November 19, 2016, in Paris, at the Reine Blanche theater, a dialogue with a Darwin robot. *Les robots humanoïdes et le Droit*. In *Festival des idées*, USPC. In collaboration with the Paul-Éluard high school in Saint-Denis, after the performance of one act of the play *Dans le plus simple appareil* ("In the simplest device"), by Juliette Malfray.

6 Even if we can hold some reserves as to the "CE marking".

7 1970 theory by Japanese roboticist Masahiro Mori.

8 Mr. Julia could tell us if "magic" and "science" can finally be compatible.

9 In particular, regarding trajectory controllers.

10 We may think, in the event of a sudden loss of altitude, that AI could summon the pilots to climb back up, when instead, they should dive the aircraft's nose in order to regain lift.

that virtual realities could be hacked and lead to serious abuses (including crimes) (Laurens 2022).

We also understand the drifts that certain types of research can lead to, for example, considering transferring real neuronal connections to a robot ("small detail"), a process which would require euthanizing the potential candidates beforehand[11]. We can be all the more suspicious when we know the supposed current maxim governing Silicon Valley: "Fake it, till you make it"[12] (Laure 2022). As researchers in neurosciences, nuclear medicine and mathematics expressed earlier this year in a remarkable column ("*En imagerie médicale, faire de l'IA une alliée*", "Making an ally of AI for medical imaging purposes"[13]), "while artificial intelligence portends major advances, its use requires multidisciplinary reflection". This is precisely what we engage in the present exchanges, and we would like to gladly add, once again, as many have said, "it also requires the use the precautionary principle".

Cybercrime, as evoked by Anne Cammilleri, remains frightening. The lawmaker has already partially intervened to avoid certain deviations (in particular, Article L. 1151-4 of the French Public Health Code now provides: "Acts, processes, techniques, methods and equipment having the effect of modifying cerebral activity and presenting a serious danger or a suspicion of serious danger to human health may be prohibited by decree, after consulting with the French High Authority for Health[14]"). That being said, it is often difficult to determine the faults of AI and to what extent it performs better than humans.

The pivotal question lies in finding out the place law could have in this general problem. As previously mentioned, the key word lies in the "confidence" these processes should inspire and the legal framework that could contribute to boosting it. Professor Anne Cammilleri and Céline Bloud-Rey helped us to think about existing rules and those that could be introduced in terms of ethics (for example, with the systematic presence of moderators). In our opinion, it is necessary to avoid the fear that due to algorithmic apprehension, truths could end up being determined not by

11 Nectome: www.nectome.com.

12 "Fake it till you make it," Silicon Valley.

13 "*En imagerie médicale, faire de l'IA une alliée*," *Le Monde*, *Sciences & Médecine*, June 1, 2022, 7.

14 Law No. 2021-1017 from August 2, 2021.

scholars, but by the law of the greatest number[15]: statistical truth does not necessarily equate to scientific truth (even though taking frequency into account is still the foundation of digital data processing). To take an example well known to jurists, it is not because the majority of courts adopt the same solution when faced with an identical problem that this solution is legally correct.

In this case, law must be the instrument of a return of the human factor, of a persistent and permanent control of the human being over the use of the data processed algorithmically (in particular, in terms of bioethics, as Celine Bloud-Rey brilliantly exposed in relation to the "ends of the law"). She advocated for encouraging the human relationship between the caregiver and the patient, so as to establish the principle of a "digital human guarantee", while making sure that in doing so, the human does not use it as an excuse to give in to the temptation of anthropocentric domination. In any case, it should already be clear that the existence of AI does not serve as a pretext to endorse a situation of medical staff shortage, in as much as "distance education" has sometimes served as a pretext not to renovate/maintain university buildings and not to create essential jobs[16].

Openness to health (lato sensu)

As we have pointed out, in our opinion, the term "health" goes beyond the sole question of care. As Céline Bloud-Rey has stated, health involves far more than the medical model. Anne Camilleri alluded to this when referring to the European Union current policy. The dictionary of the French Academy states it clearly through this definition: "Normal, satisfactory functioning state of a human or animal organism"[17]. Lautréamont even claimed that genius was the supreme health[18]. Perhaps we should carry the reflection further and think "upstream" about the possible favorable or unfavorable influence of AI over human health and particularly over human mental health (which can lead to insanity). Beyond the simple joke, should not we seriously wonder whether AI risks increasing natural imbecility?

15 Processes that can lead to affirming that our planet is not round because the majority of "data" state it is flat.

16 Dean Fauchon emphasized that this was not the case at the USPN.

17 9th edition, www.dictionnaire-academie.fr/article/A9S0401 [Accessed November 6, 2022].

18 In *Poésies* I.

Besides, university reflections are themselves frequently too anthropocentric. It is undoubtedly the health of the living[19] that should be addressed: not only animal health as the dictionary says, but also plant health. We express the hope that another symposium will extend the reflections of this one by broadening the subject in this direction.

Finally, we can see that, as often, we finally achieve presentations that evoke almost more "data" (even a "deluge of data") than AI does. Maybe the essence of the problem lies herein: what data are we talking about? How are they collected and then chosen? How have we avoided the risk of (too human[20]) a bias, etc.?

References

Carrel, A. (1935). *L'homme cet inconnu*. Plon, Paris.

Cheynet de Beaupré, A., Depadt, V., Guével, D. (eds) (2019). Colloque "Le génome en mal de droit(s) ?" *Revue juridique personnes & famille*, 14 February dossier spécial, 5 [Online]. Available at: https://www.lagbd.org/index.php/LE_G%C3%89NOME_EN_MAL_DE_DROIT(S)_%3F_De_l%E2%80%99usage_du_glaive_et_de_la_balance_quand_l%E2%80%99humain_touche_au_divin_(fr).

Ducerf, J. (2022). Web 3.0, metaverse et NFT : derrière les fantasmes, une bulle ET/OUI une révolution ? [Online]. Available at: https://medium.com/@julien_ducerf/web-3-0-metaverse-et-nft-derri%C3%A8re-les-fantasmes-une-bulle-et-ou-une-r%C3%A9volution-23cda00cd0fa [Accessed 6 November 2022].

Gautrais, V. and Mekki, M. (2018). Pour en finir avec les robots. In *Colloque "Le droit à l'épreuve du numérique"*, Wilson, C.L.R. (ed.). Faculté de droit de l'Université de Montréal [Online]. Available at: http://www.lesconferences.ca/listes/droit-a-lepreuve-du-numerique/.

Guével, D. (2016). Quel droit pour les robots ? *The Conversation France* [Online]. Available at: http://theconversation.com/quel-droit-pour-les-robots-62671.

Guével, D. (2018). Les robots humanoïdes sont-ils condamnés ? *13 en Droit*, 2.

Guével, D. (2020). Propos conclusifs et synthèse. In *Colloque "Sciences et sens de l'intelligence artificielle"*, Julia, G. (ed.). Maison des sciences de l'homme/Dalloz, Paris.

19 "To live is not to be alive, it is to be well" (Martial, Book I, Epigram 70, 15).

20 Almost in the sense of the Nietzschean formula.

Kuhn, C. and Pomart, C. (eds) (2022). *Corps humain, technologies et droit*, tome 151. Institut francophone pour la justice et la démocratie, Paris.

Laure, V.S. (2022). Les génies et les charlatans. *Le Monde*, 11 January, 31.

Laurens, V.C. (2022). Réalité virtuelle et risque de manipulation. *Le Monde*, 19 October, 3.

List of Authors

Abir BARBARA
LIPN, CNRS
Université Sorbonne Paris Nord
Saint-Denis
France

Philippe BATIFOULIER
CEPN
Université Sorbonne Paris Nord
Villetaneuse
France

Nosseiba BEN SALEM
LIPN, CNRS
Université Sorbonne Paris Nord
Saint-Denis
France

Younès BENNANI
LIPN
Université Sorbonne Paris Nord
Villetaneuse
France

Céline BLOUD-REY
IRDA
Université Sorbonne Paris Nord
Villetaneuse
France

Anne CAMMILLERI
IDPs
Université Sorbonne Paris Nord
Villetaneuse
France

Charles DACHEUX
MOVEO
LaMSN
Université Sorbonne Paris Nord
Saint-Denis
France

Nicolas DA SILVA
CEPN
Université Sorbonne Paris Nord
Villetaneuse
France

Léo DÉCHAUMET
LaMSN
Université Sorbonne Paris Nord
Saint-Denis
France

Anne FAUCHON
Université Sorbonne Paris Nord
Villetaneuse
France

Thomas GRÉGORY
MOVEO
LaMSN
Université Sorbonne Paris Nord
Saint-Denis
France

Didier GUÉVEL
IRDA
Université Sorbonne Paris Nord
Villetaneuse
France

Guilhem JULIA
IRDA
Université Sorbonne Paris Nord
Villetaneuse
France

Rushed KANAWATI
LIPN, CNRS
Université Sorbonne Paris Nord
Villetaneuse
France

Joseph KARKAZAN
Hôpital Avicenne
AP-HP
Bobigny
France

Thomas LEFÈVRE
IRIS
Université Sorbonne Paris Nord
Bobigny
France

Index

A, B

C, D

E, F

H, I

L, M

N, P

R, S

T, V, W

Other titles from

iSTE

in

Science, Society and New Technologies

2024

BARTHES Angela, CIBIEN Catherine, ROMAGNY Bruno
Biosphere Reserves and Sustainable Development Goals 1: Scientific and Practical Educational Issues in the Mediterranean
(Territory Development Set – Volume 3)
Biosphere Reserves and Sustainable Development Goals 2: Issues, Tensions, Processes and Governance in the Mediterranean
(Territory Development Set – Volume 4)

KOHLMANN Émilie
Linking with Nature in the Digital Age
(Communication, Environment, Science and Society Set – Volume 1)

2023

APCHAIN Thomas
Favela Tours: Building Otherness in the Favelas of Rio de Janeiro
(Tourism and Mobility Systems Set – Volume 6)

CARDON Alain, EL HAMI Abdelkhalak
Fundamental Generation Systems: Computer Science and Artificial Consciousness, the Informational Field of Generation of the Universe, the Sixth Sense of Living Beings
(Digital Sciences Set – Volume 4)

CURULLI Irene G., IKIZ KAYA Deniz, KHAEFI Arghavan
Heritage Education for Climate Action
(Research in Architectural Education Set – Volume 2)

ELAMÉ Esoh
The Sustainable City in Africa Facing the Challenge of Liquid Sanitation
(Territory Development Set – Volume 2)

JURCZENKO Emmanuel
Climate Investing: New Strategies and Implementation Challenges

LYUBAREVA Inna, WALDECK Roger
Diversity of Methodological Approaches in Social Sciences: Example of the Analysis of Media and Online Information
(Modeling Methodologies in Social Sciences Set – Volume 3)

PARET Dominique, CRÉGO Pierre, SOLÈRE Pauline
Smart Patches: Biosensors, Graphene and Intra-Body Communications

VENTRE Daniel, GUILLOT Philippe
Electronic Communication Interception Technologies and Issues of Power

VENTRE Daniel, LOISEAU Hugo
Cybercrime during the SARS-CoV-2 Pandemic (2019-2022): Evolutions, Adaptations, Consequences
(Cybersecurity Set – Volume 3)

2022

AIT HADDOU Hassan, TOUBANOS Dimitri, VILLIEN Philippe
Ecological Transition in Education and Research

CARDON Alain
Information Organization of The Universe and Living Things: Generation of Space, Quantum and Molecular Elements, Coactive Generation of Living Organisms and Multiagent Model
(Digital Sciences Set – Volume 3)

CAULI Marie, FAVIER Laurence, JEANNAS Jean-Yves
Digital Dictionary

DAVERNE-BAILLY Carole, WITTORSKI Richard
Research Methodology in Education and Training: Postures, Practices and Forms
(Education Set – Volume 12)

ELAMÉ Esoh
Sustainable Intercultural Urbanism at the Service of the African City of Tomorrow
(Territory Development Set – Volume 1)

FLEURET Sébastien
A Back and Forth Between Tourism and Health: From Medical Tourism to Global Health
(Tourism and Mobility Systems Set – Volume 5)

KAMPELIS Nikos, KOLOKOTSA Denia
Smart Zero-energy Buildings and Communities for Smart Grids
(Engineering, Energy and Architecture Set – Volume 9)

2021

BARDIOT Clarisse
Performing Arts and Digital Humanities: From Traces to Data
(Traces Set – Volume 5)

BENSRHAIR Abdelaziz, BAPIN Thierry
From AI to Autonomous and Connected Vehicles: Advanced Driver-Assistance Systems (ADAS)
(Digital Sciences Set – Volume 2)

BÉRANGER Jérôme
Societal Responsibility of Artificial Intelligence: Towards an Ethical and Eco-responsible AI
(Technological Prospects and Social Applications Set – Volume 4)

CORDELIER Benoit, GALIBERT Oliver
Digital Health Communications
(Technological Prospective and Social Applications Set – Volume 5)

DOUAY Nicolas, MINJA Michael
Urban Planning for Transitions

GALINON-MÉLÉNEC Béatrice
The Trace Odyssey 1: A Journey Beyond Appearances
(Traces Set – Volume 4)

HENRY Antoine
Platform and Collective Intelligence: Digital Ecosystem of Organizations

KOLOKOTSA Denia, KAMPELIS Nikos
Smart Buildings, Smart Communities and Demand Response
(Engineering, Energy and Architecture Set – Volume 8)

LE LAY Stéphane, SAVIGNAC Emmanuelle, LÉNEL Pierre, FRANCES Jean
The Gamification of Society
(Research, Innovative Theories and Methods in SSH Set – Volume 2)

RADI Bouchaïb, EL HAMI Abdelkhalak
Optimizations and Programming: Linear, Non-linear, Dynamic, Stochastic and Applications with Matlab
(Digital Sciences Set – Volume 1)

2020

ALAKTIF Jamila, CALLENS Stéphane
Migration and Climate Change: From the Emergence of Human Cultures to Contemporary Management in Organizations

BARNOUIN Jacques
The World's Construction Mechanism: Trajectories, Imbalances and the Future of Societies
(Interdisciplinarity Between Biological Sciences and Social Sciences Set – Volume 4)

ÇAĞLAR Nur, CURULLI Irene G., SIPAHIOĞLU Işıl Ruhi, MAVROMATIDIS Lazaros E.
Thresholds in Architectural Education
(Engineering, Energy and Architecture Set – Volume 7)

DUBOIS Michel J.F.
Humans in the Making: In the Beginning was Technique
(Social Interdisciplinarity Set – Volume 4)

ETCHEVERRIA Olivier
The Restaurant, A Geographical Approach: From Invention to Gourmet Tourist Destinations
(Tourism and Mobility Systems Set – Volume 3)

GREFE Gwenaëlle, PEYRAT-GUILLARD Dominique
Shapes of Tourism Employment: HRM in the Worlds of Hotels and Air Transport
(Tourism and Mobility Systems Set – Volume 4)

JEANNERET Yves
The Trace Factory
(Traces Set – Volume 3)

KATSAFADOS Petros, MAVROMATIDIS Elias, SPYROU Christos
Numerical Weather Prediction and Data Assimilation
(Engineering, Energy and Architecture Set – Volume 6)

MARTI Caroline
Cultural Mediations of Brands: Unadvertization and Quest for Authority
(Communication Approaches to Commercial Mediation Set – Volume 1)

MAVROMATIDIS Lazaros
Climatic Heterotopias as Spaces of Inclusion: Sew Up the Urban Fabric
(Research in Architectural Education Set – Volume 1)

MOURATIDOU Eleni
Re-presentation Policies of the Fashion Industry: Discourse, Apparatus and Power
(Communication Approaches to Commercial Mediation Set – Volume 2)

SCHMITT Daniel, THÉBAULT Marine, BURCZYKOWSKI Ludovic
Image Beyond the Screen: Projection Mapping

VIOLIER Philippe, with the collaboration of TAUNAY Benjamin
The Tourist Places of the World
(Tourism and Mobility Systems Set – Volume 2)

2019

BRIANÇON Muriel
The Meaning of Otherness in Education: Stakes, Forms, Process, Thoughts and Transfers
(Education Set – Volume 3)

DESCHAMPS Jacqueline
Mediation: A Concept for Information and Communication Sciences
(Concepts to Conceive 21st Century Society Set – Volume 1)

DOUSSET Laurent, PARK Sejin, GUILLE-ESCURET Georges
Kinship, Ecology and History: Renewal of Conjectures
(Interdisciplinarity Between Biological Sciences and Social Sciences Set – Volume 3)

DUPONT Olivier
Power: A Concept for Information and Communication Sciences
(Concepts to Conceive 21st Century Society Set – Volume 2)

FERRARATO Coline
Prospective Philosophy of Software: A Simondonian Study
(Technological Prospects and Social Applications Set – Volume 3)

GUAAYBESS Tourya
The Media in Arab Countries: From Development Theories to Cooperation Policies

HAGÈGE Hélène
Education for Responsibility
(Education Set – Volume 4)

LARDELLIER Pascal
The Ritual Institution of Society
(Traces Set – Volume 2)

LARROCHE Valérie
The Dispositif: A Concept for Information and Communication Sciences
(Concepts to Conceive 21st Century Society Set – Volume 3)

LATERRASSE Jean
Transport and Town Planning: The City in Search of Sustainable Development

LELEU-MERVIEL Sylvie, SCHMITT Daniel, USEILLE Philippe
From UXD to LivXD: Living eXperience Design

LENOIR Virgil Cristian
Ethically Structured Processes
(Innovation and Responsibility Set – Volume 4)

LOPEZ Fanny, PELLEGRINO Margot, COUTARD Olivier
Local Energy Autonomy: Spaces, Scales, Politics
(Urban Engineering Set – Volume 1)

METZGER Jean-Paul
Discourse: A Concept for Information and Communication Sciences
(Concepts to Conceive 21st Century Society Set – Volume 4)

MICHA Irini, VAIOU Dina
Alternative Takes to the City
(Engineering, Energy and Architecture Set – Volume 5)

PÉLISSIER Chrysta
Learner Support in Online Learning Environments

PIETTE Albert
Theoretical Anthropology or How to Observe a Human Being
(Research, Innovative Theories and Methods in SSH Set – Volume 1)

PIRIOU Jérôme
The Tourist Region: A Co-Construction of Tourism Stakeholders
(Tourism and Mobility Systems Set – Volume 1)

PUMAIN Denise
Geographical Modeling: Cities and Territories
(Modeling Methodologies in Social Sciences Set – Volume 2)

WALDECK Roger
Methods and Interdisciplinarity
(Modeling Methodologies in Social Sciences Set – Volume 1)

2018

BARTHES Angela, CHAMPOLLION Pierre, ALPE Yves
Evolutions of the Complex Relationship Between Education and Territories
(Education Set – Volume 1)

BÉRANGER Jérôme
The Algorithmic Code of Ethics: Ethics at the Bedside of the Digital Revolution
(Technological Prospects and Social Applications Set – Volume 2)

DUGUÉ Bernard
Time, Emergences and Communications
(Engineering, Energy and Architecture Set – Volume 4)

GEORGANTOPOULOU Christina G., GEORGANTOPOULOS George A.
Fluid Mechanics in Channel, Pipe and Aerodynamic Design Geometries 1
(Engineering, Energy and Architecture Set – Volume 2)
Fluid Mechanics in Channel, Pipe and Aerodynamic Design Geometries 2
(Engineering, Energy and Architecture Set – Volume 3)

GUILLE-ESCURET Georges
Social Structures and Natural Systems: Is a Scientific Assemblage Workable?
(Social Interdisciplinarity Set – Volume 2)

LARINI Michel, BARTHES Angela
Quantitative and Statistical Data in Education: From Data Collection to Data Processing
(Education Set – Volume 2)

LELEU-MERVIEL Sylvie
Informational Tracking
(Traces Set – Volume 1)

SALGUES Bruno
Society 5.0: Industry of the Future, Technologies, Methods and Tools
(Technological Prospects and Social Applications Set – Volume 1)

TRESTINI Marc
Modeling of Next Generation Digital Learning Environments: Complex Systems Theory

2017

ANICHINI Giulia, CARRARO Flavia, GESLIN Philippe,
GUILLE-ESCURET Georges
Technicity vs Scientificity: Complementarities and Rivalries
(Interdisciplinarity Between Biological Sciences and Social Sciences Set – Volume 2)

DUGUÉ Bernard
Information and the World Stage: From Philosophy to Science, the World of Forms and Communications
(Engineering, Energy and Architecture Set – Volume 1)

GESLIN Philippe
Inside Anthropotechnology: User and Culture Centered Experience
(Social Interdisciplinarity Set – Volume 1)

GORIA Stéphane
Methods and Tools for Creative Competitive Intelligence

KEMBELLEC Gérald, BROUDOUX Evelyne
Reading and Writing Knowledge in Scientific Communities: Digital Humanities and Knowledge Construction

MAESSCHALCK Marc
Reflexive Governance for Research and Innovative Knowledge
(Responsible Research and Innovation Set - Volume 6)

PARK Sejin, GUILLE-ESCURET Georges
Sociobiology vs Socioecology: Consequences of an Unraveling Debate
(Interdisciplinarity Between Biological Sciences and Social Sciences Set – Volume 1)

PELLÉ Sophie
Business, Innovation and Responsibility
(Responsible Research and Innovation Set – Volume 7)

2016

ANDRÉ Michel, SAMARAS Zissis
Energy and Environment
(Research for Innovative Transports Set – Volume 1)

BLANQUART Corinne, CLAUSEN Uwe, JACOB Bernard
Towards Innovative Freight and Logistics
(Research for Innovative Transports Set – Volume 2)

COHEN Simon, YANNIS George
Traffic Management
(Research for Innovative Transports Set – Volume 3)

EL FALLAH SEGHROUCHNI Amal, ISHIKAWA Fuyuki, HÉRAULT Laurent, TOKUDA Hideyuki
Enablers for Smart Cities

GIANNI Robert
Responsibility and Freedom: The Ethical Realm of RRI
(Responsible Research and Innovation Set – Volume 2)

GRUNWALD Armin
The Hermeneutic Side of Responsible Research and Innovation
(Responsible Research and Innovation Set – Volume 5)

LENOIR Virgil Cristian
Ethical Efficiency: Responsibility and Contingency
(Responsible Research and Innovation Set – Volume 1)

PELLÉ Sophie, REBER Bernard
From Ethical Review to Responsible Research and Innovation
(Responsible Research and Innovation Set – Volume 3)

REBER Bernard
Precautionary Principle, Pluralism and Deliberation: Science and Ethics
(Responsible Research and Innovation Set – Volume 4)

TORRENTI Jean-Michel, LA TORRE Francesca
Materials and Infrastructures 1
(Research for Innovative Transports Set – Volume 5A
Materials and Infrastructures 2
(Research for Innovative Transports Set – Volume 5B)

VENTRE Daniel
Information Warfare – 2nd edition

YANNIS George, COHEN Simon
Traffic Safety
(Research for Innovative Transports Set – Volume 4)

2015

BRONNER Gérald
Belief and Misbelief Asymmetry on the Internet

2009

VENTRE Daniel
Information Warfare

Printed and bound by CPI Group (UK) Ltd, Croydon, CR0 4YY
16/09/2026
14963081-0002